THE PRIVATIZATION PROCESS IN RUSSIA, UKRAINE AND THE BALTIC STATES

'These guidebooks to the economies of Eastern Europe offer the best description available, and – between the lines – they teach the reader how to think about the development process in the region.'

– Edmund S. Phelps,
Economic Advisory Council, European Bank for Reconstruction and Development, McVickar Professor of Political Economy, Columbia University

'Policymakers and economists engaged in the economic transformations of the former socialist countries are grappling with unprecedented problems and have no inherited wisdom to draw on. These extremely informative and valuable country surveys produced by the CEU Privatization Project ensure that they will be able to learn from each other in as timely a manner as possible.'

– Professor Axel Leijonhufvud,
Center for Computable Economics, UCLA, Former Member of Economic Expert Committee of the President of Kazakhstan

'Professors Frydman and Rapaczynski are unique. Not only are they the leading theoreticians of the privatization movement, but they are among its most experienced practitioners. Their insistence on truly opening up the privatization process to market forces and free competition may prove decisive to the ultimate success or failure of the privatization reforms now sweeping Eastern Europe. In this series of volumes, they demonstrate a wealth of knowledge and collect invaluable and otherwise unavailable information.'

– John C. Coffee Jr.,
Adolf A. Berle Professor of Law, Columbia University Law School

'Privatization of state enterprises lies at the core of effective economic transformation in previously centrally-planned economies. However, as experience shows, successful privatization is not easy and it requires a good knowledge of local and institutional constraints as well as a firm grasp of the key economic factors involved in the process. Thus, we should be grateful to the sponsors and researchers of the CEU Privatization Project for helping to provide a thorough, sharply focused and, I must say, timely report on these issues. These volumes are likely to become an indispensable reference for both policymakers involved in actual privatization processes and researchers interested in the field.'

– Guillermo Calvo,
Senior Advisor in the Research Department of the International Monetary Fund and former Professor of Economics at Columbia University and the University of Pennsylvania

'These volumes are a unique and invaluable resource for scholars and students in a variety of disciplines who need comprehensive and up-to-date information on the remarkable process of economic reorganization taking place in Central and Eastern Europe.'

– Henry Hansman,
Harris Professor of Law, Yale Law School, Dean of Yale School of Organization and Management

Roman Frydman teaches economics at New York University and **Andrzej Rapaczynski** is a Professor of Law at Columbia University. They have written on, and have been actively involved in the Eastern European privatization process from its very beginning. **John S. Earle,** who holds a Ph.D. from Stanford University, teaches economics at the Central European University in Prague. He is the author of a number of articles on the East European transition and privatization.

CEU PRIVATIZATION REPORTS | VOLUME 2

THE PRIVATIZATION PROCESS IN RUSSIA, UKRAINE AND THE BALTIC STATES

- ECONOMIC ENVIRONMENT
- LEGAL AND OWNERSHIP STRUCTURE
- INSTITUTIONS FOR STATE REGULATION
- OVERVIEW OF PRIVATIZATION PROGRAMS
- INITIAL TRANSFORMATION OF ENTERPRISES

ROMAN FRYDMAN
ANDRZEJ RAPACZYNSKI
JOHN S. EARLE
et al

CENTRAL EUROPEAN UNIVERSITY PRESS
BUDAPEST · LONDON · NEW YORK

First published in Great Britain 1993 by
Central European University Press
25 Floral Street, London WC2E 9DS

British Library Cataloguing in Publication Data

A CIP catalogue record for this book is available from the British Library

ISBN 1 85866 003 3 Hardback
ISBN 1 85866 001 7 Paperback

ISSN 0968–5278

Library of Congress Cataloging in Publication Data

A CIP catalog record for this book is available from the Library of Congress

Typeset by Mayhew Typesetting, Rhayader, Powys
Printed and bound by SRP, Exeter

CONTENTS

CONTRIBUTORS

The following persons contributed to the preparation and writing of the first two volumes of these reports:

Project officers and staff
Joel Turkewitz
Dana Săpătoru, Sina Toussi
Alexander Dreier, Roger East, Georgy Feher, Tatiana Nemeth

Regional project participants
Bulgaria
Todor Gradev – Project Coordinator
Center for the Study of Democracy, Sofia

Reneta Indjova – Research Fellow
Agency for Economic Coordination and Development

Spartak Keremidchiev – Project Coordinator
Center for the Study of Democracy, Sofia

Stephan Kyutchukov – Research Fellow

Vesselin Pasev – Economic Advisor
Council of Ministers

Todor Popov – Senior Expert
Agency for Privatization

Todor Radev – Research Fellow
Institute of Economics, Bulgarian Academy of Sciences

Dimiter Stefanov – Deputy Chairman
Agency for Privatization

Czechoslovakia
Alena Buchtíková – Research Fellow
Institute of Economics, Czechoslovak State Bank

Richard Bureš – Information Manager
Federal Ministry of Finance

Eva Macourková – Research Fellow
Institute of Economics, Czechoslovak Academy of Sciences

Michal Mejstřík – Acting Director
Center for Economic Research and Graduate Education Charles University

Vladimir Rudlovčak – Deputy Minister
Federal Ministry of Finance

Estonia
Ardo Kamratov – Deputy Minister
Ministry of Economy

Alar Kein – Research Fellow
Institute of Economics, Estonian Academy of Sciences

Erik Terk – Director
Estonian Institute of Future Studies

Veiko Tali – Research Fellow
Institute of Economics, Estonian
   Academy of Sciences

Liina Tõnisson – Deputy Chairman
Parliamentary Committee of Economy

Hungary
Lajos Csepi – Managing Director
State Property Agency

Mária Móra – Deputy General Manager
Kereskedelmi Bank RT

Erika Katona – Research Fellow
Central Statistical Office

Erzsébet Lukács – Counsellor
State Property Agency

Gabriella Pál – Research Fellow
Rajk Lászlo College

Lászlo Urbán – Director
Center for Parliamentary Management

István Zsoldos – Research Fellow
Rajk Lászlo College

Latvia
Inga Auzina – Chief Specialist
Antimonopolies and Competition Policy,
Ministry of Economic Reforms

Eduards Dimitrovičs – Consultant
Permanent Commission of the Supreme
   Council

Natalija Gračova – Engineer
Latvian Institute of National Economy

Natalija Jackovicka – Chief Specialist
Ministry of Economics

Normunds Luste – First Deputy Minister
Ministry of Economic Reforms

Ilma Ruduša – Department Head
Antimonopolies and Competition Policy,
Ministry of Economics

Lithuania
Jonas Čičinskas – Professor
Economics Department, Vilnius University

Giedrius Jankauskas – Specialist
Ministry of Foreign Economics Relations

Atanas-Zenonas Kaminskas – Director
Privatization Department, Ministry of
   Economy

Antanas Merčaitis – Deputy Minister
Ministry of Economics

Nijole Žambaite – Expert, Member of the
   Board, Lithuanian Free Market
   Institute

Poland
Joanna Debska – Director
Foreign Affairs Bureau, Ministry of
   Privatization

Jaroslaw Gora
Foundation Center for Privatization

Janusz Lewandowski – Minister
Ministry of Ownership Transformation

Wojciech Maciejewski – Dean and Professor
Department of Economics, Warsaw
   University

Piotr Makowski – Research Fellow
Department of Mathematics, Warsaw
   University

Krzysztof Rybinski – Research Fellow
Department of Economics, Warsaw
   University

Wanda Wojciechowska – Director
Department of Programming and
   Statistical Surveys
Central Statistical Office

Romania

Ion Andrei – Vice President
National Agency for Privatization

Luoana Dana Dulgheru – Researcher
National Institute for Economic Research

Elena Gheorghiu – Senior Researcher
National Institute for Economic Research

Costea Munteanu – Director General
Romanian Development Agency

Dan Dimitru Popescu – Deputy Secretary
of State
Ministry of Economy and Finance

Ladislau Randjak – Information Technology
Expert
National Agency for Privatization

Theodor Stolojan – Prime Minister

Russia

Alexander S. Bim – Head of Department
Institute of Market Economy, Russian
Academy of Sciences

Anatoli Chubais – Deputy Prime Minister
and Chairman, State Committee for
the Management of State Property

Gennady R. Margolit – Senior Research
Associate, Institute of Market
Economy, Russian Academy of
Sciences

Yelena A. Nickulina – Research Associate
Institute of Economic Forecasting,
Russian Academy of Sciences

Vladimir T. Tolkushkin – Vice Chairman
Statistical Committee of Commonwealth
of Independent States

Dmitry V. Vasilyev – Deputy Chairman
State Committee for the Management of
State Property

Yury A. Yurkov – Deputy Director
Center for Economic Situation &
Forecasting, Ministry of Economy of
Russia

Edward Yu. Zhydkov – Research Associate
Institute of Economic Research, Ministry
of Economy of Russia

Ukraine

Volodymyr Lanovoy – Minister
Ministry of Property, Transformation and
Entrepreneurship

Olena Manninen – Research Fellow
Institute of Economics, Ukrainian
Academy of Sciences

Oleksander Paskhaver – Head Scientific
Fellow, Institute of Economics,
Ukrainian Academy of Sciences

Victor Rodionov – Department Head
Macro-Economics Department, Ministry
of Statistics

Inna Shovkun – Senior Research Associate
Institute of Economics, Ukrainian
Academy of Sciences

Vadim V. Vasilyev – Administrative
Director, State Property Fund of
Ukraine

Oleksander Zavada – National Advisor
Cabinet of Ministers of Ukraine

ABOUT THE CEU PRIVATIZATION PROJECT

The volume of reports presented here is the second in a series to be produced by the Privatization Project of the Central European University. The Project is designed to create a regional framework for the promotion and improvement of public policies in the area of privatization in Eastern Europe (including former Soviet republics). In particular, the Project aims at the following four objectives:

- the creation of a forum for the collection and exchange of information concerning privatization in all the countries of the region;
- the training of local government and academic personnel, as well as other forms of contribution to the human capital required for a successful completion of the privatization process;
- the creation of a research and advising facility making the services of experts from both the Western world and other countries of the region available to the regional governments;
- the definition and elaboration of the emerging corporate governance issues in Eastern European economies, including the development of standards for professional and ethical conduct of corporate directors in the private sector.

It is the policy of the Project to involve local personnel in its activities, as much as possible. This policy is based on the belief that local participants have special access to information and unique knowledge of the conditions in the region, which, when conjoined with the Western expertise provided by the Project, will greatly enhance the understanding of East European privatization.

The headquarters of the Project are located in Prague, with offices in New York and all of the countries of the region. The Central European University in Prague provides facilities for some of the educational and training programs of the Project. It also serves as a informational clearing house and as a meeting place for participants.

At this stage, the Project conducts research and other activities in Bulgaria, Czechoslovakia, Estonia, Hungary, Latvia, Lithuania, Poland, Romania, Russia, Ukraine, and has approximately sixty Eastern European participants and collaborators. The participants in each country include high level government officials, two to three part-time senior researchers (often working in ministries, national statistical offices, and specialized institutes), and one or two full-time junior researchers. They collect and process information, conduct Project-related research, and maintain contact with the headquarters in Prague and New York.

The activities of the Project

1. CEU Privatization Reports

The *CEU Privatization Reports* present the results of research and analysis conducted by Project participants. The purpose of the *Reports* is to provide policymakers and analysts in Eastern Europe, as well Western official, academic, and professional circles, with reliable and comprehensive information concerning the state of privatization in the region.

The individual *Reports* are based on research carried out by the Project teams in each country. The information is collected on the basis of a questionnaire containing a large number of standardized categories. The preparation of each report involves several iterations during which issues and answers are further clarified. The final version of the *Reports* is written by the Project Directors, with the help of the staff in Prague and New York.

Following the first two volumes of the *Reports*, providing an overview of the whole privatization process, future issues will cover specific areas, including leasing, management contracts, small, large, and mass privatization, the privatization of banking and agriculture, and the effects of privatization on labor-market dynamics.

2. Educational and training programs

The Project is engaged in several educational programs, both in the public and the private sector, aimed at upgrading the human capital necessary for a successful execution of the ambitious privatization plans in the region. In particular, the Project is now involved in the following initiatives:

- The Privatization Project, together with the Committee for the Management of State Property of the Russian Federation, established the Institute of Privatization and Management in Moscow, which is in the process of providing a massive program of training for the personnel of the Committee, involving approximately 5,000 officials of the territorial and local offices of the Committee.
- The Privatization Project, jointly with the Center for International Private Enterprise of the U.S. Chamber of Commerce, is running the Corporate Governance Training Program, which trains members of the boards of directors of the newly formed East European joint-stock companies in the state and private sectors. The program is also preparing a general model of corporate governance standards for the region. Pilot courses involving present and future company directors from Czechoslovakia, Hungary, Poland, and Romania were conducted during the summer of 1992.
- The Privatization Project is working closely with the Economics Program of the Central European University in Prague on a joint program designed to integrate the general teaching of economics to Eastern European postgraduate students with practical research- and policy-oriented experience in the field of privatization.

3. Short-Term research and technical assistance projects

The Privatization Project is equipped to provide, upon request from government officials in the participating countries, special targeted short-term research and technical assistance for Eastern European policy-makers dealing with particular problems of the moment. The following initiatives have been undertaken by the Project in this connection:

- At the request of governments considering the implementation of

mass and voucher privatization programs, the Project organized a
workshop on voucher privatization in Versailles, France, in June
1992. The workshop provided a forum for exchange of ideas
between decision makers in the region and top Western experts on
voucher privatization.

- At the request of the Polish government, the Project has been
  involved in the evaluation of the design and the legislative
  framework of the Polish mass privatization program.
- At the request of the Latvian government, the Project has
  participated in the implementation of the Latvian privatization
  program.

4. Other Project publications

In addition to *CEU Privatization Reports*, the Privatization Project also
sponsors the publication of the results of research conducted under its
auspices. Among the forthcoming books by Project authors are:

R. Frydman and A. Rapaczynski, *Markets By Design: Privatizing
Privatization in Eastern Europe*, forthcoming, 1993

J. S. Earle, R. Frydman, A. Rapaczynski (eds.), *Privatization in the Transition to a Market Economy*, Pinter Publishers and St. Martin's Press,
1993

A list of other publications sponsored by the Project is available
upon request.

**The Privatization Project is a part of the Central European University,
which is a private, independent, and non-partisan educational
institution. Although some Project participants are government
officials, the opinions expressed in the *CEU Privatization Reports* and
other Project publications are exclusively those of the authors, and do
not reflect the views of the respective governments or other organizations.**

ACKNOWLEDGEMENTS

The Privatization Project is grateful to Mr. George Soros for his unfailing and generous support. Mr. Soros's vision of open societies in Eastern Europe has provided a source of encouragement for the Project participants. The Project also gratefully acknowledges support received from The Pew Charitable Trusts.

The interest of Prime Minister Theodor Stolojan of Romania in the early activities of the Project was in part responsible for its continuation. The staff of the Soros Foundations in the countries of the region has provided valuable logistical support for the Project.

Roman Frydman and Andrzej Rapaczynski thank C.V. Starr Center for Applied Economics at New York University and Columbia University School of Law, respectively, for institutional support. The authors would also like to thank Dr. Frances Pinter for her extraordinary efforts in coordinating and expediting the publication of this volume.

RUSSIA[1]

CONTENTS

[1] The authors would like to thank Professor Andrei Shleifer for comments on the first draft of this chapter.

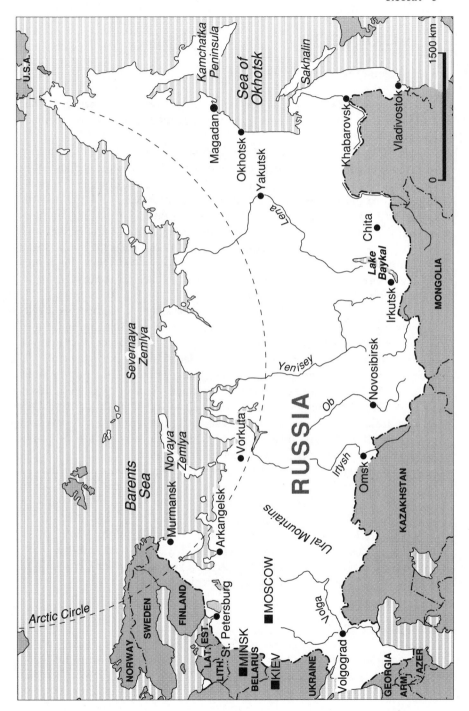

1. INTRODUCTION

Brief history of reforms

The Russian Federation was the largest republic of the former Soviet Union, accounting for 51 per cent of its population and 76 per cent of its territory.

Until 1990, the republics, including Russia, had neither the authority nor the instruments to conduct independent economic policy. Key decisions were made by the union ministries and committees. In addition to formulating economic policy for all republics and the Union, union and party authorities repeatedly attempted to introduce changes in the overcentralized and highly distorted structure of the Soviet and republican economies. Following the proclamation of *perestroika*, some economic decision-making power gradually devolved from the center to the more assertive republics, while the pace of partial reforms initiated by the center accelerated.

In 1988, 40 per cent of state enterprises were classified as "self-supporting." The rigid, centralized control over their financial and production decisions was replaced by a system of indirect instruments, attempting to link enterprise spending decisions to performance.

The center also tried to reform the price system. After half-hearted attempts in 1990, the first steps toward price liberalization were taken in 1991. This liberalization involved a relaxation of state control over a substantial proportion of wholesale and retail prices. However, it was only after the dissolution of the Union that any radical attempts were made to transform the Soviet price system.

After the failed coup attempt in August 1991, Russia quickly moved to assume control over the property and functions of the former union ministries and other governmental institutions. The Central Bank of Russia took over the Soviet State Bank, Gosbank, and the Soviet Foreign Trade Bank, *Vneshekonombank*. Together with seven other republics, Russia also took over responsibility for Soviet external debt. By December 1991, all Soviet ministries, except those for defense and atomic energy, were placed under direct Russian control.

Main points of the reform program

In December 1991, President Yeltsin chose a new group of individuals, committed to radical transformation of the Russian economy, to lead his government. He also gained authority from the parliament to serve as his own Prime Minister and to govern by decree. It was through such decrees that Mr. Yeltsin and Mr. Gaidar, the chief architect of the Russian reform program, sought to restrict credit and monetary growth, and introduced fiscal and price reforms.

A radical reform program, liberalizing most wholesale and retail prices, was launched on January 2, 1992. However, some prices, especially those charged by state wholesalers, were subject to centrally imposed ceilings, and prices of basic foodstuffs, energy, and some other consumer and producer goods continued to be fixed by the authorities. Nevertheless, these prices were raised by at least 300 per cent.

The budget prepared by the new government called for a sharp drop in the budget deficit, from 20 per cent of GDP in 1991 to 1 per cent in the first quarter of 1992. The budget envisaged reductions in subsidies, military and investment expenditures, and a shift from turnover and sales taxes to value-added and export taxes.

The Central Bank of Russia introduced a number of standard monetary instruments to control the growth of credit and monetary aggregates. However, the monetary and fiscal disarray, and the inherited configuration of interests of state commercial banks and enterprises have stood in the way of financial stabilization.

The January 1992 program also included the partial liberalization of exchange rates and foreign trade. The commercial exchange rate of the ruble was drastically devalued and import tariffs were abolished. However, the system of multiple exchange rates (dependent on transaction type), export quotas, and licensing requirements remained in effect.

Additional components of the reform program, including large-scale privatization and the provision of a social safety net, were elaborated and approved by the government in June and July 1992.

2. ECONOMIC ENVIRONMENT

The structure of output

According to the Central Statistical Office, *Goskomstat*, and the International Monetary Fund (IMF), the net material product (NMP) of the

Russian Federation, in current prices, was Rb 444.6 bln[2] in 1990, and Rb 810.0 bln in 1991.

PlanEcon's estimate of Russia's gross national product (GNP) for 1990, in current prices, is Rb 611.7 bln. The IMF's estimate of the Russian GDP in 1991, in current prices, is about Rb 1,120.3 bln.

The structure of net material product reflects the dominant role of industry in the Russian economy.

Table 2.1 The structure of net material product in 1990 (in per cent of the total)

Industry	42
Agriculture	20
Construction	13
Foreign trade	10
Transport and communications	7
Other	8

Source: *Goskomstat*

The industrial structure of the Russian Federation has been extremely concentrated. In 1988, 9 per cent of enterprises produced about 76 per cent of the value of net material product (NMP) (see Table 2.2).

Output

The GNP of Russia, in 1990 prices, declined 2.4 per cent in 1990. The decline accelerated to 7.6 per cent in 1991. NMP is estimated to have fallen by at least 11 per cent in 1991, led by a 19 per cent drop in construction. Industry, agriculture, and transport declined by about 10 per cent each.

As reported by *Goskomstat*, NMP continued to drop in 1992, by 14 per cent during the first quarter, 18 per cent for the first six months,

---

[2] According to *PlanEcon*, the average "commercial" ruble–dollar exchange rate was 1.76 in 1990, 1.74 in 1991, and ranged between 140 in January and 390 in October of 1992. It should be noted that pre-1992 rates are distorted and thus dollar equivalents of local statistics are useful only for superficial illustrative purposes.

Table 2.2   Industrial enterprises in 1988

	Number of enterprises	Output (Rb bln)	Employment (thousands)
Enterprises by number of employees			
fewer than 100	7,511	8.327	386
101–200	4,666	14.767	678
201–500	5,582	37.025	1,806
501–1,000	3,308	48.454	2,338
1,001–2,000	1,997	66.690	2,789
more than 2,000	2,176	291.397	12,733
Totals	25,240	466.660	20,730

Source: *Goskomstat*

and 20 per cent between January and September, as compared with the same periods of 1991. GNP declined 17 per cent in the first nine months of 1992.

Investment

After remaining unchanged in 1990, gross investment in fixed capital fell by 11 per cent in 1991. Nevertheless, the share of net investment in NMP remained high, at 23 per cent. Investment continued to drop in 1992. In the second quarter, total investment was 48 per cent less in real terms than in the corresponding period of 1991.

Price liberalization

The new Russian government initiated massive price liberalization on January 2, 1992. Although the government relinquished control over about 80 per cent of wholesale and 90 per cent of retail prices, it set ceilings for some of the remaining prices. In an inflationary environment, these ceilings have rapidly become too low, and have even been reported to have fallen below production costs in some cases. The authorities also continued to fix prices of basic foodstuffs, energy, some services (for example, airfares), and a number of other consumer and industrial products.

Prices of some basic foodstuffs (bread, milk, and a few others) were liberalized in March 1992. They were then drastically increased in May 1992. Subsequently, in September 1992, the price ceilings for these products were replaced by special excess profit taxes.

Inflation

Inflation accelerated in Russia during 1990 and 1991, as the government monetized the increasing budget deficit. The GDP deflator increased by approximately 8.5 per cent in 1990, and almost doubled in 1991, the change in the consumer price index averaging about 8.4 per cent per month. Centrally administered, wholesale price adjustment in April 1991 resulted in a 56.5 per cent increase in prices in state stores, while the market prices of foodstuffs rose only 7.5 per cent. For the whole of 1991, the average monthly increase of market prices was 5.15 per cent, much below the 8.6 per cent increase registered for prices in state retail outlets.

Following price liberalization, the consumer price index jumped by 245 per cent in January 1992. The index of food products increased 300 per cent, while prices of particular foodstuffs sold in local markets were reported to have risen as much as 1,000 per cent. Prices of non-food items increased 150 per cent, and prices of services jumped 130 per cent. The wholesale price index of industrial goods rose by close to 400 per cent in January 1992. The consumer price index continued to increase by over 10 per cent per month between January and September 1992 (see Table 2.3).

Behavior of wages

Following the retail price reform of April 2, 1991, all state employees received a lump sum monthly increase of Rb 60 ($34). In October 1991, the Law on Indexation of Incomes and Savings was adopted. This law provided for graduated, partial indexation of wages and bank deposits. At the time of this writing, there exists no formal indexation mechanism. The government sporadically revises employee compensation, funded

Table 2.3 Consumer price index (previous month = 100)

	1991					
	Jan	Feb	Mar	Apr	May	June
Aggregate index including: prices in state	106.6	104.8	106.4	154.4	102.4	100.0
stores	106.2	104.8	106.4	156.5	102.6	100.8
market prices of foodstuffs*	113.2	114.9	109.3	107.5	94.7	78.8
	July	Aug	Sept	Oct	Nov	Dec
Aggregate index including: prices in state	99.3	99.8	101.3	104.4	109.0	112.6
stores	100.3	100.8	101.4	104.0	108.0	111.1
market prices of foodstuffs	79.9	82.3	95.2	113.5	133.2	139.3
	1992					
	Jan	Feb	Mar	Apr	May	June
	345	138	130	122	112	117
	July	Aug	Sept			
Aggregate index	110	110	112			

* This is an index of prices of roughly 80 goods produced and sold directly by the cooperative farms (*kolhozes*).

Source: Goskomstat

directly from the national budget. Wages in the enterprise sector are basically set through negotiations between enterprise managers and employees.

The average nominal monthly wage increased from Rb 297 in 1990 to Rb 530 in 1991, while the average monthly industrial wage rose from Rb 311 to Rb 580. Although nominal wage increases outpaced inflation in the fourth quarter of the year, average real wages for the year fell by about 6 per cent in 1991.

The average nominal wage in industry rose by 45 per cent in January 1992, implying a further sharp drop in the real wage. Monthly percentage increases in nominal wages for the remainder of the first eight months of 1992 were also much smaller than the inflation rate.

Table 2.4   Average nominal wages in industry, 1992 (month-to-month per cent change)

Jan	Feb	Mar	Apr	May	June	July	Aug
45	39	36	12	20	19	8	8

Source: *Goskomstat*

Employment and unemployment

According to *Goskomstat*, employment fell by only 0.3 per cent in 1991 despite a 7.6 per cent drop in GNP. After a 2 per cent decline to 63.8 mln in 1990, employment in the state sector remained virtually unchanged in 1991. However, officially recorded employment in the private sector increased from 1.1 mln in 1990 to 1.4 mln in 1991, and to 1.8 mln in 1992.

Unemployment benefits cover 100 per cent of the last wage during the first three months after the job loss. This amount is paid by the last employer of the newly unemployed. For the next three months the unemployed person can register at a special labor exchange and receive 75 per cent of his or her former wage. This percentage declines to 60 per cent for the next four months, and to 45 per cent for the subsequent five months. Benefits can be denied to unemployed persons refusing to accept jobs found for them by the exchanges.

Since unemployed persons must wait three months after termination of their employment to register, the number of registered unemployed lags three to six months behind actual unemployment. Thus, while data on registered unemployment are available (see Table 2.5), the measure of unemployment which is most internationally comparable, is the total number of persons "out of employment," defined as persons not working, but available for work and seeking employment. Data on persons "out of employment" are available only since January 1992. This figure reached slightly under 900,000 persons or 1.3 per cent of the labor force, by the end of August 1992.

Table 2.5 Unemployed (in thousands, end-of-period)

	Registered	"Out of employment"
1991		
July	16.1	
Aug	25.3	
Sept	46.5	
Oct	51.3	
Nov	63.7	
Dec	59.3	
1992		
Jan	69.6	484.4
Apr	151.0	695.4
July	203.0	842.7
Aug	294.3	888.2

Source: Goskomstat

"Out of employment" is defined above. This category includes registered unemployed.

State budget

In the former Soviet Union, the budgets of the republics were subordinated to the consolidated budget for the Union. At the same time, state enterprises in each republic were subject to either union or republican budgetary authority. In the second half of 1991, union enterprises, located on the territory of Russia, were given special financial incentives to move from Union to Russian jurisdiction. Furthermore, in November 1991, Russia took over most of the other budgetary responsibilities of the Soviet Finance Ministry. This substantially increased the Russian republic's budget deficit. The 1991 deficit, including deposit compensation for administered price increases in April, totalled about 31 per cent of GDP. (This compensation was originally deferred, in part, until 1994, but it was eventually unfrozen at the end of March 1992.)

The 1992 budget envisaged a reduction of the budget deficit to 1 per cent of GDP. It was intended that fiscal contraction would result from further reductions in expenditures, including defense spending and subsidies to enterprises, and increases in tax revenues. However, after posting a slight surplus in the first quarter of 1992, the consolidated budget balance showed a deficit of about Rb 250 bln by the end of June

1992. Moreover, this figure underestimates the deficit, because it does not include some expenditures – such as subsidies to the enterprises for losses due to price controls – which are recorded only on an annual basis. Another estimate of the budget deficit is given by the value of credits extended by the Central Bank to the Ministry of Finance. This amounted to Rb 401 bln for the first six months of 1992.

The budget deficit increased dramatically during the summer of 1992. As reported by the Ministry of Finance, it reached Rb 820 bln by the end of August. Credits extended by the Central Bank to the Ministry of Finance amounted to Rb 1,050 bln for the same period.

TAXATION

Value-added and excise taxes replaced sales taxes as part of the January 1992 package of reform measures. Value-added tax (VAT) is paid at the rate of 28 per cent. The rate is reduced for goods with controlled prices and for some foodstuffs. A limited number of transactions are exempt from VAT.

The range of goods subject to excise taxes is similar to that of other countries, and includes alcohol, tobacco, and luxury goods. The excise tax rates range from 14 to 90 per cent.

The basic profit tax rate is 32 per cent, but higher rates are charged on enterprise incomes from selected activities. In addition, enterprises are charged a 15 per cent tax on dividends and interest derived from holding securities and shares of other enterprises. Employers also pay an excess tax on wages that are greater than four times the minimum wage, out of after-tax profits.

The wage (payroll) tax is levied at 39 per cent. Payroll tax revenues are contributed to different insurance funds according to the following formula: Pension Fund – 28 per cent, Social Insurance Fund – 5.4 per cent, Employment Fund – 2 per cent, Medical Insurance Fund – 3.6 per cent.

The tax reform also introduced a unified tax on personal income. The current rate ranges from 12 per cent on incomes up to Rb 200,000 per annum, to 40 per cent on incomes exceeding Rb 600,000 per annum. Also, employers are required to withhold one per cent of salary for contribution to the Pension Fund.

Monetary policy

MONEY SUPPLY AND CREDIT

According to the International Monetary Fund, nominal M2 increased by 77 per cent in 1991, while currency and time and demand deposits grew by 100 per cent and 72 per cent, respectively. Broad money (M2) growth averaged about 14 per cent per month for the first six months of 1992.

The 127 per cent growth in the stock of credit exceeded the inflation rate in 1991. Furthermore, the maturity structure of credit shortened. Short-term credit to enterprises rose by 175 per cent, while long-term credit declined by 9 per cent. The growth in short-term credit has continued in 1992. It is reported to have exceeded 25 per cent per month during January and February 1992. By the end of August, short-term credits constituted 95 per cent of the stock of outstanding credits (Rb 2,100 bln).

INTEREST RATES

During 1991, commercial banks had to pay 12 per cent interest on funds borrowed from the Soviet State Bank, and 1 to 9 per cent (depending on the use of resources) on funds borrowed from the Russian Central Bank. There was a 25 per cent ceiling on bank lending rates. In January 1992, the rate charged by the Russian Central Bank rate was raised to a uniform 20 per cent, and all ceilings on the lending rates were removed. The refinancing rate was further increased to 50 per cent in April and 80 per cent in May 1992.

The average lending rates charged by commercial banks in the Moscow region during the first eight months of 1992 were as follows: January – 28 per cent; February – 37 per cent; March – 50 per cent; April – 57 per cent; May – 72.2 per cent; June – 84.8 per cent; July – 99.4 per cent; and August – 109.3 per cent.

INTER-ENTERPRISE DEBT

According to *Goskomstat*, the total volume of gross inter-enterprise and short-term bank debt of enterprises was Rb 1,430 bln at the end of April 1992. This amount was greater than the country's GNP during the first quarter of 1992. By the end of June, the total volume of gross inter-enterprise debt reached Rb 3,197 bln. However, net inter-enterprise debt is only a fraction of this amount.

President Yeltsin signed a decree on the normalization of settlements between enterprises in June 1992. Inter-enterprise debts incurred before July 1, 1992 are to be frozen and tough measures are to be used against enterprises which fail to pay their bills after that date. The introduction of these measures reduced inter-enterprise debt to Rb 1,800 bln in July and Rb 1,200 bln in August.

Debt

In December 1991, Russia agreed to assume 61 per cent of the foreign debt obligations of the former Soviet Union. According to the IMF, in October 1991 this amounted to $37.2 bln. Debt service (on principal and interest) was estimated at $12.3 bln for 1992.

Foreign trade

In mid-November 1991, President Yeltsin signed a decree on liberalization of foreign trade. Reform of foreign trade and partial liberalization of the exchange rate were initiated in January 1992. Although import tariffs were abolished, exports were subject to quotas, and licensing requirements. Moreover, uncertainty concerning the foreign trade settlement mechanism impeded trade among former republics.

In 1990, Russia's exports to other republics constituted about 70 per cent of its total exports, while the share of inter-republican imports was 47 per cent. After the dissolution of the Soviet Union, trade among former republics has been conducted on the basis of bilateral agreements, specifying a list of goods to be exchanged, with the goal of achieving a balance of trade at world market prices. This principle applies to Russia's trade with most of the other former republics.

Russia's exports to the other former republics fell from $157 bln in 1990 to $142 bln in 1991, while imports declined from $120 bln to $99 bln. Exports to other countries dropped sharply from $51 bln in 1990 to $37 bln in 1991. Although Russia's exports to former Comecon countries plummeted by about 60 per cent, the switch to hard currency trade among the former socialist countries helped lift Russia's convertible currency exports by about $3 bln. Russia's imports from former Comecon countries dropped from $46 bln in 1990 to $14 bln in 1991. Nevertheless, convertible currency imports did not increase correspondingly, and in fact declined in 1991, relative to 1990.

During the first nine months of 1992, exports fell by 35 per cent, while imports declined by 17 per cent, as compared with the same period in 1991.

The Russian ruble is a non-convertible currency. Its commercial exchange rate was sharply devalued in January 1992. However, the exchange rate was not unified; and different, centrally set, exchange rates were used to fulfill the foreign currency earnings surrender requirements. The ruble became internally convertible in June 1992.

Importers are free to buy hard currency. However, organizations buying centralized imports continued to receive their foreign exchange at below market price.

At the end of June, the ruble was set at 125.26 to the U.S. dollar, the market average during June.

Since the July 2 currency auction, the ruble has been floating. It depreciated sharply during the summer and early fall. By the end of October 1992, the exchange rate fell to 390 rubles to the U.S. dollar.

3. PRESENT FORMS OF OWNERSHIP

3A. Legal framework of economic activity

The legal situation in Russia is complicated by a plethora of often overlapping and conflicting laws and decrees emanating from a number of jurisdictions. Prior to the demise of the Soviet Union, in December 1991, the Russian Federation had asserted, since June 1990, the supremacy of its laws over conflicting Soviet legal norms, but the Soviet laws continued to have validity in Russia to the extent that they were not in conflict with Russian laws. (This state of affairs will end in 1993.) Moreover, legislative practice in Russia often seems to be not to amend or repeal old laws, but rather to pass new ones, with an injunction that they should be read in conjunction with the old ones. Finally, the executive branches of both Russia and former Soviet governments have had far-reaching decree powers[3], which they have used extensively. Other legal acts of considerable importance have been passed by legislatures, decreed by the Council of Ministers, or even issued by particular ministries. As a result, the same subjects are often covered by many different and mutually contradictory normative pronouncements, and it is sometimes difficult to ascertain their ultimate validity.

The following are the more important laws and regulations concerning property rights, forms of business organization, and privatization in Russia:

---

[3] The decree powers of President Yeltsin were based on a special grant by the parliament, expired at the end of 1992. In a reversal of the usual legislative practice, the parliament had veto power over presidential decrees, which became automatically valid if not reversed by the parliament.

— Decree of the President of the Soviet Union: Fundamentals of Legislation of the USSR and the Union Republics on Lease ("Fundamentals") (1989);
— Decree of the Presidium of the Supreme Soviet of the USSR on Lease and Lease Relations in the USSR (1989);
— Law on Enterprises and Entrepreneurial Activity ("Enterprise Law") (1990);
— Law on Property (1990);
— Statute on Joint-Stock Companies, promulgated as the Decree (No. 601) of the Russian Council of Ministers ("JSC Statute") (1990);
— Law on Cooperatives in the USSR (1988, amended in 1989 and 1990);
— Order No. 131 of the former USSR Ministry of Finance: Provisional Guidelines on the Evaluation of the Property of State Enterprises (1990);
— Civil Code (1991);
— Land Code (1991);
— Law on Foreign Investment (1991);
— Housing Privatization Act (1991);
— Law on Privatization of State and Municipal Enterprises in the Russian Federation ("Privatization Law") (1991, amended 1992);
— Presidential Decree on Commercialization of Trade Utilities (1991);
— Presidential Decree on the Liberalization of Foreign Economic Activity on the Territory of the Russian Federation (1991);
— Presidential Decree (No. 323) on Urgent Measures for the Implementation of the Land Reform in the RSFSR (1991);
— Basic Provisions of State Program for Privatization of State and Municipal Enterprises in the Russian Federation in 1992 ("Basic Provisions") (1991);
— Law on Consumer Cooperatives in the Russian Federation (1992);
— Presidential Decree (No. 66) on Accelerating Privatization of State-Owned and Municipal Enterprises ("Acceleration Decree") (1992) *including*:
— Supplement No. 1: Interim Regulations on the Procedure for the Submission, Registration, and Processing of Applications for the Privatization of State and Municipal Enterprises in the Russian Federation;
— Supplement No. 2: Interim Methodological Guidelines for the Valuation of Properties Targeted for Privatization;
— Supplement No. 3: Interim Regulations Concerning Reorganization

of State and Municipal Enterprises into Open Joint-Stock Companies;
— Supplement No. 4: Interim Regulations on the Privatization of State and Municipal Enterprises in the Russian Federation by Auctioning;
— Supplement No. 5: Interim Regulations on Competitive Privatization of State and Municipal Enterprises in the Russian Federation (tenders);
— Supplement No. 6: Interim Regulations on the Procedure for Using Incentive Funds and Profits of Privatization of State and Municipal Enterprises during Privatization in 1992; and
— Supplement No. 7: Interim Regulations on Privatization Commissions.
— Presidential Decree (No. 322) on Additional Measures on Implementing the Guidelines of the Program of Privatization of State and Municipal Enterprises in the Russian Federation in 1992 (1992);
— Presidential Decree (No. 631) On Approving the Order of Sale of Land Plots During Privatization of State Enterprises (1992);
— Presidential Decree (No. 914) on Introducing a System of Privatization Vouchers in the Russian Federation ("Decree 914") (1992), *supplemented by* Statute on Privatization Vouchers ("Voucher Statute") (1992);
— Presidential Decree On Measures to Support and Rehabilitate Insolvent State Enterprises and the Application to Them of Special Procedures (1992);
— Presidential Decree (No. 721) on Organizational Measures for Transforming State Enterprises and Voluntary Associations of State Enterprises into Joint-Stock Companies (1992) ("Decree 721") *and the accompanying* Statute on the Commercialization of State Enterprises and Their Simultaneous Transformation into Publicly-Held Joint-Stock Companies ("Commercialization Statute") (1992);
— Presidential Decree on Russian Federal Property Fund (1992);
— Presidential Decree (No. 301) on The Sale of Land Plots to Individuals and Legal Entities During Privatization of State and Municipal Enterprises (1992);
— State Program for Privatization of State and Municipal Enterprises in the Russian Federation in 1992 ("State Program") (1992);
— Finance Ministry Rules of Issue and Registration of Securities on the Territory of the Russian Federation (1992).

Recognized forms of business organizations

STATE ENTERPRISES

While the extensive process of corporatization and privatization is expected gradually to decrease the number of state enterprises in Russia, the overwhelming majority of economic units in the state sector are still organized in the form of state enterprises. Moreover, the current legal framework does not envision the extinction of all state enterprises; indeed, the official 1992 privatization program and the regulations concerning corporatization prohibit the transformation or privatization of state enterprises in certain strategic areas of activity and require special permission from an appropriate governmental agency for a whole range of other enterprises. In addition, enterprises below a certain size cannot be corporatized (transformed into joint-stock companies), and many others have a choice in this matter. (See below, Sections 4B and 5.) Thus, a large number of state enterprises will continue to exist in Russia in the foreseeable future.

The overarching norm governing all business activity in Russia is the Law on Enterprises and Entrepreneurial Activity of December 1990 (the "Enterprise Law"). The most interesting aspect of this law is that it brings both private businesses and state and municipal enterprises under the same legal regime, with only a few special provisions concerning state enterprises. Moreover, while there exist other legal acts in addition to the Enterprise Law, which provide more detailed rules for the governance and organization of certain specific forms of business activity (such as joint-stock companies), no separate legal act establishes similar rules for state enterprises. And since at the same time all Soviet laws in this matter have been repealed, the legal provisions governing Russian state enterprises are extremely general in nature.

The Enterprise Law lists state and municipal enterprises as two among a number of other forms of business organization, distinguishing them by the fact that their assets are contributed to by an organ of the state (including its regional bodies) or by a municipality. The law establishes state enterprises as separate juridical persons, and limits state liability for their actions to the amount of enterprise assets. The only other significant provisions specifically addressing the regulation of state enterprises concern the appointment of managers and loosely define the rights of the collectives. Thus, the actual governance of Russian state enterprises today is largely a result of the previous legal regime and practices that have developed, often informally, in the last few years.

After a long period of stagnation, during which the central branch ministries, backed by the powerful *nomenklatura*, wielded the predominant power over the whole productive sphere, the governance structure of state enterprises during the last period of communist rule underwent a rapid succession of reforms. But since these reforms were at bottom rather timid and half-hearted, their effects were often perverse, and amounted to the strengthening of special interests at the local and enterprise levels. On the organizational level, these reforms often resulted in a number of hybrid enterprise forms, involving rather peculiar leasing arrangements, various forms of inter-enterprise associations, concerns, etc.

Prior to Russia's assertion of sovereignty over state enterprises, most enterprises were governed by the 1987 Soviet Law on State Enterprises and later by the 1990 Soviet Enterprise Law. These laws specified a rather elaborate three-tier governance structure, giving considerable powers to the general meeting of the labor collective and a partly elected Enterprise Council. At one point, power seemed to be shifting significantly toward the workers, who could elect enterprise managers, subject to confirmation by the founding body. In the end, however, managerial interests remained predominant, and the focus of the political struggle shifted to the conflict between the so-called "industrial lobby," composed of enterprise insiders (dominated by management) and the old economic bureaucracy (both on the central and intermediate levels), and the efforts of the reformers aiming at subjecting the enterprises to the discipline of the market and ultimately opening them to external control (through privatization).

Viewed from this perspective, the Russian Enterprise Law is essentially a transitional document, reflecting a stage in this process during which the "industrial lobby" was still rather firmly in control. The Enterprise Law retains the institution of the general meeting of the labor collective and replaces the Enterprise Council (which was in part appointed by the state) with a council representing the labor collective. But the law is quite unclear on the subject of who exercises ultimate power in the enterprise, since it gives a number of important rights, such as appointing the manager and determining the terms of his employment, as well as the right to amend the enterprise charter, to "the founding body together with the labor collective." The law also mandates collective agreements between all forms of enterprises and their labor force, and many issues relating to the mutual obligations of the labor force and management of state enterprises are apparently decided in this way as well.

LEASE ENTERPRISES

The laws of the Soviet Union, which have not been fully repealed in Russia, established a special entity, called the "lease enterprise," distinct from both the standard state enterprise and a genuinely private business organization. The official purpose of introducing the lease enterprises was to readjust the incentives of the people in charge of state enterprises and to improve the performance of the state sector. The stated intent was also to facilitate the breakup of large economic units in wholesale and retail trade, and to increase the efficiency of both the distribution of goods and the delivery of services to the population. In practice, the new system was an important stage in giving insiders control over a substantial portion of smaller state enterprises in the former Soviet Union, and constituted the first step toward insider ownership of these enterprises.

The leasing program began in April 1989, initiated by the Decree of the Presidium of the Supreme Soviet of the USSR on Lease and Lease Relations in the USSR. The decree was then amplified in November of the same year by another act issued by President Gorbachev, under the name "Fundamentals of Legislation of the USSR and the Union Republics on Lease" ("Fundamentals"). The program was first implemented in 1990 and gained force in 1991, the Fundamentals stipulating that state organs were under an obligation to develop leasing arrangements to the utmost of their abilities.

The assets of an enterprise could be leased either in their entirety or in part, but a part of the assets of an enterprise or of an amalgamation of enterprises[4] could not be split from the rest without the parent enterprise's consent.[5] The leasing arrangement could be proposed by any party qualified to become the lessee (collectives, state enterprises, and organizations of individuals, among others). The appropriate state authorities were obliged to respond within thirty days. The law was unclear as to when such applications could be denied, but refusals could not be "unmotivated."

The lease was supposed to be awarded on a competitive basis, but the Fundamentals gave explicit priority to work collectives of existing enterprises, which could, by a vote of two-thirds of their members,

---

[4] These amalgamations are discussed in the next subsection (on industrial associations).

[5] This rule, unlike the new Russian rules promoting the division of large enterprises during corporatization without the consent of their other divisions (see the subsection on the privatization of lease enterprises in Section 4B below, as well as Section 5 below), imposed an effective limit on the process of deconcentration. In effect, large units could always condition the splitting off of the smaller ones on the preservation of old ties (usually stipulated in great detail in the lease agreement).

organize themselves as separate units and enter into a lease agreement with the appropriate authorities (the larger enterprise, association, or governmental body). In practice, no competitions were ever held. The lease would run for a relatively long period, usually no less than five years and often as long as fifteen (the time might correspond to the period during which the value of the leased equipment was scheduled to depreciate to zero). In most cases, the lease would also contain a redemption provision, allowing the lessees to purchase the property during or at the end of the term. Upon registration, the resulting "lease enterprise" would become a legal entity separate from the state enterprise out of which it had been carved, but it might preserve the name of the old enterprise and take the assets with all or a part of the old liabilities.

The Fundamentals contain a number of vague provisions concerning the governance structure of lease enterprises. They do not stipulate any particular set of organs, but mandate that the statutes of the new enterprise be approved by its work collective and that its organization conform to the principles of self-government, democracy, and worker participation. The property of a lease enterprise is said to be shared among the "members of the enterprise" on the basis of each member's contribution through work or monetary investment. Membership shares may be issued in the form of securities.

In practice, nearly all leases were awarded to insiders of state enterprises, and created significant opportunities for profitable arrangements for the *nomenklatura*. Where the lease enterprises were not *nomenklatura* schemes designed to produce potentially huge profits from the arbitrage of goods and materials in short supply, they remained state enterprises under a new name. In many respects the leases were closer to what a Western observer knows as a profit sharing arrangement, rather than a genuine lease. First, the lease nearly always specified that the new enterprise had to continue to operate within the framework of the state enterprises and associations to which it had belonged, to provide specified products for the group, play its previous role in the production chain of the larger group, and take its supplies from the same sources as before. Moreover, the rent on the lease was not often fixed. Instead, it depended on profits, interest rates, and depreciation of assets. In effect, then, any increase in the efficiency and productive potential of the leased unit was constrained by its continued dependency on the old network of the state enterprise system.

The attitude of the Russian authorities to lease enterprises inherited from the Soviet past has vacillated between acceptance and hostility. The 1990 Russian Enterprise Law originally retained the institution of lease enterprises, and gave labor collectives the right to decide upon enterprise transformation. (The Soviet laws on leasing also remained in force.) However, lease enterprises had an indelible stamp of insider control that the new Russian government increasingly came to see as threatening its vision of privatization. Leasing also did not lead to a genuine separation of small units, such as shops, workshops, and service outlets, from the old system of large state enterprise networks. Thus, the new government faced the particularly difficult issue of deciding whether the redemption clauses contained in most leases should be honored (giving insiders ownership title), and whether they should be added to leases not containing such clauses. (For more information, see the subsection on privatization of small enterprises in Section 4B below.) The government ultimately found a compromise solution, and forbade new leasing arrangements in 1992, but the size of the existing lease sector is large enough to have lasting effects on the future structure of ownership in the Russian Federation.

By the beginning of 1991 over 2,400 enterprises, employing 1.5 mln people, had been leased, and accounted for 5.2 per cent of industrial output. In the service sector, approximately 2,000 retail organizations and trusts, 33,000 shops, as well as a large number of service outlets were under lease. By the end of February 1992, the number of lease enterprises grew to 9,451; their industrial output amounted to 13 per cent of total production, and their share of annual turnover reached 33 per cent in the retail trade and catering sector, and 44 per cent in the service and repairs sector. Employment in lease enterprises reached 8 per cent of total employment (11.3 per cent in industry).

INDUSTRIAL ASSOCIATIONS

Other groupings of state enterprises, known as "associations," "concerns," "corporations," etc., have also played an important role in the state sector in Russia. The particular legal forms taken by these amalgamations (which we will refer to as "associations") were frequently adopted in an *ad hoc* fashion, and were scheduled to disappear together with most state enterprises during the mandatory corporatization process in the fall of 1992 (see Section 5 below). Nevertheless, associations have been among the most important special interests in the powerful industrial lobby in Russia. The underlying groupings of enterprises are likely to remain major players in the politics of corporate governance and privatization, regardless of their concrete legal forms.

Many of the existing associations were formed by the enterprises themselves, acting under the 1989 amendments to the Soviet Law on State Enterprises and the Russian Enterprise Law. Many others were formed on the basis of decisions of local governmental bodies. But the most powerful associations bring together industrial enterprises organized on the basis of special resolutions of the executive branch of the former Soviet Union, such as the Council of Ministers or a particular ministry, which implemented decisions of the Central Committee of the Communist Party. The enterprises involved usually had pre-existing links, having been under the common administration of a particular branch ministry. The formal foundation of an association among them was then designed to make them largely independent of the former administrative structure, thus also making them immune to the successive administrative decisions of the government and the ever-new restructuring attempts characteristic of the last years of the Soviet regime. As a practical matter, in creating the associations, concerns, etc., the old sectoral structures of the Soviet industrial establishment were attempting to "privatize" or at least to "commercialize" themselves, and to acquire a legal form separate from the government. Thus, for example, the old Ministry of Machine-Tool and Instrument-Making Industry of the USSR transformed itself in a wholesale fashion into a new "state joint-stock association" known as "Stankoinstrument," leaving the former industrial leaders firmly in control, with the former minister duly becoming the president of the new joint-stock association.

The enterprises were meant to enter into these new arrangements voluntarily. In fact, they had very strong incentives to join, since the associations offered the benefits of essentially monopolistic cartels, representing and protecting the interests of their members *vis à vis* the governmental authorities. In addition, in the conditions of a chronic "shortage economy," enterprises that did not join associations risked losing access to state credits and subsidies, raw materials, supplies, the results of research conducted by institutes affiliated with associations, the services of design organizations, etc.

Most enterprises entering associations retained their former legal status as state enterprises, but some took on new legal forms. Occasionally this involved a conversion into a joint-stock company (most often of a closed type).[6] More often, though, they were transformed

---

[6] The conversions usually took place in conformity with the Soviet law on joint-stock companies, but the enterprises involved must now conform to the Russian law.

into lease enterprises. (See the subsection on lease enterprises above.) The associations themselves were organized as corporate bodies under the laws of the Soviet Union, usually closed joint-stock companies. Their ownership and governance structure often (especially in the case of concerns created by the central authorities) resembled the mythical snake eating its own tail. A typical statute of such an association might, for example, assign half of the shares of the association to the constituent enterprises, while the other half would be retained by the association acting as a trustee for the state.[7] At the same time, the association would hold the state-owned shares of the constituent joint-stock companies, as well as being the body charged by the state with the responsibility for the property of the member state enterprises, and the lessor of the property leased out to work collectives of the constituent "lease enterprises." The statutes might further specify that the role of the general meeting of the shareholders of the association would be played by the enterprises and companies comprising the association, with each member having one vote. The general meeting would then be given, among others, the right to elect all the members of the Management Board and half of the members of the Supervisory Council, to approve the annual plan of the activities of the association, and provide its budget and the number of employed personnel. The only formal role of the state would be its right to appoint half of the members of the Supervisory Council of the association, a watchdog body with very limited powers. The real leadership of the association would be in the hands of the president and the Management Board (chaired by the president). The Board, elected for five-year terms, would be charged with protecting the interests of the member-enterprises and representing them before state administrative organs, as well as with coordinating their various activities (such as organizing material and technical supply systems, setting up sales organizations, providing research and information services, advertising and promotion, specialization of production, new product design, etc.). In addition, the Board would be given the task of elaborating and implementing the organizational structure of the association, and – to close the loop – would delegate members to sit on the boards and councils of the constituent companies and enterprises.

---

[7] The concrete structure described here is based on the statutes of the already mentioned *Stankoinstrument*, but they are said to be representative of associations formed on the basis of the decisions of the central Soviet authorities.

The creation of associations as a shield from political changes of the moment has turned out to be quite successful: they have survived the demise of the Soviet Union and still comprise the umbrella organizations of a very substantial part of the Russian industry. According to the reports of the State Committee on Statistics, there existed in Russia, at the end of 1991, 227 concerns, sixteen inter-industry State groupings, 3,076 associations, and 123 consortia organized on the basis of various legal acts allowing such amalgamations. Of these, fifty-three were associations, comprising 4,162 enterprises, established on the basis of decisions of the central authorities. These associations, grouping between two and 901 constituent enterprises and between 1,700 and 1,334,000 employees, accounted for 38.3 per cent of industrial production and over 6.4 mln employees. They are mostly horizontal structures, and constitute extremely powerful cartels. Thus, for example, one concern (Rosneftigas) controls 99.8 per cent of Russian oil production, while another (Gasprom) controls 93 per cent of natural gas production. Yet another (Ugol Rossiyi) controls 97.7 per cent of coal production, and the already mentioned Stankoinstrument controls 88.7 per cent of machine tools and 81.6 per cent of forge presses. One association (Avtocelhozmash-Holding) controls the production of 87.6 per cent of tractors and 99.8 per cent of combines, while another (Norilsky Nikel) controls 87 per cent of nickel and cobalt production. Even the production of such things as clocks and watches is 72.1 per cent controlled by one association (Chasprom).

The authorities of the Russian Federation have made several attempts to reassert control over the associations. Thus, for example, the resolution of the Russian Parliament of October 10, 1991, stated that the associations were not authorized to represent the state in the disposition and management of state-owned property, and that they could not conclude contracts with the leaders of constituent state enterprises, approve the charters of these enterprises, or create new enterprises. This resolution was confirmed in another act (the Resolution of December 27, 1991, on Property Differentiation in the Russian Federation), which made the State Property Committee and its local equivalents (see Section 4A below) the sole bodies entitled to dispose of state property. At the same time, however, the State Property Committee has a right to delegate its authority to other state management establishments, and the Presidential Decree of December 3, 1991, granted the associations some of the rights barred to them by the parliamentary resolutions. As a result, the legal status of the associations has been rather uncertain, although their role may be somewhat regularized in the process of the implementation of the new laws concerning corporatization. (See Section 5 below.) Nonetheless, the political and economic power of the associations may be a serious obstacle to privatization.

COOPERATIVES
As in all communist countries, Russia had a very large pseudo-cooperative sector during the Soviet period. Unlike a number of other countries, however, the Soviet cooperative movement was limited to agriculture and consumer services, and was not active in the area of production. The pseudo-cooperatives were run in much the same way as the rest of the state sector, with a hierarchy of cooperatives headed by central "union" organizations. The movement thus had little to do with real cooperatives, evidenced in part by the way in which its profits were distributed: only 3.2 per cent of the profits of the consumer cooperatives, for example, was distributed to cooperative members, while over 40 per cent went to the higher organizations and centralized funds controlled by the state bureaucracy.

A new act, the Law on Cooperatives in the USSR, enacted on June 1, 1988, and amended in 1989 and 1990, changed the situation somewhat, in that it allowed the creation of production cooperatives, and introduced a new governance structure in the cooperative sector. Until recently, the law had no effect on existing agricultural cooperatives and very little impact on existing consumer cooperatives. But in the absence of other legal forms of independent economic activity, new cooperatives became a common form of private business activity in Russia in the last years of Soviet rule. With time, and the enactment of other laws permitting private business activity, the Law on Cooperatives lost much of its significance for new businesses, but it is still in force in Russia today, except in the area of consumer cooperatives, where it was replaced by the new Law on Consumer Cooperatives in the Russian Federation (1992). Perhaps its greatest impact is felt in agriculture, where a series of recent laws and decrees forced the old collective (pseudo-cooperative) and state farms to convert into new legal forms. Many of them have chosen to reconstitute themselves under the Law on Cooperatives into genuine cooperative institutions. (See the subsection on the privatization of land and agriculture in Section 4B below.)

The Law on Cooperatives established a governance structure involving a general meeting of the members, and an executive body composed of one or more persons. The general meeting (or a committee of representatives), at which each member has one vote, regardless of his or her contribution, decides on charter amendments, admission and expulsion of members, election of officials, distribution of profits, mergers, liquidation, and the size of membership fees. The executive body of the cooperative is constituted by the Chairman or a Board of Directors, and the law specifies no membership requirement for these officials. An auditing commission is also required.

Of particular importance is the fact that this law does not adopt the principle of profit allocation according to capital contributions, though it does not exclude it either. Concretely, the law sets the rule of distribution according to "labor contribution" as a default, but also allows distribution in proportion to capital contributions "when specifically provided in the charter." The law also gives to members of production cooperatives the right to employment in the cooperative.

All cooperatives engaged in production and services are required to establish an insurance reserve fund, into which must be paid no less than 5 per cent of the after-tax profits of the cooperative. In order to raise capital, a cooperative may also issue shares of stock (with value not to exceed annual gross revenue) to its members, its contractual employees, or to other enterprises. Cooperative members have preferential rights to purchase the shares of stock.

The executive committee of a local soviet may decide to liquidate a cooperative that has been insolvent for six months. The committee may also act on a petition of a bank to which the cooperative fails to make timely debt payments. Prior to such a petition, the bank may also declare the insolvency of a cooperative and determine the payment schedule of its creditors, until measures to secure the financial health of the cooperative have been taken.

The new Russian Law on Consumer Cooperatives replaced the pertinent provisions of the Soviet Law on Cooperatives, but it has been criticized for not changing the old system radically enough. Apart from specifying the rights of the general meeting of the members (similar to the old law, including the one-person-one-vote rule), it does not specify the executive governance of the cooperatives. Also, the new law does not commit the cooperatives to any particular allocation of its profits, leaving the matter to the general meeting. The strongest criticism of the new law concerns its failure to break up the old structure of the all-Russian consumer cooperative union, i.e., the central body dominating the cooperative sector under the old regime.

COMMERCIAL ENTERPRISES

In a decisive break with the past system, which was dominated by state ownership, the 1990 Russian Law on Property introduced the principle of equal treatment for all forms of property, which the law divided into private, state, municipal, and collective. Private individuals are allowed to own productive property and engage in business, either individually or in association with other physical and legal persons. The general principles governing both privately and publicly owned businesses were established in the Enterprise Law, and special provisions concerning corporations are contained in the Statute on Joint-Stock Companies ("JSC Statute"), promulgated as Decree No. 601 of the Russian Council of Ministers in December 1990. In addition, the Civil Code, enacted by the Soviet Union in May 1991, still provides binding operative rules when the Enterprise Law is silent. Among the general rules set forth in the Enterprise Law and applicable to all forms of business entities, the following should be noted:

- The law requires registration of all enterprises, but registration may not be denied, except for non-compliance with the proper procedures, or submission of documents at variance with official requirements.
- Non-state-owned enterprises can engage in any activity not prohibited by law. Entry into specially regulated economic areas, determined by the Council of Ministers and the councils of ministers of the constituent republics, may require a license. In addition, private enterprises are excluded from the manufacturing of weapons or ammunition, the production and marketing of narcotics or poisonous substances, the processing of precious metals, and the production of tobacco and alcoholic beverages.
- The law grants certain rights to labor collectives in all enterprises (including private ones); among them the right to a collective labor agreement and the right to regulate the activities of political parties and other public organizations in the enterprises.

Individual entrepreneurship. Individual entrepreneurs who are not using hired labor may register as being engaged in "individual labor activity" and obtain official status for their business. Businesses employing hired labor, on the other hand, are termed "enterprises," and can take the forms discussed below (in addition to cooperatives and state and municipal enterprises).

Sole proprietorship. The simplest form of enterprise is the sole proprietorship, termed "individual" (family) private enterprise in the Enterprise Law. The name of the company must contain the name of the owner. The law limits this form of activity to "citizens," without defining the meaning of this term. The law is also somewhat ambiguous about the extent of the liability of the owner of a sole proprietorship, saying that he is responsible "within the limits stipulated in the charter of the enterprise." This suggests the possibility of limited liability, which would be very unusual.

General partnership. An entity corresponding to general partnership is termed a "full partner-company" in the Enterprise Law. It is an association (without legal personality) of citizens or juridical persons for the purpose of engaging in joint economic activity, and its name must contain the name of at least one partner. Partners (called "participants") bear full liability for the obligations of the enterprise.

Limited partnership. An entity corresponding to limited partnership is termed "mixed partner-company" in Russian law, with general partners referred to as "actual members" and limited partners referred to as "contributing members." While the general partners are personally liable for the obligations of the company, the liability of limited partners is limited to their contributions. A limited partnership is a juridical person.

Joint-stock companies (open and closed). The Enterprise Law distinguishes between "closed joint-stock companies," which it also terms "partner-companies with limited liability," and "open joint-stock companies," but both of these entities are covered together by the JSC Statute.[8] Since most provisions apply to both types of companies, they will be discussed together, except when differences between them must be noted.

The main difference between the open and closed joint-stock companies (JSCs) relates to the way their shares are traded. Closed companies are private, limited to 100 shareholders, and their shares cannot be publicly traded. By contrast, open JSCs may issue shares to

---

[8] The JSC Statute never explicitly states that its closed joint-stock companies are indeed the same as the limited-liability companies listed in the Enterprise Law, which raises the issue of whether a separate third type of corporate entity with limited liability could exist under Russian law, as it does in some other countries (e.g. Ukraine).

the public. Furthermore, shares of an open JSC can be traded without any restrictions, while the shares of a closed company cannot be sold without the consent of the majority of the shareholders, unless company bylaws provide otherwise. The authorized capital of a closed JSC must be Rb 10,000 or more; that of an open company Rb 100,000 or more.

All JSCs are juridical persons, and may be founded by one or more physical or juridical persons. The founders of a JSC must draw up its bylaws, ratify them by a three-quarters majority, and elect the company's governing bodies. The company comes into legal existence upon its registration by the Ministry of Finance, which must respond to the application within thirty days (joint-stock banks and other credit institutions must be registered by the Central Bank). A permanent certificate of registration is granted when the company receives 50 per cent of its authorized capital. Contributions in kind are valued by a joint decision of the founding members, and the entire authorized capital must be paid up within one year of the company's existence.

A JSC may issue several classes of shares or bonds,[9] but all shares must be registered (debentures may be bearer securities). The issuing of shares is regulated by the Finance Ministry Rules of Issue and Registration of Securities on the Territory of the Russian Federation (March 1992), which allow both private placements and public offerings, but the latter may be made only by companies already in existence (i.e., private placement must be used at the time of the founding for both closed and open JSCs; only later can an open JSC make offerings to the public). Private placements cannot bring the holders of a given class of shares to more than 100 or its volume to more than Rb 50 mln; the rules concerning public offerings – requiring appropriate disclosures, publication of a prospectus, etc. – apply to all issues above these thresholds.[10] The bylaws of a JSC or a decision of the shareholders may grant employees the right to purchase shares at reduced prices.

The Enterprise Law provides that a purchase on secondary markets of over 15 per cent of the company stock by any person other than a founder requires the consent of the Ministry of Finance. Additional

---

[9] Bonds must be for a term of no less than one year. No provisions for short-term paper seem to have been made.

[10] The Enterprise Law also allows "unallotted shares ...› be issued; these remain at the disposal of the company's Board of Directors.

approval from the State Committee on Antimonopoly Policy and Promotion of New Economic Structures is required for any purchase of more than 50 per cent of the company's shares.

Payment of dividends is made on the recommendation of the Board of Directors, and the annual shareholder's meeting may decrease, but not increase, the recommended amounts. Dividends can be paid in rubles, or if the bylaws so provide, in shares or goods. Taxes must be withheld at the source.

All stock companies are required to maintain a business reserve with a value of not less than 10 per cent of the authorized capital.

The governing bodies of a joint-stock company are the shareholders' meeting, the Board of Directors, the Governing Board, and the Auditing Committee.

The shareholders'meeting has the exclusive right to alter the bylaws, increase or decrease the authorized capital, elect the directors, confirm the annual returns, decide to establish or close branches, and to liquidate the company. The meeting must be held at least once a year. Extraordinary general meetings may be convened to consider particular subjects. Shareholders' meetings are duly constituted when attended by individuals owning or representing at least one-half of the shares. Decisions are made by a majority of the voting stock, except for amendments to the bylaws, and reorganization or liquidation of the company, which must be supported by three-quarters. Proxy votes seem to be unrestricted.

The Board of Directors, elected by the general meeting from among the shareholders for renewable two-year terms, is empowered to make decisions on all matters concerning the company's business not exclusively reserved for the general meeting. The number of directors must be odd, with at least three directors in a closed JSC and at least five directors in an open JSC (unless the number of the company's shareholders is smaller). Unless the bylaws specify otherwise, the board must meet at least once a month, and the quorum is two-thirds of the directors.

The general or executive director of the company is selected by the board from among its members. The general director is the president of the company and is entitled to act in the company's name. The general director proposes, and the Board of Directors approves, the members of a Governing Board, composed of the executives in charge of the main divisions of the company. The Governing Board, presided over by the general director, is the executive body responsible for managing the company's business between the meetings of the shareholders and of the Board of Directors.

An Auditing Committee, composed of shareholders other than the executive directors, is elected by the general meeting to inspect the company's business and financial activity. The committee may investigate matters on its own initiative or on a demand received from more than 10 per cent of the shareholders. Members of the committee are required to call a general meeting if the interests of the company require it.

Joint-stock companies organized prior to the passage of the Enterprise Law were required to re-register with the Ministry of Finance before April 1, 1991. The 1992 State Program for Privatization of State and Municipal Enterprises in the Russian Federation makes all companies with authorized funds containing state-owned or municipal property subject to transformation into open joint-stock companies.

Bankruptcy and liquidation

Russia still does not have a bankruptcy law. A draft has existed since 1990 but the parliament has refused to adopt it; the last rejection came in June 1992 when the bill fell three votes short of passing in the Chamber of Nationalities. The resistance to the bankruptcy law came primarily from the industrial lobby, fearful that bankruptcies might lead to a massive closing of state enterprises. In fact, the draft law is quite lenient, since it would allow a declaration of bankruptcy only when a company's liabilities are greater than its assets. Since enterprises are allowed to count the ubiquitous (and often uncollectable) inter-enterprise debts among their assets, the new law would be unlikely to lead to dramatic changes.

In response to parliament's intransigence, President Yeltsin issued, on June 15, 1992, a Decree "On Measures to Support and Rehabilitate Insolvent State Enterprises (Bankrupts) and the Application to Them of Special Procedures," setting down the rules of bankruptcy for enterprises in which the state holds a capital interest of 50 per cent or more. This decree allows for a declaration of bankruptcy when an enterprise is unable to fulfill its obligations to the budget or to its creditors within three months of their becoming due, or when it has long-term debts outstanding with the value equal to two times the enterprise's assets. The bankruptcy petition may be brought by ministries and other state organs, banks, creditors, and the debtor itself. In addition, banks and taxing authorities are obliged to inform the appropriate committee for the management of state property (see Section 4A) about any facts that might constitute a basis for a bankruptcy declaration.

The decree gives no significant role to any judicial organs in bankruptcy proceedings. Instead, the decision to declare an enterprise bankrupt rests with the appropriate committee for the management of state property.[11] Prior to the declaration, the committee requests from the enterprise information concerning its assets and liabilities, and a list of debtors and creditors, but the law, interestingly, does not contain any rules concerning creditor priorities. Within a month of the initiation of the process, the committee must recognize the solvency of the enterprise or declare it bankrupt.

The management of a bankrupt enterprise is assumed by the committee for managing property. Within a month of the declaration of bankruptcy, the committee must make a decision whether to reorganize or to liquidate the enterprise. If reorganization is selected, an auction takes place for the right to manage the reorganized enterprise. Any investor, domestic or foreign, taking part in the auction must deposit 10 per cent of the book value of the enterprise (if positive). The right to manage the enterprise goes to the highest bidder. If there are no bidders, the appropriate property management committee will run the enterprise directly.

The winner of the auction (which can be the work collective) must maintain at least 70 per cent of the jobs at the enterprise, take responsibility for paying off the debts of the bankrupt, and guarantee the rights and interests of fired workers. At least 80 per cent of any funds deposited by the winner or received from the sale of selected enterprise assets must be used to finance renovations and the paying of debts.

If the restructuring is successful, the property committee will declare the enterprise solvent. The organization responsible for the restructuring (the auction winner) becomes a partial owner of the enterprise. Its ownership share is determined by the size of the funds invested in the enterprise during restructuring and the profits of the enterprise at the time of the declaration of its solvency. The deposit, if any, is also returned to the managing organization, and may be used to increase its ownership share. Special provisions are also made for the

[11] The decision of the committee may be appealed, but the appeal does not stay the proceedings.

remuneration of the administrative director during the restructuring process (including a one-off payment equal to twenty monthly salaries).

If the restructuring fails or the enterprise becomes bankrupt for a second time within one year of rehabilitation, the property committee can liquidate the enterprise, and the investor in charge of the restructuring loses its deposit. The assets of the liquidated enterprise are sold at an auction. The committee may impose conditions on the sale of the assets, such as a restriction that no more than 30 per cent of the workers may be fired, or that the buyer must continue producing the main product. However, if such conditions prevent a sale, they are removed in subsequent auctions.

No data are yet available on the effect of the decree on bankruptcies of state enterprises. According to the estimate of one high official in the regional Moscow administration at the time of its issuance, the decree would affect 90 per cent of the enterprises in the Moscow region, which were said to owe over Rb 1.4 bln in back pay to their employees.

Regulations governing foreign ownership

Foreign investment in Russia is largely regulated by the Law on Foreign Investment of 1991 and the Presidential Decree of November 15, 1991, on the Liberalization of Foreign Economic Activity on the Territory of the Russian Federation. In addition, laws and regulations concerning currency, as well a number of other laws, in particular the Land Code of April 1991 and the 1992 State Program for Privatization of State and Municipal Enterprises in the Russian Federation, contain important provisions concerning foreign investment.

The Law on Foreign Investment allows foreign investors (including Russian citizens domiciled abroad) to invest in Russia by means of founding a Russian commercial entity with a Russian partner, founding a fully-owned Russian commercial entity, setting up a branch or a subsidiary in Russia, or purchasing shares in an existing enterprise or the right to use land and other natural resources. Recent presidential decrees also allow foreigners to acquire property in nonagricultural land in connection with the privatization of state enterprises. (See the subsection on privatization of land and agriculture in Section 4B below.)

Foreign investors may participate in all forms of business organizations, and enterprises with foreign participation are in principle regulated by the same rules as domestic commercial enterprises. Foreign investors who established their activities in accordance with the older, Soviet laws have been granted certain exemptions, though "joint ventures" established under Soviet law are no longer registered in Russia. Companies with foreign investment above specified thresholds are also entitled to exemptions from certain import and export regulations, and to tax privileges. In particular, companies registered prior to January 1, 1992, and engaged in material production are entitled to a profit tax exemption for the first two years (three years in the Far East) of their operation in which they show profits.

Companies with foreign participation must be registered with the Ministry of Finance, or a duly authorized state agency, and registration of enterprises with foreign participation in excess of Rb 100 mln requires the permission of the Council of Ministers. (This figure, rapidly eroded by inflation, is expected to be adjusted upwards in the forthcoming amendments to the Law on Foreign Investments.) Applications for registration must include a notarized document attesting to the foreign investor's solvency, and a certified proof of the foreign investor's registration in his home country.

Enterprises with foreign participation can conduct business in any area not prohibited by law, but the Ministry of Finance must approve a special license for companies involved in providing insurance or in brokering security transactions. Also, the Central Bank must grant a special license for companies involved in banking. The Council of Ministers may specify other sectors in which similar licenses will be required.

In principle, legal rules regulating the commercial activity of organizations with foreign participation may not be less favorable than the rules applied to domestic business entities, and provisions in international treaties signed by the Russian Federation concerning the treatment of foreign investment take precedence over Russian law. Protection of foreign investment includes standard guarantees against nationalization and confiscation, and a right to "swift, adequate, and effective" compensation. Foreign investors can also sue state agencies or their officials for damages caused by the improper performance of their duties, and compensation is to be paid by the state agency responsible for the damages.[12]

---

[12] According to press reports, a group of foreign casino investors brought an action under this provision against local police forces and the Ministry of Finance for lost profits. The casinos had been closed down because they could not obtain the necessary license, for which the Ministry of Finance had failed to work out the required procedure.

Upon payment of appropriate taxes, foreign investors can transfer abroad foreign currency received from their investment in the form of profits, dividends and interest, licensing and commission fees, and contractual payments, but a 20 per cent transfer tax is apparently imposed. A myriad of other currency regulations have been simplified by the introduction of a uniform rate of exchange, and appropriate amendments to the Law on Foreign Investments have been proposed.

Most restrictions on foreigners' rights to participate in the privatization of large enterprises in Russia have been eliminated by the 1992 State Program for Privatization of State and Municipal Enterprises. The only exceptions are the following:

- the permission of local authorities is required for foreign participation in the privatization of small enterprises (below 200 employees or Rb 1 mln in fixed assets) involved in industry, construction, and transport, enterprises involved in trade and public catering, and consumer companies;
- approval from the government of the Russian Federation (or, depending on the form of state ownership, of the government of the appropriate republic) is required, for foreign participation in the privatization of facilities and enterprises in the fuel and energy sector, or in the mining and processing of precious metals and radioactive and rare earth elements.

3B. Structure of ownership

Traditional state enterprises in Russia still employ a large fraction of the labor force and produce most of the country's output. However, the recent data show significant growth of employment in leased enterprises (which are described in Section 3A above), and some growth of employment in the emerging private sector. Between January and September of 1992, the number of employed persons in the private sector increased three times, as compared with the same period of 1991.

In addition to state and lease enterprises, cooperatives have played an important role in the Russian economy. They were established in the countryside in order to meet the consumer needs of their members. The number of cooperatives grew substantially in the late 1980s, after the passage of the new 1988 law on cooperatives (see the subsection on cooperatives above). The output of this sector almost

Table 3B.1 Distribution of employment by type of organization (in millions)

	1990	1991*
State enterprises	61.3	56.8
Cooperatives	4.1	4.2
Lease enterprises	2.8	5.1
Joint-stock companies	0.2	0.8
Joint ventures	0.1	0.1
Collective farms	4.0	3.9
Private sector**	1.2	1.7

* provisional
** includes private, family farms and individually-owned businesses

Source: International Monetary Fund and *Goskomstat*

Table 3B.2 Gross output (in Rb bln)

	1985	1990	January–June 1992
State and cooperative sectors	798.64	933.2	4,693
cooperative sector	54.3	109.9	
Private sector	26.4	36.2	226
private, family farms	26.4	35.4	
individually-owned businesses	–	0.8	

Source: *Goskomstat*

doubled between 1985 and 1990, and cooperatives are now selling their output to the population through a system of cooperative stores.

Foreign investors have traditionally participated in the Russian economy through joint ventures. Although the number of joint ventures has grown in recent years, their output and employment has remained relatively small, especially in comparison with the traditional state sector. Most joint ventures have been set up in the industrial sector of the economy.

Table 3B.3 Joint ventures

	1989	1990	1991
Number	322	620	1,145
Output (in Rb bln, current prices)	0.6	3.2	18.4
Employment	17,300	66,000	137,400

Source: Goskomstat

Table 3B.4 Distribution of joint ventures by sector in 1991 (in per cent)

Industry	43
Construction	6
Trade and catering	9
Science and research	9
Other	33

Source: Goskomstat

4. THE PRIVATIZATION PROCESS

The legislative background of Russian privatization

The first serious proposals to privatize state property in Russia date back to the days of the Soviet Union and the famous 500 Days Program, outlined in mid-1990 by Grigory Yavlinsky and Stanislav Shatalin. While the 500 Days Program was ultimately rejected after much vacillation, the more cautious reform proposals submitted, in October 1990, by Soviet Prime Minister Nikolai Ryzhkov and his deputy, Leonid Abalkin, and the later plan, put forward in 1991 by Ryzhkov's successor, Valentin Pavlov, contained some provisions for privatization, although no detailed program was ever proposed. The common thread in the Ryzhkov–Abalkin and the Pavlov plans was the retention by the central ministries of full control over the privatization process.

There were also various separate proposals at the Russian republican level, culminating in the adoption, in June 1991, of the Law on

Privatization of State and Municipal Enterprises in the Russian Federation ("Privatization Law").[13] The law's adoption was preceded by the formulation of a liberal-oriented Russian economic reform program, associated with the then republican Minister of the Economy, Yevgeny Saburov. Saburov's proposals contained very optimistic forecasts on privatization, including some barely realistic timetables. They envisaged the division of all Russian state property into three groups. The first group, which included housing and agricultural enterprises, was to be privatized in 1991, with some important facilities to become private in time for the 1991 harvest season. The second group, including wholesale and retail trade enterprises, repair workshops, and other services, was to be auctioned off in short order. Finally, the third group, comprising medium-sized and large enterprises in all branches, was to be divided into between seventy and eighty smaller groups, each of which was to become a separate holding company temporarily acting as the representative of the state. A large proportion (35 per cent) of the shares of the holding companies was then supposed to be distributed, free of charge, using vouchers, among all adult Russian citizens.

Even though Saburov's proposals were never developed into a fullfledged program, the 1991 Privatization Law constituted a watershed in the Russian privatization process. It set up a special agency, the State Committee for the Management of State Property (often referred to by its Russian acronym "Goskomimushchestvo," and called the "State Property Committee" in this report), to organize the privatization process and to represent the interests of the state governmental bodies. The chairman of the State Property Committee is given ministerial status and is an *ex officio* deputy chairman of the Council of Ministers. (For further information on the structure and role of the State Property Committee, see Section 4A below.) The Privatization Law also envisaged the conversion of most large state enterprises into joint-stock companies, and the establishment of federal and local "property funds," designed as the trustees of corporatized state property. Finally, the law prescribed a series of privatization procedures to be followed in all privatizations. Although some provisions of the Privatization Law have been amended by subsequent presidential decrees, it remains the basis for the present attempt at ownership transformation in Russia.

In the wake of the demise of the Soviet Union and the subsequent

---

[13] The Privatization Law was extensively amended on June 5, 1992.

reorganization of the government structure of the Russian Federation (which took over all the functions of the former Soviet Union and incorporated many Soviet ministries), Russian leaders focused on macroeconomic reform and the introduction of radical price liberalization in January 1992. As a result, the implementation of the Privatization Law, including the issuing of the necessary regulations and the adoption of the state privatization program mandated by the law, was somewhat delayed. Nevertheless, on January 29, 1992, President Yeltsin issued his Decree No. 66 on Accelerating Privatization of State-Owned and Municipal Enterprises (the "Acceleration Decree"), which included seven interim regulations, specifying procedures for the submission of applications for privatization, principles of valuation, rules for conducting auctions and competitive tenders, and guidelines for the operation of enterprise privatization commissions. In December 1991, the President also issued a document called "Basic Provisions of State Program for Privatization of State and Municipal Enterprises in the Russian Federation in 1992" (the "Basic Provisions"), constituting a draft of the first annual privatization program required by the Privatization Law. The Basic Provisions outline various categories of enterprises and the order of their privatization, with a special emphasis on the immediate privatization of wholesale and retail trade facilities and other smaller enterprises. The Basic Provisions also postponed the issuance of vouchers to the population, and imposed a series of obstacles to foreign participation in the privatization program.

The enactment by the parliament of the final "State Program for Privatization of State and Municipal Enterprises in the Russian Federation for 1992" (the "State Program") did not take place until June 11, 1992. The battles raging over the program were centered mostly around the role of workers and management in the privatization process. A number of parliamentary deputies, the old sectoral ministries, enterprise associations, and the powerful industrial interests lobbied for ever more preferential terms for insiders and for the retention of ministerial control. In opposition to this coalition, the team of reformers around the acting Prime Minister, Mr. Gaidar, and the leaders of the State Property Committee defended the idea of privatization which included participation of outsiders and a change in the basic governance system of the Russian enterprises. The existing State Program is a compromise between the two positions. Insiders gained very great advantages in the purchase of state assets and, in many cases, the ability to retain control of large enterprises (see the subsections on the privatization of large enterprises and on small-scale privatization in Section 4B below). On the other hand, ministries are kept out of the process and free transferability of the workers' shares is instituted to facilitate further ownership changes through secondary markets.

The last important legislative enactment at the time of this writing was the President's Decree No. 721 on Organizational Measures for Transforming State Enterprises and Voluntary Associations of State Enterprises into Joint-Stock Companies ("Decree 721") containing the Statute on Commercialization of State Enterprises and their Simultaneous Transformation into Publicly-Held Joint-Stock Companies (the "Commercialization Statute"). This law mandates an extremely accelerated procedure for the conversion of state enterprises into joint-stock companies (called here "corporatization"), which amounts to their imminent removal from the control of sectoral ministries and other organs of state administration. (See Section 5 below.) The Commercialization Statute also significantly amends the privatization procedure for large and selected medium-size enterprises previously specified in the Privatization Law. The new procedure leaves not only corporatization, but also the preparation of the privatization plan for each enterprise, much more under the control of the enterprise insiders. (See Section 4B below.) Also, following corporatization and prior to any further transfers of the shares of the privatized enterprises, shares not acquired by insiders become controlled (and can be partially voted) by the federal and local property funds, which are, to a far greater extent than the State Property Committee, controlled by appropriate legislatures. (See the subsection on privatization organs other than the State Property Committee in Section 4A below.) These legislatures, and in particular the Federal Parliament, are in turn under the powerful influence of the industrial lobby. Moreover, the property funds are further "advised" by Decree 721 to transfer temporarily (on a contractual basis) the shares held by them to potential investors approved by the work collectives. While the effect of this provision is yet to be seen, enterprise insiders and commercial structures allied with the industrial lobby may very well become the trustees of these shares (see Section 5). The struggle for control over Russian industry thus continues, and the direction of future developments is not yet clear.

4A. Organizational structure of state regulation of privatization

The Property Committees

The main organ charged with the organization, management, and supervision of the privatization process in Russia is the State Committee for the Management of State Property, or "Goskomimushchestvo R.F." This body is a ministerial office, and its chairman (at this time of writing Mr. Anatoly Chubais) is a member and *ex officio* Deputy Chairman of the Council of Ministers of the Russian Federation. The State Property Committee, created by the mandate of the Privatization Law, is responsible for:

- the preparation of annual state privatization programs (to be approved by the Council of Ministers and adopted by the parliament) and the drafting of all legal acts concerning privatization;
- the supervision of the implementation of the annual programs;
- the preparation of forms and documents to be used by other state bodies involved in privatization;
- the enforcement of privatization legislation on the territory of the Federation, including prosecution of judicial actions on behalf of the Federation;
- the direction and control, through its territorial agencies, of the entire privatization process;
- the establishment of privatization commissions responsible for the preparation of privatization plans of individual enterprises (except when they are set up according to Decree 721 and the Commercialization Statute – see the subsection on the initial privatization procedures in Section 4B below);
- the final resolution of decisions concerning the privatization of individual enterprises owned by the Federation; and
- the promotion of investment funds involved in voucher privatization.

The central office of the State Property Committee (located in Moscow) employs over two hundred people. It is divided into departments dealing with the privatization of particular sectors of the economy (such as construction and transportation, real estate, agriculture, military industry, food processing, services, fuel and energy) and special departments charged with the preparation of state programs, legal matters, information, foreign investment, state property registration, external relations, etc.

The "territorial agencies" of the State Property Committee are attached to local governments, but their personnel is directly accountable to the Moscow office. While this sometimes creates tensions with local authorities, it ensures a clear sense of direction in the implementation of the federal program at a level where local authorities often have their own special interests.

Parallel to the structure of the State Property Committee, the Privatization Law also calls for the creation of a series of local committees for the management of local state property (local property committees), attached to the administrations of the constituent republics, territories, regions, autonomous regions, autonomous areas, districts (except city districts), and certain cities. Altogether there are eighty-two such local committees. Although most state property in Russia belongs to the Federation (89 per cent of enterprises responsible for 95 per cent of output), the role of local governments will be quite important in the early stages of the program, since they own many individual units, such as shops, service outlets, and small workshops, which are scheduled for early privatization. Therefore, the local authorities are obliged to adopt their own privatization programs, consistent with the federal program. Local property committees are charged with the preparation and implementation of local programs, and are responsible for all of the tasks parallel to those of the State Property Committee (setting up privatization commissions, making transformation decisions, etc.). The local property committees are also empowered to send their representatives to the privatization commissions set up by the State Property Committee. In addition, the State Property Committee can authorize the local committees to effect the privatization of federal property.

The organizational structure of local committees is left to the approval of local soviets, but the Privatization Law stipulates that the chairman of the committee must be an *ex officio* deputy of the most senior person in the local administration. Unlike the State Property Committee, which is financed from the federal budget, the local property committees are intended to be self-financing (using the proceeds of privatization).

Finally, on the level of individual enterprises, the most important bodies charged with privatization are the privatization commissions. The procedure for establishing a privatization commission and its composition are described in the subsection on initial privatization procedures in Section 4B below. Once formed, the commissions are responsible for the valuation of each enterprise, the preparation of its conversion into a joint-stock company, the preparation of a privatization plan specifying the types of benefits to be conferred on the insiders, and the techniques to be used in selling the shares or the assets of the enterprise, etc.

Other state organs

In addition to the State Property Committee, its territorial agencies, the local property committees, and the privatization commissions, a number of other state organs are also involved in the privatization process. It is sometimes difficult, however, to specify their involvement with precision, since Russian laws and decrees often remain without effect or contradict each other. The following are some functions of the most important of these other organs, as stipulated in the relevant legislative enactments:

1. The President of the Russian Federation has been the prime mover in matters of privatization, and has issued a number of important decrees regulating the privatization process. Given his vast legislative powers, the president can, and often does, issue decrees that change or modify the laws adopted by the parliament, including the basic Privatization Law of 1991.

2. The parliament of the Russian Federation and the local soviets have significant functions in addition to their normal role as legislatures and administrative bodies. They approve the annual Privatization Programs in their jurisdictions and the annual reports of the appropriate property funds (see below). Furthermore, according to the Privatization Law and Supplement No. 7 (Interim Regulations on Privatization Commissions) to the Acceleration Decree, local soviets were given the right to be represented on privatization commissions charged with developing privatization plans for individual enterprises within their jurisdiction and could object to these plans, although the ultimate decision as to the adoption of the plan was left to the State Property Committee. This role of the soviets has been modified, however, by the Commercialization Statute of June 1992, which put the privatization commissions in large enterprises under the mantle of the enterprises themselves. The earlier procedure applies only in

smaller enterprises (not following the corporatization route) or in those larger enterprises in which the enterprise insiders fail to act within a specified period. (See the subsection on initial privatization procedures in Section 4B below.)

The praesidia of the federal and local legislatures are charged by the Privatization Law with the establishment of property funds in their jurisdictions.[14] Furthermore, in accordance with the State Program, local soviets or bodies authorized by the soviets must approve foreign participation in the privatization of trade and consumer-service facilities, and of small enterprises (below two hundred employees or book value below Rb 1 mln) in the area of industry, transport, and construction. Finally, the State Program stipulates that special permanent commissions of the appropriate local soviets will be responsible for control of the implementation and the legality of privatization transactions.

3. The Council of Ministers of the Russian Federation is charged with a variety of functions in the privatization process. Among others:

- it proposes the annual privatization programs to the parliament and can unilaterally make some changes in the programs after their adoption;
- it is entitled to set the procedures for auctions and competitive tenders to be used in the privatization process (although the actual regulations were issued by the president) and to confirm other normative acts (such as the statute on investment funds) regulating the privatization process (see the subsection on small-scale privatization in Section 4B);
- it can confer special preferential benefits for insiders in the privatization of individual enterprises (but this matter has in practice been handled by the president);
- it authorizes foreign investment in certain sectors listed in the State Program (see also the subsection on foreign investment above); and
- it approves the privatization of the types of enterprises listed in a special category in the Privatization Program (see the subsection on the scope of privatization envisaged by the State Program in Section 4B below).

---

[14] The Statute on the Russian Federal Property Fund, promulgated by the President in July 1991, refers to the property fund as being established by a decision of the RSFSR Supreme Soviet (the predecessor of the Russian parliament), rather than of its Presidium.

4. According to the Privatization Law, shares of joint-stock companies owned by the state are transferred to special federal and local property funds, set up by the praesidia of the appropriate legislatures. The property funds are then instructed to exercise ownership rights on behalf of the state during the general meetings of shareholders, sell the shares held in the funds in accordance with state privatization programs, act as founders and purchasers of future state-owned joint-stock companies, and process the revenues from state-owned companies. While the funds are essentially trustees administering and implementing, rather than formulating, privatization policies, they will play an important role in the privatization process. The Russian fund, created by the Presidential Statute on Russian Federal Property Fund, in June 1992, will have a number of local branches (distinct from local property funds[15]), and is to be governed by the Fund Board, composed of a chairman, two deputies, and six members. The board in turn is to be assisted by a Council of the Fund, composed of the heads of the local branches. The board is responsible for the activities of the fund and must submit annual reports to the parliament, including a statement of profits and losses.

5. It is significant to note that sectoral ministries of the Russian Federation have a very minor role in the privatization process (since they are the centers of the industrial lobby in Russia). They are charged with assisting the State Committee of the Russian Federation for Antimonopoly Policies and Support of New Economic Structures in the preparation of recommendations, concerning special conditions obtaining in their sectors, to be submitted to the State Property Committee. In fact, the ministries and local administrative bodies are specifically barred by the State Program from having any role in administering the state enterprises in the wake of the adoption of the privatization decision concerning these enterprises, even if a local property committee attempts to delegate such power to them.

6. Among important bodies promoted by the state will be the investment funds participating in the voucher privatization program. These funds, however, will be private institutions, rather than state organs.

---

[15] The local property funds hold the shares of companies owned by local and municipal authorities, while the federal fund (including its local branches) holds the shares owned by the federal government.

Distribution of proceeds from privatization

According to the State Program, the proceeds from the privatization of state and municipal enterprises are distributed in specified proportions among the federal and local budgets, with small percentages also going to institutions involved in the administration of the privatization process. The rules of division are somewhat different for municipal and all other state property (including federal, republican, territorial, regional, etc.). In the latter case, the federal budget receives 35 per cent of the proceeds, the municipal budgets 10 per cent, and the budgets of the intermediate units 45 per cent. In the case of municipal property, on the other hand, municipalities receive 45 per cent of the proceeds, the federal budget 25 per cent, and the other budgets 25 per cent. A special set of rules governs the privatization of military property, in which 70 per cent of the proceeds go to the federal budget, 5 per cent to municipalities, and 15 to other units, but 50 per cent of the total (coming from the federal share) must be deposited in a special social security fund for military personnel.

4B. Overview of privatization programs

The scope of privatization envisaged in the State Program

The State Program divides all state enterprises, according to their eligibility for privatization, into the following categories:

- Facilities and enterprises which are prohibited from being privatized in 1992. This wide category includes, among others, the Pension Fund of the Russian Federation, radio and television centers, pipelines, enterprises involved in monitoring and protecting the environment, highway maintenance organizations, enterprises producing narcotic and toxic substances, ports, waste disposal enterprises and equipment, gold and diamond reserves, public utilities, most of the nuclear industry, specialized hospitals, nurseries, and sanatoria, water resources, resources of the continental shelf, minerals, objects of historical and cultural heritage, etc.
- Facilities and enterprises which can be privatized only by the decision of the government of Russia. These include the armaments industry, parts of the atomic industry, enterprises processing precious metals, the energy sector, commercial banks,

communications enterprises, the printing and publishing industry, remaining sanatoria, etc. Applications for the privatization of enterprises in this category must be processed in one month, and the decision to allow privatization is made by the deputy chairman of the government of the Russian Federation on the recommendation of the State Property Committee.

- Facilities and enterprises which can be privatized only by the decision of the State Property Committee, in consultation with the branch ministries. These include enterprises with a dominant market position, enterprises with more than 10,000 employees or fixed assets with a book value (as of January 1992) of more than Rb 150 mln, surplus military property, rail, air, and sea transport enterprises, large construction enterprises (including materials for construction), animal breeding farms, educational and research institutions, the medical and pharmaceutical industry, liquor and tobacco production, the baby food industry, petroleum products, folk arts and crafts, etc. When enterprises in this and the preceding category are privatized, the State Property Committee can retain a controlling block of shares for up to three years.

- Facilities and enterprises which may be privatized only in keeping with local privatization programs. These include municipal and public service enterprises (baths, waste treatment plants, licensed pharmacies, and institutions of "socio-cultural significance"). Decisions concerning these enterprises are to be made by local state property committees. Local governmental bodies cannot introduce additional restrictions.

- Facilities and enterprises subject to mandatory privatization. These include wholesale and retail trade establishments, restaurants, construction, agricultural enterprises other than state farms, the food production and processing industry, light industry, all enterprises operating at a loss (with the exception of those listed in the first category), uncompleted facilities, motor transport enterprises, and the property of liquidated enterprises.

The State Program predicts revenues from privatization to amount to Rb 72 bln in 1992, Rb 350 bln in 1993, and Rb 470 bln in 1994. However, the main sources of funds used in privatization during these years are expected to be vouchers and privatization funds (accounts) of the enterprises. While sale proceeds may not be large, if the program is implemented to the extent expected by the Russian authorities, the amount of state property transferred into private hands will be considerable. According to the deputy chairman of the State Property Committee, Dmitri Vasilyev, the government aims to privatize about 30 per cent of the economy by the end of 1993, and a further 30 per cent by the end of 1995, which, as officials are quick to point out, would make the Russian economy more "private" than those of some Western European countries, such as Austria.

Methods of privatization envisaged by the State Program

The State Program divides all enterprises to be privatized into three categories:

- small enterprises – with up to 200 employees and book value of fixed capital (as of January 1, 1992) of less than Rb 1 mln;
- large enterprises – with more than 1,000 employees or book value of fixed capital over Rb 50 mln;
- all other enterprises.[16]

Enterprises in the third category can be privatized by any means permitted in the State Program, and their privatization may or may not involve prior corporatization (the Commercialization Statute leaves

[16] The State Program and the Commercialization Statute are rather cavalier with respect to their use of such connectives as "and" and "or." If the use of these connectives is to be taken as intentional (which is not always possible, since it is at times inconsistent), the third category of enterprises, as defined in the State Program, would include all enterprises with (1) assets valued at less that Rb 50 mln *and* employment of fewer than 1,000 persons, *and* (2) assets valued at more than 1 mln *or* employment of more than 200 persons. The Commercialization Statute, in turn, modifies this definition, at least for some purposes, since the corporatization procedure it prescribes applies to large enterprises, defined as employing "on the average" over 1,000 persons *or* having assets over Rb 50 mln, and to other enterprises, defined as having a workforce "averaging" over 200 persons *and* assets between Rb 10 (not 1) and 50 mln. (To add to the confusion, the next sentence of the Statute allows separate corporatization of divisions of enterprises if these divisions have the workforce "averaging" over 200 persons *or* assets between 10 and Rb 50 mln.)

Apart from the question of what "average" employment means, the Commercialization Statute excludes from its coverage enterprises with over 200 employees and between one and 10 mln in fixed assets. It is thus unclear whether, in violation of the State Program, enterprises in this bracket are prohibited from following the corporatization route, or whether they can still corporatize, but have to follow the procedures in effect prior to the Commercialization Statute. (For an explanation of the new procedures introduced by the Commercialization Statute, see the following subsection on initial privatization procedures and Section 5 on corporatization, below.)

the transformation decision to the work collectives and the management committees[17]). Privatization of small enterprises is to proceed without prior corporatization, by means of an auction, tender, private placement, or liquidation followed by a sale of assets. Large enterprises must all be converted into joint-stock companies, and their shares must be sold or distributed in the manner described in the State Program, the Privatization Law, and the Voucher Statute. (For more details, see the appropriate sections below.)

The initial privatization procedures

The Privatization Law and the subsequent amending acts specify the first stages of the privatization procedure that is common, in part, to all state enterprises subject to privatization.

The Privatization Law had originally envisaged an individual, enterprise-by-enterprise decision concerning the initiation of the privatization process. The proposals could come from the State Property Committee and its territorial agencies, local property committees, enterprise insiders (the general manager or the work collective), potential investors, banks, creditors, or even 'allied' enterprises. Within one month of the application, the appropriate property committee is required to announce its decision (which had to be positive, unless some legal provision restricted the privatization of the enterprise), and to set up a special enterprise privatization commission.[18] The privatization commission, according to the Privatization Law, was to include representatives of the appropriate property committee, the local soviet, officials of financial agencies, the management, and the council of the work collective. The privatization commission was charged with preparing, within six months, a detailed privatization plan for the enterprise, coordinating it with the local soviet and the work collective, and obtaining approval from the property committee. If the work collective rejected the plan presented by the commission, the commission was to modify its plans. In the event of another rejection by the work collective, the plan was supposed to be considered by the local soviet. If the local soviet twice

---

[17] But see the preceding footnote for possible problems of interpretation.
[18] It is important to distinguish privatization commissions (charged with the privatization of individual enterprises) from (federal and local) property committees (charged with overseeing the privatization process in a given jurisdiction).

rejected the plan, the final decision was to be left to the State Property Committee.

The procedure specified by the Privatization Law was modified in minor ways by the Interim Regulations for Privatization Commissions, issued as Supplement 7 to the Acceleration Decree, which specified that the commission be chaired by the representative of the property committee. It also eliminated the cumbersome procedure for consulting with the work collective of the enterprise.

More serious modifications were subsequently included in Decree 721 and the Commercialization Statute with respect to the privatization commissions of the enterprises subject to corporatization. These presidential enactments abandoned the *ad hoc* mode of initiation of the privatization process of large enterprises, and replaced it with an obligatory transformation procedure within a rigid timetable (to be completed by November 1, 1992), accompanied by the preparation of a full-fledged privatization plan. In addition to large enterprises, smaller enterprises (with between 200 and 1,000 employees and fixed assets between Rb 10 mln and Rb 50 mln), in which work collectives so decide, may also follow the same procedure. Moreover, in all enterprises subject to Decree 721 and the Commercialization Statute, both the composition and the *modus operandi* of the enterprise privatization commissions differ from those specified by provisions of the Privatization Law. These commissions, to be composed of between three and five members, are now to be set up by the chief executive of the enterprise, and the only requirement is that they must include a representative of the work collective. If within seven days of the entry into force of Decree 721, the chief executive failed to set up a privatization commission, one may be established by the work collective, without the participation of the management. Only if the work collective, in turn, fails to set up a commission by October 1, 1992, does the procedure revert to the one specified in the Privatization Law, and the commission is then established by the appropriate property committee in conformity with the Interim Regulations of the Acceleration Decree.

The job of preparing a privatization plan of an enterprise involves the valuation of the enterprise in accordance with the Interim Methodological Guidelines for the Valuation of Properties Targeted for Privatization, issued as Supplement 2 to the Acceleration Decree, which specifies the book-value method, without adjustment for inflation, as obligatory.[19] On the basis of this valuation, the privatization commission subsequently determines the starting price of the enterprise at an auction or the authorized capital of the joint-stock company into which the enterprise will be transformed. The commission, with assistance from outside experts if necessary, was also empowered by the Supplement 7 to the Acceleration Decree to propose a reorganization of the enterprise.

The basic function of the privatization commissions remains the same after Decree 721 and the Commercialization Statute, but the valuation mandated by the Commercialization Statute is more perfunctory than that stipulated in the Acceleration Decree, and the time provided for the privatization commissions to complete their work has been shortened from six months to a few weeks. The deadline for the property committees' approval of privatization plans is also extremely, not to say unrealistically, short: seven days from the filing of the documentation prepared by the privatization commission. Given the fact that privatization commissions will now be dominated by the insiders interested in obtaining the lowest possible valuation of the company, this is likely to lead to abuses.

The extremely short deadlines imposed by Decree 721, make it also unlikely that privatization commissions will be able to prepare well thought-out privatization plans for their enterprises. Instead, the plans will probably follow a general model prepared in advance by the central authorities, such as the model of state-owned joint-stock statutes attached to Decree 721 and the Commercialization Statute (see Section 5 below). Unlike the case of the model company statutes, privatization plans cannot be easily standardized across all industries, since they should realistically reflect the specific conditions pertaining to the particular enterprise. Still, the saving grace of this hasty pace may lie in the fact that, again unlike corporatization, the original privatization plan is not likely to be realized immediately, so that in most cases there will be time for future revisions which take into account the special circumstances of the individual enterprises.

Once the privatization plan prepared by the privatization commission is approved by the appropriate property committee, it functions

---

[19] The Privatization Law originally envisaged a valuation procedure more closely reflecting the market value of the assets. The change of method, which was retroactively permitted by the June 1992 amendments to the Privatization Law, was clearly due in part to the difficulty of market valuation under Russian conditions. For the reasons why no adjustments are made for inflation, see the subsection on the privatization of large enterprises, below.

as a prospectus for the share issue of the new joint-stock company, and the commission is dissolved. In order to protect the employees of the enterprise, no dismissals or transfers can be made between the day the privatization commission is created and the day the transformation is accomplished.

Privatization of large enterprises

This category, comprising ca. 4,000 enterprises,[20] constitutes – together with those remaining state enterprises that elect to privatize through corporatization and the sale of the shares of the new state-owned joint-stock company – the greater part of Russian industry. It is this part of Russian industry over which the greatest battles have been fought. Initially, the Privatization Law had foreseen a rather traditional program of sale for these enterprises, involving their valuation according to the discounted-future-cash-flow method, their transformation into joint-stock companies, and a sale of shares "on the securities market" over an extended period of time.

An important provision (Article 9) of the Privatization Law prohibits the sale of shares of privatized enterprises to any juridical person more than 25 per cent owned by any state body. The purpose of this provision, in addition to ensuring that privatization is not merely spurious, was to end the practice, common under the laws of the Soviet Union, in which some enterprises or their parts were transformed into joint-stock companies and their shares were acquired by other state enterprises. This practice created a network of cross-holding that further obfuscated the ownership and control situation, and gave managerial insiders firmer control over a portion of the state sector. (See the subsection on associations of state enterprises above, and Section 5 below.)

According to the Privatization Law, the employees of new state joint-stock companies were entitled to a 30 per cent discount on their purchases of shares, up to a limit specified by the (then still non-existent) state privatization program. Installment purchases by employees (with up to three-year terms and a minimum 20 per cent down payment[21]) were also envisaged, as was a three-year limit on

---

[20] There are actually about 6,000 enterprises with more than 1,000 employees and assets above Rb 50 mln, but 2,000 of them are in the category of enterprises not subject to privatization. See the subsection on the scope of privatization envisaged in the State Program above.

[21] Changed to 15 per cent by the June 1992 amendments to the Privatization Law.

secondary sales of preferentially acquired shares.[22] Finally, the workers could use for their share purchases the income from the specially set up "incentive" or profit-sharing funds at their enterprises.

With time, the balance between the state as formal owner of the enterprises and insiders clamoring for control shifted decisively toward the insiders. To begin with, the Interim Methodological Guidelines for the Valuation of Properties Marked for Privatization, issued as Supplement No. 2 to the January 1992 Acceleration Decree, departed from the "market" valuation principles of the Privatization Law, and provided a uniform method of valuation according to a "residual" or book value of the assets, with the nominal value of the shares issued equal to the net book value of the enterprise. To be sure, certain assets, such as unfinished objects, obsolete equipment, uncollectable loans to other enterprises, or assets located previously within the Soviet Union, but now outside Russian jurisdiction, may have considerable book value (measured by their purchase price less depreciation) and no real market value. But as a rule, the book value of the assets of Russian enterprises is far below their market value (provided they have any), primarily because no inflation-related adjustments have been made.[23] A good example of such undervaluation was given recently by the head of the State Property Committee, Anatoly Chubais, in his press conference concerning the Russian program: the residual value of a Volga taxi cab in August 1992 was between Rb 2,000 and Rb 3,000, i.e. between 10 and 15 U.S. dollars!

The change in favor of book value pricing and the decision not to adjust the valuation for inflation greatly increased, of course, the value of any preferential discounts to insiders. Indeed, given the rates of inflation in Russia during 1992, it is quite possible that all sales at nominal prices, even without any preferential terms, will amount to giveaways. But the preferential terms themselves were also changed very significantly in favor of insiders by the time the June 1992 State Program was enacted, both in terms of the direct subsidies

---

[22] The Council of Ministers was given the right to grant additional privileges (including gratuitous distributions) in connection with the actual privatization of particular enterprises. The restrictions on resale of preferentially acquired shares were eliminated in the 1992 amendments to the Privatization Law.

[23] There is also no provision for valuing such intangibles as trade secrets (unless patented or registered as trademarks), goodwill, etc.

granted to insiders and in terms of their ability to acquire large, often controlling, stakes in privatized enterprises and prevent any dramatic changes in the way they are run. Finally, the voucher program announced in August 1992 gave each citizen a direct Rb 10,000 subsidy for the purchase of the privatized assets and enterprises, which the insiders can use to purchase the shares of their enterprises at extremely depressed nominal prices.

The growth of special benefits for insiders pre-dates the adoption of the State Program. In the earlier Basic Provisions (the presidential blueprint of the State Program), the workers of large enterprises had already been offered up to 25 per cent of enterprise shares free of charge, and the right to purchase up to an additional 10 per cent at a 30 per cent discount (with an upper limit defined in terms of multiples of minimum wages and further privileges for top management). But the Basic Provisions also limited the effect of the proposed giveaways on the future corporate governance of corporatized (and ultimately privatized) enterprises by stipulating that shares distributed without payment to employees had to be preferred, nonvoting stock, thus limiting employees' influence on decisions affecting the new joint-stock company.

Insiders' options have been still further expanded in the final version of the State Program, which gives enterprise work collectives a choice among three variants of preferential terms:

● *Variant I*, essentially taken over from the Basic Provisions, allows workers to receive, without payment, 25 per cent of the shares of their enterprise (but with a value of no more than twenty times the minimum wage per worker) in the form of preferred, nonvoting stock, and to purchase an additional 10 per cent of the shares (with full voting rights, but with the value amounting to no more than six times the minimum wage per worker) at a 30 per cent discount off the nominal price. Although the State Program does not specify the rights enjoyed by the preferred shares, additional information is contained in the model joint-stock company statutes appended to the Commercialization Statute (see Section 5 below). According to this document, the preferred shares distributed to workers (denominated "class A") will receive fixed dividends equal to 10 per cent of the company's net profit for the preceding financial year. If, however, during a given year, the dividends paid out to common-share owners are greater (on a per share basis) than those paid to the owners of preferred stock, the latter will have to be increased to the same amount.[24]

In addition to these insider benefits, the high administrative officials of the enterprise (the manager, his deputy, the head engineer, and the head bookkeeper) are also granted an option to purchase a total of up to 5 per cent of the shares at the nominal price (but not more than 2,000 times the minimum wage per person). The procedure for distributing free shares is to be determined by the general meeting of the collective.

• *Variant II* does not grant any discounts, but allows the employees to purchase up to 51 per cent of the shares at the nominal price, with no additional restrictions.[25]

• *Variant III*, available only to enterprises with more than 200 employees and fixed assets between Rb 1 mln and Rb 50 mln, combines discounts to all workers with special privileges for a smaller group of insiders who gain the approval of the whole collective and undertake special responsibilities for the future of the enterprise. The special group enters into an one-year, nonrenewable agreement stipulating the commitments and liabilities of its members, with the members obliged to put up a collateral equal to no less than 200 times the minimum wage. In exchange, the group immediately receives the voting rights to 20 per cent of the shares from the appropriate property fund. If it adheres to the terms of this agreement, the group can purchase these shares at their nominal price (without any further restrictions) on the expiration of the one-year period. When this variant is chosen, all of the workers can also purchase up to 20 per cent

---

[24] In effect, the provision prevents significant accumulations of profits within the enterprise, and forces a significant annual dividend payment. The forced payment is more than the stipulated 10 per cent of the annual profits payable to the preferred shareholders, since the owners of the common stock cannot recoup any profits not paid out in the past years without sharing them with the owners of the preferred stock. Thus, since all shares have the same nominal value, the stipulation practically assures that at least 40 per cent of the profits will be paid out annually (since this is the percentage of profits attributable to the preferred shares that must be paid out). Given the conditions of chronic shortage of capital characteristic of Eastern Europe, and the need to retain profits for the purpose of restructuring, this is potentially a problematic provision.

[25] While the State Program seems to envisage purchase at the nominal price, the State Property Committee established that the price at which the workers will be able to purchase their shares under Variant II will be equal to 1.7 of book value (and thus higher than in the other variants). Given the rate of inflation, however, this difference may not be significant.

of the shares at a discount of 30 per cent from the nominal price (but the purchase price cannot exceed twenty times the minimum wage per person).

In order to elect Variant II or III, the work collective of the enterprise must vote for it with at least a two-thirds majority; in all other cases, the "default" is Variant I.

In addition to the already described advantages granted to insiders, the State Program provides that 10 per cent of the proceeds from the sale of the remaining shares to outside investors will be paid to the employees' "personal privatization accounts," which the enterprises may establish for their employees in 1992 in accordance with the Interim Regulations issued as Supplement No. 6 to the Acceleration Decree, and into which they can transfer the balance of the incentive (profit-sharing) funds and up to 10 per cent of 1992 after-tax profits.[26] These accounts, which are vested, transferable by gift and inheritance,[27] and which the State Program makes tax exempt, can be used to purchase any property (state and municipal) being privatized in Russia.

The remaining shares of commercialized enterprises will be placed in the state and local property funds, which will be charged with selling them to outside investors. The procedures for these sales are prescribed by the Privatization Law and elaborated upon in Supplement No. 4 to the Acceleration Decree. The prescribed mode of sale will be an auction using either open or sealed bids. The initial offer is to comprise 10 per cent of the total company shares, followed by further offerings every month.[28] Presumably, a large portion of these sales will be to individuals and investment funds using the vouchers distributed to the population, and the rest might be sold for cash to domestic and foreign investors, as originally envisaged in the Privatization Law. But the sales for cash cannot be expected to be very large, and the State Program does not envisage large proceeds from such sales.

As evidenced by some of their public comments,[29] the authors of

---

[26] These personal privatization accounts should be distinguished from the funds made available through the voucher program which, according to some documents, are also said to involve such accounts.

[27] Transferability by gift was added in the State Program.

[28] Apparently a single auction for all the shares of each enterprise is now being contemplated.

[29] For example the interview given to Reuters by the deputy chairman of the State Property Committee, Dmitri Vasilyev, on June 19, 1992. For evidence of the pressures exerted by managers opposing the "going public" of their enterprises, see also the August 21, 1922 press conference of the Committee's chairman, Anatoly Chubais, and his deputies.

the State Program were clearly aware that the modifications introduced since the original provisions of the Privatization Law were
largely a victory for enterprise insiders and the industrial lobby, and
that they had to alter their original vision of the control structure
expected to emerge from the privatization program. As a result, the
distribution of large, often controlling blocks of shares to insiders
raises a serious question with respect to the governance arrangements
of the enterprises privatized through this program. Unless most of the
enterprises choose Variant I as their preferred route, or unless the
shares distributed to insiders are widely traded in secondary markets,
control of the privatized enterprises is bound to remain in the same
hands as it is now. In situations in which a selected group of insiders
(such as the special insider group in Variant III or perhaps the high
management insiders in Variant I) concentrates a significant block of
shares in a few hands, the State Program evidently anticipates that
partial management buy-outs will strengthen the present management
and sufficiently adjust its incentives to result in increased efficiency.
Also, the concentrated stakes of the current management may facilitate
further ownership changes, since the desire of the new holders to cash
in on these gains may lead to the inclusion of significant outside
investors. Nevertheless, in most situations, but especially in Variant II,
significant insider holdings are likely to be spread among a large
number of employees, which may make further secondary transfers
more difficult, and may obstruct the sale of remaining shares (held in
property funds) to outside investors. Probably with this in mind, the
State Program eliminated all of the earlier transferability restrictions
with respect to preferentially acquired shares, and the Voucher Statute
stipulates that vouchers are freely transferable as well. It is evidently
hoped that the secondary markets will be robust enough, and the
concentration of holdings in the hands of the investment funds sufficiently great, to lead to a new structure of control, capable of
counteracting some of the most obvious problems of insider control,
such as the maximization of wages and employment, resistance to
change, etc. (See also the subsection on the voucher program below.)

Small-scale privatization

Privatization of small economic units, such as shops and service
establishments, and significant reform of the operation of small state
enterprises in other areas, have been on the economic agenda of

all recent reformers in Russia, and also occupied the authors of the various reform projects in the Soviet Union. The standard wisdom on this subject was that the break-up of the monopolistic structure of the Soviet distribution, retail trade, services, and consumer-oriented production was a prerequisite for the improvement of the living standards of the population. The focus here was not so much on property as on decentralization and the introduction of rudimentary market institutions. While the growth of the private and cooperative sectors played a role in this respect, the most significant result of these developments in the last years of the Soviet Union was the widespread creation of so-called lease enterprises. (See the subsection on lease enterprises above in Section 3A.)

One of the most serious obstacles to the success of reform programs contemplated in the Soviet period, whether they involved privatization, leasing, or some other form of decentralization, was the existence of price controls which made marketization impossible. As long as the price of bread, for example, was held at ridiculously low levels, any attempt to release bakeries from state control would have immediately resulted in their conversion into other types of shops where prices were not as strictly controlled. On the other hand, if new owners or tenants were forced to maintain the same line of business, it was impossible to conduct it without being integrated into the old supply and distribution networks, since otherwise there was no way of obtaining the necessary inputs and goods and adhering to mandated prices.

Serious changes became possible only when price liberalization was introduced in January 1992 (see the subsection on price liberalization in Section 2 above). But even then, the problem had aspects of a vicious cycle, since in the absence of genuine decentralization, price liberalization often led to an enormous increase of monopoly profits for many enterprises, and created very few of the initial benefits of competition. A quick destruction of the state enterprises' lock on the market infrastructure came to be seen, therefore, as essential for the success of the more fundamental reforms of the Russian economy.

Even prior to privatization, the Russian government attempted to break up the large enterprises in the consumer sector. Accordingly, in November 1991, the Presidential Decree on Commercialization of Trade Utilities granted independent legal status to all retail trade and public catering facilities, and established January 1, 1992 (when the new price liberalization was to come into effect) as the deadline for full implementation. However, only a small portion of the affected units, approximately 21,000, became separate legal entities by the beginning of 1992, and only 21 per cent of stores in Russia became separate juridical persons by the end of March of the same year.

Not surprisingly, privatization of small enterprises and other small economic units carved out of existing enterprises became the first priority of Russian privatization, both because of its potential impact on consumers and because the task of small privatization was seen as less daunting than the job of transforming the ownership structure of heavy industry. Consequently, the State Program singled out wholesale and retail trade establishments, restaurants, the food production and processing industry, and light industry as areas subject to immediate mandatory privatization. Indeed, the earlier Basic Provisions were even more specific on this subject, envisaging for 1992 the privatization of 50 per cent of small enterprises involved in wholesale trade and public catering, 60 per cent of enterprises involved in the food industry, agriculture, and retail trade, and 70 per cent of enterprises in light industry, construction, and motor transport and repair. Regional privatization programs had even more ambitious objectives: For example, Moscow planned to privatize 90 per cent of enterprises in trade, catering and consumer services, and the goals for privatization in St. Petersburg were only slightly less optimistic.

AUCTIONS AND TENDERS

According to the Privatization Law, all enterprises not subject to corporatization (see subsection on the methods of privatization envisaged by the State Program above) and all assets of liquidated enterprises are to be sold at auctions or through competitive tenders. Neither the Privatization Law nor the State Program seem to leave any room for the possibility of private placements with a restricted number of prospective buyers.[30] The Privatization Law also contains a number of provisions governing auctions and tenders, which are in turn supplemented and elaborated in Supplements No. 4 and 5 to the Acceleration Decree.[31] All auctions and competitive tenders are organized by the appropriate (federal or local) property funds, but the initial prices, whether an auction or a tender is to be used, are determined on the basis of the enterprise privatization plan approved by

---

[30] An exception was made for certain enterprises in areas inhabited by small ethnic groups, particularly in northern Russia. Foreign investors can participate in small-scale privatization sales only by a decision of the local authorities.

[31] According to the Privatization Law, the implementing regulations were supposed to have been issued by the Council of Ministers. In fact, they took the form of a presidential decree.

the State Property Committee or an appropriate local property commit-tee.[32] With respect to both procedures, the sale price cannot fall more than 30 per cent below the initial price determined on the basis of the book value of the enterprise.[33] Originally, the laws required that the auction or tender be canceled if there was only one bidder, but a special Presidential Decree (Decree No. 322 on Additional Measures on Implementing the Guidelines of the Program of Privatization of State and Municipal Enterprises in the Russian Federation in 1992) allowed sales in such cases if the only bidders were employees of the enter-prise. In such cases the price would be determined according to Order No. 131 of the former USSR Ministry of Finance (Provisional Guidelines on the Evaluation of the Property of State Enterprises) of November 29, 1990, which stipulated the procedure for adjusting the book value for inflation. The State Program relaxed this even further, admitting sales to all bidders qualified as buyers within the meaning of the Privatization Law, and leaving the price setting to a later regula-tion of the State Property Committee.[34] Prior to all auctions and tenders, prospective buyers must make a deposit equal to 10 per cent of the initial price.

While the procedures for auctions are straightforward, those for competitive tenders may be of further interest. Such tenders are to be organized in cases where the buyer must comply with certain condi-tions following privatization. Permissible conditions may stipulate that the enterprise must continue for a certain period of time to produce specified goods; that no staff reductions can be made for a period of up to one year; that the buyer must maintain certain levels of invest-ment in the privatized object; or that the buyer must finance certain social programs. Interestingly, no other conditions are allowed to be imposed. The winner of the competitive tender sale is the person submitting the bid most closely satisfying the sale conditions and with the highest monetary offer. The administration of the tender and the

---

[32] The regulations permit either open or sealed bid auctions. The former are used for small and the latter for large enterprises (with over 200 employees).

[33] Given the unreliability of book valuation in the communist system of accounting, this potentially could create serious difficulties. In other countries, such as Poland, the majority of the assets of liquidated enterprises have been sold at much higher discounts. But the decision not to adjust book values for inflation (see the subsection on the privatization of large enterprises above) makes this limitation meaningless in any case.

[34] If employees are the bidders, they will not qualify for the usual preferential terms (see this subsection, below), but the price will presumably be set at an appropriately low level.

choice of the winner is entrusted to a special "competition commission" created by the appropriate property fund and composed of five persons with the chairman representing the property fund, and the other members appointed by the appropriate property committee, and unspecified "financial organizations." The work collective of the privatized enterprise and the state antimonopoly office might also be represented upon their own initiative. Each commission member must submit a written report explaining his choice of the winner, and the chairman makes the decision (to be approved by the property fund) "on the basis of conclusions of members of the competition commission." (It is unclear whether this phrase requires that the chairman follow the majority of the commission.)

INSIDERS' BENEFITS

As with privatization of larger state enterprises, the employees of smaller state enterprises or parts of enterprises sold at auctions and through competitive tenders have also been granted a series of preferential terms. These terms have also been gradually made more generous over time, although they have never become as generous as the benefits given to employees of larger corporatized enterprises.

The original preferential terms specified in the Privatization Law were rather modest: they offered insiders, if at least one-third of them formed a special company for this purpose and outbid other prospective purchasers, the possibility of buying their enterprise on an installment plan, with full purchase payment due within three years and an initial downpayment of no less than 30 per cent.[35] The employees were also permitted to use their profit sharing accounts for the purchase (for the use of these funds and of the personal privatization accounts, see subsection on the privatization of large enterprises above), and they were given priority if their offer during a competitive tender was of the same quality as the offers coming from other bidders.

Privileges for insiders were expanded significantly in the Basic Provisions: employees were given a 30 per cent discount off the purchase price, with a shorter-term installment plan of one year, and they were given 10 per cent of the purchase price outright, if the purchaser was an outsider. Finally, the State Program

---

[35] This figure was changed to 25 per cent by the 1992 amendments to the Privatization Law.

restored the three-year term for the installment plans available to workers and lowered the minimum down payment amount to 25 per cent of the purchase price. The State Program also increased the portion of the purchase price paid by outsiders which is to be distributed among insiders who do not become purchasers. These insiders will now be entitled to receive up to 30 per cent of the purchase price, but no more than ten times the minimum monthly wage, in the case of a sale at an auction, and up to 20 per cent of the purchase price in the case of a competitive tender, but no more than fifteen times the minimum monthly wage. (Tenders will presumably be used to sell larger enterprises.)

THE PRIVATIZATION OF LEASE ENTERPRISES

In the last years of the Soviet Union a special problem related to small privatization emerged as a result of the proliferation of lease enterprises. (See Section 3A above.) More than 80 per cent of the leases giving rise to these enterprises contained an option for the lessees to purchase the leased enterprise, which guaranteed "insider privatization of these enterprises." Quite apart from the fact that this contradicted the intention of the new authorities to make privatization an open process and that a number of leases had a distinct *nomenklatura* flavor, the redemption provisions of existing leases usually did not contain any adjustments for inflation, and did not reflect the real value of the enterprises. While the same can be said about the principle of valuation used to determine the price at which insiders can purchase shares of their enterprises in the case of corporatization (see the subsection on the privatization of large enterprises above), the State Program never permitted an *entire* enterprise to be sold on such favorable terms, nor were such terms ever the basis for the sale of small enterprises.

Soon after its creation, the State Property Committee prohibited new leasing contracts which included redemption clauses, a restriction which was reiterated in the Basic Provisions. The State Program adopted the policy of allowing redemptions on the terms specified in leases entered into prior to the passage of the Privatization Law. If the lease provides for redemption but does not specify clear terms, the enterprise can be converted into an open joint-stock enterprise and the leaseholders will then be given an unspecified "priority" in purchasing the shares belonging to the state. In neither of these cases are insiders given any preferential terms if they happen to be the leaseholders exercising their right of redemption. A special exception is made, apparently to encourage the division of enterprises engaged in trade, public catering, and consumer services, if one-half of the work collective of any division of a lease enterprise in these areas decides to purchase its division. In such cases the insiders are given the right to purchase their division (a shop, restaurant, or a service outlet) at the appropriate proportion of the redemption price (calculated on the basis of the proportion of the overall volume of sales or production), with an additional discount of 30 per cent off the purchase price. Finally, even if a lease entered into prior to the enactment of the Privatization Law does not contain a redemption clause, a partnership created by the work collective of a division of such an enterprise will also have the right to purchase its division, although no preferential (or other) purchase terms in such a case are specified in the State Program. In all cases in which the State Program permits lease redemptions, such permission is made conditional on the conversion of the entities involved into legal forms recognized in Russian legislation (thus eliminating all special arrangements made under Soviet law).[36]

By implication, all lease enterprises created after the effective date of the Privatization Law, regardless of whether or not they contain a redemption clause, are to be privatized in the same way as ordinary state enterprises.

PRELIMINARY RESULTS
It is very difficult to obtain reliable estimates of the progress of small privatization to date. Different sources apparently use different defini-tions of privatized units, and various local governments (which own a large proportion of the small enterprises and facilities) being privatized fail to maintain a clear line between fact and fiction. In addition, the numbers seem to be changing so fast that they are apt to become out of date before they are published. The State Property Committee, on the basis of information provided by sixty-seven (of eighty-two) regional property committees estimates that there are, in all of Russia, over 175,000 enterprises and other economic units subject to mandatory privatization under the Basic Provisions and the State Program. Of these, 60 per cent are scheduled to be privatized in 1992, but only 23,500 submitted privatization applications by May 1 (the most recent date for which central data are available). The revenues from small privatization until that time were said to amount to Rb 3,185.4 mln.

---

[36] The provisions concerning the privatization of lease enterprises were also incorporated into the Privatization Law as a result of the amendments of June 5, 1992.

The brightest local privatization spot is often said to be the program of Nizhny Novgorod. By August 1, 1992, over 200 facilities in the city, primarily trading outlets, and 377 enterprises in the surrounding region are reported to have been successfully privatized. Nizhny Novgorod has been held up as a model by Minister Chubais, who suggested that its example might become the prescribed model throughout Russia. Much of the city's success can be traced to the openness of the process, the absence of restrictive sale conditions, and the city's assumption of the debts of the privatized enterprises. The Nizhny Novgorod auctions were closed to foreigners, but this limitation was removed as of October 1992.

The pace of privatization in Moscow is reported to have picked up dramatically in 1992. The city government claims that 7,533 businesses were sold by July 30, 1992, including 3,853 retail trade businesses, 1,440 public catering establishments, 2,195 consumer service outlets, forty-three transport businesses, sixteen local industrial units, and six construction organizations. The proceeds are reported to be over Rb 3 bln.

The program in St. Petersburg seems to be among the most feeble in the main Russian cities. Only 112 municipal businesses and five federal enterprises were reported sold, as of the end of June 1992. The municipality is said to have responded to only 389 out of a total of 1,375 requests for privatization.

Not surprisingly, initial valuations of the privatized units, based on unadjusted book values, have turned out to be widely off the mark. Actual sale prices routinely reached twenty to fifty times higher than the starting price. (In Nizhny Novgorod, one store initially valued at Rb 62,000 was ultimately sold for Rb 4.2 mln, an increase of 7,260 per cent!) Government officials also often retain discretionary prerogatives over privatization procedures. For example, the Moscow city government, the mayor, or the head of the municipal property department can circumvent the competitive auction procedures by allocating non-housing premises to individuals engaged in activities which "serve the long-term interests of the Moscow region." Questions also persist concerning the continuation of former price-setting practices and the maintenance of the old networks among the now formally independent trade and service establishments.[37]

---

[37] The next CEU Privatization Report will deal in detail with the program of small privatization, and will contain more systematic data concerning its results.

The voucher program

The Russian privatization program has a very important component of artificial capital, created by the voucher program. The intentions of the Russian authorities with respect to the use of vouchers have vacillated somewhat since the adoption of the Privatization Law (which is silent on the matter). While the Basic Provisions did not foresee any use of vouchers in 1992 and contained only vague references to their use in 1993, the Presidential Decree No. 322, issued in April of 1992, announced that vouchers would be distributed to the population in the fourth quarter of 1992. There followed, in August 1992, another Presidential Decree, "On Introducing a System of Privatization Vouchers in the Russian Federation" ("Decree 914"), supplemented by the Statute on Privatization Vouchers (the "Voucher Statute"), specifying the details of the program. Among other things, these acts set the timetable for the process, according to which the first tranche of privatization vouchers will be issued to every Russian citizen, regardless of age, between October 1 and December 1, 1992.

The rationale behind the Russian voucher scheme is to generate demand for shares of privatized enterprises, to insure a greater degree of fairness in the distribution of resources through the privatization process, and to generate political support for the privatization process, both among the enterprise insiders and ordinary citizens.

Unlike some other voucher programs, such as the Czechoslovak or the Polish ones, the Russian scheme did not create a separate program for the sale of shares and assets for vouchers. Rather, it integrates voucher payments with purchases for cash, and preferential sales to enterprise insiders. Consequently, all vouchers will have a nominal value expressed in rubles and will be accepted at face value by the privatization authorities, although their market value is apt to be different from their nominal value, and is likely to change over time. Again, unlike a number of other voucher programs, the Russian scheme makes vouchers freely and unambiguously alienable, creating a separate market for these certificates, and allowing their concentration in fewer hands.

The program envisages the issuance of several consecutive tranches of vouchers, each with an expiration date (which cannot be less than one year or more than two years from the date of issue) designed to reduce the likelihood that vouchers would become an alternative form of general currency. Once used to purchase shares or assets of privatized enterprises (their acceptance as means of payment for other purposes is prohibited), the vouchers will be extinguished and not reintroduced into circulation. The nominal value of each voucher issued in the first tranche (starting October 1, 1992) will be Rb 10,000, and its validity will be from December 1, 1992, to December 31, 1993. The initial date was set to coincide with the expected completion of the wholesale corporatization of large and medium-size Russian enterprises and the creation of a very large supply of securities issued by newly created state-owned joint-stock companies. But the very tight schedule of the corporatization program raises the possibility that vouchers will have become available long before it is known which companies' shares will be available, thus creating a disturbing element of uncertainty. (See the subsection on privatization of large enterprises, above, and Section 5 on corporatization, below.)

The only body empowered to issue privatization vouchers is the federal government; local authorities are specifically prohibited from issuing their own. Apparently, the fear of inflationary effects and a loss of confidence in the program due to the possibility of the circulation of an uncontrolled number of vouchers persuaded the Russian authorities to restrict the program in this way. The voucher program will also be funded by the federal government: it is designed to cover the sale of 35 per cent of all shares of all privatized enterprises. The proportion of privatization proceeds will be channelled to the federal budget. (See the subsection on the distribution of proceeds from privatization in Section 4A, above.)[38] Local authorities also can, but are not required to, accept vouchers in part payment of their share of the privatization proceeds.[39] In effect, then, the federal government is giving up its share of the proceeds of privatization in 1993, in favor of a free distribution to the Russian citizens.

The distribution of vouchers will be handled by the State Savings Bank, which has branches in all the localities. The recipients must pay

---

[38] Apparently, the proportion of assets sold for vouchers is to be increased.

[39] The decree leaves unclear what happens when local governments do not want to receive vouchers as a part of their share of the privatization proceeds (in effect, refusing to distribute a part of their budgetary allotment to the population). Other provisions of the decree seem to make it clear that vouchers must be accepted as payment in full during the privatization process. If they are therefore used to acquire more than the federal share of the proceeds, and local authorities do not want to take part in the free distribution, the federal budget would be bound to make up the difference.

a Rb 25 handling charge. A list of all eligible recipients will be provided to the Bank by the authorities in charge of issuing residence permits, with special provisions being made for unusual cases.

Once citizens receive their vouchers, they will be able to use them in the following ways: 1) to purchase shares of any corporatized state enterprise on the same terms as if the payments were in cash (see the subsection on the privatization of large enterprises above); 2) to purchase state assets at auctions (see the subsection on the privatization of small enterprises above); 3) to exchange them for shares of special investment funds created in connection with the voucher program (see below pp. 70–71); 4) to sell them for cash without any restrictions. An additional rule, now apparently changed, required that any buyer of shares or assets from the state had to pay at least 35 per cent of the price in vouchers.[40] This last rule ensured that the entire share of privatization proceeds due the federal budget would indeed be converted into a free distribution, and that the value of vouchers could not fall much below the value of 35 per cent of all the assets to be privatized during the period of the vouchers' validity. (It also ensured that the market value of the vouchers would automatically adjust for inflation.) What was not guaranteed was that the markets in which vouchers are used would clear: it remained possible that a significant portion of the vouchers would remain unused before the expiration of their validity, or that shortages of vouchers could develop in the later stages of the program (perhaps even slowing down the privatization process). The latter possibility was particularly disturbing in light of the fact that vouchers, on the one hand, have nominal value and, if used together with money, had to be accepted as means of payment at face value, and, on the other hand, had to be used to cover at least 35 per cent of the purchase price of a whole range of assets. If these assets were to be sold exclusively at some artificial price not subject to inflation (as is the case when shares are sold to employees at book value), the problem would not be very serious. But to the extent that the assets sold during privatization are sold at market prices (as will be the case when auctions or

---

[40] See the transcript of the August 21, 1992 press conference of Minister Chubais. There is nothing in the decree or official discussions that would exclude foreigners from this requirement, nor is there anything in them that would preclude foreigners from buying up vouchers.

public tenders are used), the nominal sale prices are likely to skyrocket during the next year, as inflation erodes the value of the ordinary ruble. This means, however, that in order to satisfy the requirement that 35 per cent of the purchase price must be paid in vouchers, average buyers would need to buy a huge number of vouchers with nominal values of Rb 10,000 each, resulting in a severe shortage of vouchers.

The consideration just raised is only a special case of the general problem arising when the use of vouchers is combined with the use of money. Since prices of privatized assets and shares must be expressed in rubles, it becomes necessary to assign a monetary value to the vouchers as well (something that has been avoided in Czecho-slovakia, for example), and it would be difficult (although not impossi-ble) to rely on their market value alone. The authors of the Russian program have therefore decided to give the vouchers a nominal value. Even they have no reliable way of ensuring that this number even approximately corresponded to the market value of the vouchers. This was bound to create some problems and a degree of confusion among the recipients, who might lose confidence in the program if the market price of the vouchers falls far below their nominal value or if they sell their vouchers prematurely, not realizing that the real value greatly exceeded the nominal price.

Apparently as a result of this type of consideration, the State Property Committee has abandoned the idea of mixing vouchers with money in the same auctions, and now intends to run separate auctions for a certain percentage of the shares, in which only vouchers will be used.[41] But vouchers will still be used together with money in the initial stages of the program, when enterprise insiders will purchase shares offered to them on the preferential terms specified in the State Program. This fact also makes the nominal value of the vouchers particularly problematic. Since, as discussed in the subsection on the privatization of large enterprises, the value of shares sold to the insiders in the Russian privatization program is determined on the basis of the company's book value unadjusted for inflation, the vouchers are apt to acquire tremendous purchasing power in the hands of lucky insiders whose enterprises have some positive value. We have mentioned already that Volga taxi cabs may be valued

---

[41] The question still remains as to whether vouchers would have to be accepted in lieu of cash in the remaining auctions.

at Rb 2,000 to Rb 3,000. On the basis of such data, the chairman of the State Property Committee, Mr. Chubais, has also stated that one voucher will have the real worth of Rb 150,000 to 200,000.[42] Indeed, in an enterprise employing 1,000 people, the value of the vouchers distributed to insiders and their families might easily come to Rb 30 or 40 mln (counting three to four persons per family). Since the State Program seems to associate the number of 1,000 employees with the book value of Rb 50 mln of fixed assets,[43] one can conjecture that the insiders who choose Variant II for their preferential treatment (see the subsection on privatization of large enterprises above) will easily be able to use their vouchers to purchase the full 51 per cent of the shares of their state enterprise (to which the State Program makes entitled them) and still have vouchers to spare.[44] In effect, then, the voucher program seems to give the controlling blocks of state enterprises to the insiders free of charge.[45,46]

The Russian voucher program also contains provisions concerning the creation of special investment funds, which will be able to collect vouchers from the population in exchange for their own shares, and use the vouchers to purchase shares or assets of privatized enterprises. These shares or assets will then be held by the funds in trust for the funds' shareholders. Investment funds of this kind are common to many large-scale free distribution schemes and can fulfill two important functions. First, the investment funds allow an average investor to diversify his modest assets and rely on the expertise of the fund to determine the best method of investment. Second, they can lead to a

---

[42] *Izvestia*, August 31, 1992. Mr. Chubais has at one point referred to his informal calculations as "figures of speech backed up by real calculations." Press conference of August 21, 1992.

[43] These two figures are the interchangeable benchmarks defining "large" enterprises.

[44] This will be true even if the price is 1.7 of the book value. See above, footnote 25.

[45] Decree 914 specifically states that vouchers may be used to pay "in full" for the privatized assets and that refusal to accept vouchers as a means of payment during privatization is forbidden. This seems to preclude a limitation on the proportion of shares that may be purchased with vouchers. See also footnote 39 above. But documents drafted by the State Property Committee mention a limitation that would allow workers using Variant II to pay for only 50 per cent of their shares with vouchers.

[46] Another feature of the Russian program, contained in the State Program, additionally strengthens the position of insiders who must come up with some purchase funds in addition to vouchers: the program allows the existing commercial banks (though not the Central Bank) to lend without restrictions for the purpose of privatization. Given the established relations between commercial banks and the enterprise *nomenklatura*, this provision may turn out to be a source of unlimited credit.

concentration of holdings which may be used to exert influence on the management of the privatized enterprises. It is unlikely that a very large number of small investors, facing serious collective action problems, could do the same.

At the time of this writing, the Russian investment funds are expected to be private institutions, governed by a special set of regulations, which will be issued in September 1992. These regulations will provide a simplified registration procedure for participating investment funds (as distinct from normal mutual funds, which will not be able to purchase vouchers in exchange for their shares), and will require that they are organized as open joint-stock companies, with at least 50 per cent of their shares exchanged for vouchers. The draft regulations also require that the funds be invested in at least ten companies, which has been criticized as insufficient for proper diversification under Russian conditions. But even if the investment funds are able to provide the means of diversification and expert advice to the beneficiaries of a Russian voucher program,[47] they are unlikely to be very effective in fulfilling the second of the functions we have mentioned, namely, assuring the presence of an active owner in the corporate governance structure of the privatized enterprises, since the draft regulations also prohibit the funds from buying more than 10 per cent of the shares of any given enterprise.[48]

Privatization of land and agriculture

Russia's land reform has been very slow, and a number of laws and decrees repeatedly addressed the problem of the transformation of the huge but hopelessly inefficient agricultural sector. Solutions advanced in recent years have all tended to increase the size of private farming and convert the remaining collective and state farms into more business-oriented institutions. As with privatization elsewhere, however, government officials and bureaucrats in charge of the state farming sector have opposed most centrally-advanced measures. It is only

---

[47] Interestingly, the first deputy chairman of the State Property Committee, Alexander I. Ivanenko, speaking in his official capacity on Russian television (on August 28, 1992), stated that "the most appropriate way of using the privatization vouchers is to acquire shares in state enterprises," rather than putting them in an investment fund.

[48] A Decree on the Organization of the Securities Market was issued by President Yeltsin on October 7, 1992. Attached to it, as Annex 2, was a statute on specialized privatization investment funds defining the procedure for the constitution and activities of investment funds accumulating privatization vouchers.

very recently that the radical measures undertaken by President Yeltsin have begun to yield significant results.

During their early stages, the main purpose of the new laws was to provide recognition of the very concept of private property in land. The 1990 Property Act introduced the principle of equality of all types of property, including private ownership of land. The act also recognized the right of all natural persons to acquire plots of land for possession and enjoyment (usufruct). Concrete steps to introduce private ownership of land were taken in the 1991 Land Code, which provided that the local soviets would sell or, below a stipulated minimum, distribute *gratis* land to persons who apply for it in connection with certain types of economic activity and housing construction. An important restriction remained, however, in the form of a ten-year moratorium on the alienation of land acquired by private persons.

The changes effected by this legislation, until the end of 1991, were very modest: 40,000 private farms created in 1991 amounted to only one per cent of all arable land. Although the cost of farm machinery may have deterred some individuals from establishing their own farms, the main obstacle was resistance from local authorities. Conservative officials in charge of collective and state farms either refused requests for private land or parcelled out barren and undeveloped plots.

In December of 1991, President Yeltsin responded to this problem with an aptly titled decree on "Urgent Measures for the Implementation of Land Reform in the RSFSR," which calls for mandatory reorganization of all state and collective farms before the end of 1992. By that time, all farms were to bring their legal form into conformity with the Enterprise Law and other normative acts of the Russian Federation. Workers on existing farms had to decide by March 1992 on one of the following three reorganization paths: (a) to dissolve the collective and state farms and acquire their share of the land; (b) to transform the collective into a joint-stock company; or (c) to re-register the collective as a cooperative with a share form of ownership.

As of August 1992, 8,000 farms completed their transformation under the new decree. Five thousand of these decided to stay as collective farms with a share form of ownership, more than 300 became open joint-stock companies, and many others split up into closed joint-stock companies, mixed partnerships, and other kinds of cooperatives. The number of private farms increased to over 135,000, the average size of which was equal to 41 hectares. To support this process, Rb 6.5 bln has been allocated from the central budget for aid to private farming. While progress has been achieved, complaints are often heard in Russia that the managers of many of the newly reorganized large farms have succeeded in including a number of restrictive provisions in the bylaws of the new farming entities, thus preserving much of the *status quo ante*.

Whatever modest success has been achieved is partly due to special provisions in the "Urgent Measures" which force collective and state farm managers, under threat of loss of pay, to identify land for private farming as a first priority, and to approve farmers' requests for private land within one month of application. The titles to land previously allocated for subsidiary farming, gardening, and housing construction were freely transferred to farmers who previously had only the right of possession. Farmers were also granted, for the first time, the right to mortgage their land and receive bank credits.

Despite these changes, the "Urgent Measures" failed to remove the most important restrictions on the sale of land. Under the new decree, land can only be sold if: (a) the owner is retiring; (b) the owner inherits the land; (c) the owner is resettling with the aim of organizing a private farm on land made available through another redistribution scheme created under the same decree; or (d) the proceeds from the sale of land are being invested in food processing, trade, or construction services in rural areas. An anachronism for most Russians,[49] the restriction on land sales has provoked much controversy. The Russian parliament, which is influenced by a strong agrarian lobby dominated by the old guard, repeatedly blocked attempts to amend the Russian Constitution (written in 1978, under Soviet rule) to allow unrestricted sale of land, despite President Yeltsin's threat to resolve the matter in a national referendum.

A separate chapter in the story of land privatization concerns nonagricultural land. The Presidential Decree No. 301 on "The Sale of Land Plots to Individuals and Legal Entities During Privatization of State and Municipal Enterprises", issued in March 1992, sanctioned the right to privatize land plots during privatization of state enterprises, but failed to specify a detailed procedure. This was accomplished in a separate act, Decree No. 631 "On Approving the Order of Sale of Land Plots During Privatization of State Enterprises" (1992). In this way, restrictions contained in the Land Code, which allowed private acquisitions of only leasing and usufructual interests, have been removed. But the right of land acquisition (which is open to foreigners

---

[49] An August 25, 1992 poll found that almost 55 per cent of all Russians believe that free sale of land should form the basis of privatization.

as well) must still be exercised after the acquisition of a privatized enterprise, and the government may impose additional restrictions. Moreover, land is still subject to a ten-year moratorium on sales. Finally, acquisition of land not connected with the privatization of a state enterprise is also allowed, but only for the purpose of expansion of an existing business. Sales of land for this purpose are to be made by competitive bidding, or by an auction open only to the owners of privatized enterprises.

Privatization of housing

Housing privatization in Russia is regulated by the Housing Privatization Act of July of 1991. The act was the first uniform law on housing privatization, and replaced several ineffective 1988 decrees. Though incomplete, the act goes a long way in privatizing the 2.4 bln square meters of state-owned housing. Through a combination of gratuitous transfers and sales, the act created over 400,000 privatized apartments in the first five months of 1992, amounting to 20 mln square meters of living space. Combined with the October 1991 elimination of residence permits, housing privatization has made substantial progress towards a free market system.

Under the act, Russian citizens and families who live in state-owned apartments are permitted to acquire legal title to their apartments, including the right to sell, lease, and bequeath them. The act grants a certain amount of living space free of charge, leaving the exact space limit for gratuitous transfers to the discretion of local governments (though it does not stipulate that this limit cannot be less than eighteen square meters per person and nine extra meters for families). With respect to additional space, the act prescribes a more complicated procedure, allowing residents to purchase the remainder at a price determined by a government official who must assess the quality and size of the apartment. Money collected in this way is earmarked for improving housing conditions. (As of May 1992, only 25 per cent of privatized living space had generated any revenues.)

The success or failure of housing privatization under the act depends on the initiative of the appropriate local bureaucracy. In Moscow, for example, government officials have aggressively pursued housing privatization and provided generous free housing allotments. In fact, Moscow accounts for 40 per cent of all gratuitously privatized apartments in Russia. On the other hand, government bureaucracy and corruption have stifled housing privatization in St. Petersburg, where a mere 1,841 apartments have been privatized as of June 1992, amounting to only Rb 5 mln in revenues.

One of the problems with the existing law is that it confers a legal sanction on existing inequalities resulting from the system through which Soviet authorities distributed housing stock among their supporters. However, the fact that the law gives the old *nomenklatura* the opportunity to convert their privileged housing allotments into valuable legal titles provides a significant incentive for the bureaucracy to proceed with greater speed with the privatization of housing, and thus ensures an effective and quick market allocation of the existing stock of housing. At the same time, the freeing of rents and maintenance costs necessary for such a market is also apt to lead to a dramatic rise in housing costs for the average family. This, together with the legal sanctioning of the existing inequalities, might make housing privatization very unpopular.

Spontaneous privatization

In purely quantitative terms, it is possible that the greatest part of privatization has been unofficial, informal, spontaneous, and of dubious legality. We have alluded at various points to the mechanisms through which *nomenklatura* insiders have been able to convert their controlling positions in many enterprises into legal titles of one kind or another. Other mechanisms through which state assets have been converted into private ownership involved joint-venture arrangements with foreign participants receiving state assets at a very low price in exchange for kickbacks to insiders in the form of ownership participation, bribes, and jobs with special privileges. Siphoning assets from state enterprises, through phony sales and other contractual arrangements, is also said to be very common. Having said all this, however, it is important to note that, despite the wealth of anecdotal evidence and the mythical dimensions of spontaneous privatization, no genuine data are available on the size of this phenomenon, nor do we have a systematic overview of its forms.

5. CORPORATIZATION

Corporatization, i.e., the conversion of state enterprises into joint-stock companies, is often referred to in Russia as "commercialization," since the transformed enterprises become governed by a new legal regime of commercial law, common to both public and private business organizations. The origins of this process in Russia antedate the demise of the Soviet Union, and go back to the practice of transforming sectoral and branch ministries. During this process, governed not by a well-defined set of procedures, but mostly by *ad hoc* decisions of the Council of Ministers, the branch ministries themselves would often be abolished and transformed into one or more "associations" of enterprises, organized as closed joint-stock companies under the Soviet joint-stock company law of 1990. Following the creation of an association, a number of its constituent enterprises would also be transformed into joint-stock companies. (For more information, see the subsection on industrial associations in Section 3A above.)

The purpose of these early conversions was quite distinct from that which became dominant in the Privatization Law and subsequent Russian legal norms governing corporatization. The aim of the more recent Russian legislation on corporatization has been to make enterprises managerially more independent from ministerial administration, while at the same time clarifying the ownership relations in the state sector and reasserting the rights of the state as proprietor of state enterprises. By contrast, the earlier corporatizations were usually motivated by the desire to perpetuate the power of the industrial *nomenklatura* by transforming ministerial structures into new legal forms governed by commercial law, while at the same time obfuscating further the question of state ownership and making it more difficult for political branches to push through a more radical program of structural reform. An additional incentive for corporatization under the old regime was the possibility it raised for the *nomenklatura* in control of the new structures to follow up a conversion into joint-stock company form with a maze of self-dealing transactions, as a result of which a good portion of the shares might end up in the hands of a few privileged insiders.

The basic principle of corporatization introduced by the Privatization Law of 1991 and the subsequent decrees and regulations was to impose the control of the State Property Committee and its local equivalents over the conversion process and to create well defined bodies – the property funds of the federal and local governments – authorized to exercise ownership rights on behalf of the state. At the same time, the transformed enterprises would be removed from their dependence on the old branch ministries and enjoined to act in accordance with the same norms of commercial law as the private sector.

The Privatization Law and the Acceleration Decree, which contained special Interim Regulations Concerning Reorganization of State and Municipal Enterprises into Open Joint-Stock Companies (Supplement No. 3), set a uniform procedure for corporatization, but did not make the conversion of all state enterprises, even those subject to eventual privatization, automatic. Instead, corporatization could proceed on an enterprise-by-enterprise basis on the initiative of the State Property Committee, its local equivalents, or other parties specified in the Privatization Law (the work collective, potential investors, etc.)[50] In addition, the government of the Russian Federation and the local governments could also initiate the conversion process. The decision concerning corporatization was left to the territorial agencies of the State Property Committee and its local counterparts, and the property committees were made the exclusive founders of state-owned joint-stock companies.

The procedure prescribed by the earlier legislative enactments has been significantly modified by Presidential Decree No. 721 and the accompanying Commercialization Statute. These acts abandoned the old enterprise-by-enterprise approach, and specified in general terms which enterprises must be corporatized, and a rigid timetable for their simultaneous conversion. With the exception of those enterprises prohibited from privatization by the State Program (see the subsection on the scope of privatization envisaged in the State Program in Section 4B, above), the decree makes corporatization mandatory for all state enterprises with more than 1,000 employees or fixed assets valued at more than Rb 50 mln. With respect to state enterprises with fewer than 200 employees and Rb 10 mln of fixed assets, the choice of whether to follow the corporatization route specified in the decree is left to their work collectives. The ability of some of the remaining enterprises to corporatize is left somewhat unclear.[51] The timetable prescribed for

---

[50] For more information, see the subsection on initial privatization procedures in Section 4B above.

[51] See the subsection on the methods of privatization envisaged by the State Program in Section 4B above, and especially footnote 16.

mandatory conversions requires that the process be completed by November 1, 1992, and very strict time periods are prescribed for particular phases of the entire operation. The prescribed deadlines are sometimes extremely short. For example, property committees are given seven days from the filing of the appropriate documents to examine them and confirm the proposed privatization plans. Given that several thousand enterprises will be converting at the same time, and that the privatization proposals involve such complex matters as enterprise valuation, the pressure on the committees is likely to be enormous. (See also the subsection on initial privatization procedures in Section 4B above.)

All conversions must result in an open joint-stock company and must be prepared by the enterprise privatization commissions form involved (which means that corporatization always involves the preparation of a privatization plan). But the Commercialization Statute is much more specific in this respect, and provides a model joint-stock company statute that the privatization commissions must use. The new joint-stock company is to take over all assets and liabilities of the state enterprise, except for assets the privatization of which is subject to special conditions, and certain "social and cultural facilities" which are entrusted to the new company, but not counted as part of its initial authorized capital.

Upon the completion of the corporatization process, the property committee responsible for the conversion must convey all shares owned by the state to the appropriate (federal or local) property fund, which becomes the body representing the state as the owner of the new company. (See Section 4A, above, for more information concerning the role and the governance structure of property funds.)

An interesting feature of the Russian corporatization program is the attempt to limit the influence of property funds on the governance of companies remaining partially in the state sector. The original limitation, contained in the Privatization Law, permitted the property funds to vote only 20 per cent of the shares of any given company. All remaining shares held by the funds, regardless of their nominal status, had the provisional status of preferred shares with a fixed dividend equal to the bank discount rate. This provision was clearly designed to diminish the power of the state over companies even prior to their full privatization, and to assure that as the fund begins to sell its shares private buyers can acquire more power *vis à vis* the state than they would normally be entitled to on the basis of their percentage of ownership. The sense of this provision shifted, however, when it became clear that under all variants of insider preferences specified in the State Program, the corporatization of Russian enterprises would immediately be followed by a distribution of shares (with or without payment) to workers and other insiders.[52] The percentage of voting shares acquired by insiders under Variants II and III of the Russian large-scale privatization plan is immediately greater than 20 per cent, and it is likely to stand at 15 per cent in the case of Variant I.[53] Under the new conditions, the "20 per cent rule" would give insiders immediate voting control of the enterprise,[54] and the state could not realize its goal of asserting itself as owner. Moreover, the arrangement would give a clear incentive to insiders to try to prevent real privatization, since the remaining state equity, receiving dividends at a fixed rate equal to the bank discount rate, would in fact be a low-interest loan (without guaranteed interest payments), while it would be converted into full-fledged common stock upon sale to private parties.[55]

Most likely for reasons of this kind, the model joint-stock company statute attached to Decree 721 seems to have changed the earlier provisions of the Privatization Law and provided that the state will receive 25 per cent of the authorized capital in the form of a special class of preferred shares (denominated "class B") and the rest in ordinary (voting) common stock. These preferred shares will be nonvoting and

---

[52] In this the Russian system of preferential treatment of insiders is different from the Polish one, for example, which mandates the sale of shares on special terms to the insiders only at the time the company is actually privatized. The decision to distribute the shares to the insiders directly following corporatization, and without regard to when the rest of the shares will be sold, was first made in the Privatization Law, and is also embodied in the Commercialization Statute. With the unfortunately common inconsistency of Russian legislative enactments, the State Program for some reason speaks of the distribution to insiders "when shares are sold."

[53] This is the proportion of common shares the workers and the managers are entitled to purchase under Variant I, in addition to the preferred shares distributed free of charge. For more information, see the subsection on the privatization of large enterprises in Section 4B above.

[54] Even under Variant I, 20 per cent of the shares of the property fund would represent only 12 per cent of the authorized capital (since including the freely distributed shares, 40 per cent of the authorized capital would go to the insiders).

[55] Of course, if the enterprise were to bring positive profits below the discount rate, the insiders would have an incentive to bring in an outside investor in order to diminish the interest payments on the "loan" from the state. But this incentive would not be very strong, and the outside investor would probably be reluctant to come in at a time when profits are low.

will be entitled to a fixed dividend equal to 5 per cent of the preceding fiscal year's profits, with the proviso that if the dividends on the common stock are greater than those on the preferred shares, the latter will be increased to the point of equality. (For some considerations pertaining to this arrangement, see the discussion of class A preferred shares in the subsection on the privatization of large enterprises in Section 4B.) Upon sale to a private investor, these shares will automatically be converted to ordinary common stock. The fund will be able to vote its common stock in the same way as any other investor, and as long as it holds over 50 per cent of the common stock, it will also be able to make a number of important decisions, such as deciding upon the liquidation or division of the company, specifying the contracts (and presumably appointments) of all administrative officers, and setting the salaries for all board members, without a general shareholders' meeting. There are also no provisions as to the order in which the state must sell its holdings, so that it may begin by selling the preferred shares and hold on to its common stock in order to establish a voting alliance with outside investors.

Another noteworthy feature of the legislative framework of corporatization is the provision for the possibility of delegation of the ownership rights enjoyed by the property funds. The earlier provision, contained in the Interim Regulations on corporatization (Supplement 3 to the Acceleration Decree), stated that the property fund could, under certain circumstances, invite representatives of ministries to exercise the powers of the proprietors at shareholders' meetings of companies controlled by the state. Decree 721 takes a somewhat different tack, without mentioning the earlier provisions. Instead, it states that the property funds "shall be advised" (the decree does not say by whom) to enter into contracts with investors qualified under Article 9 of the Privatization Law (i.e., individuals and institutions, with less than 25 per cent of equity in the hands of the state, including companies and partnerships formed by work collectives), making those investors trustees of blocks of shares, pending the sale of these shares during privatization. Presumably these contracts would go to prospective buyers of the company shares who would get a sort of management contract prior to the actual purchase. According to press reports, the arrangement would also allow the "trustees" to use the enterprise profits to purchase new shares unconditionally. At the same time, however, the decree gives work collectives a veto power over any such contracts, thus making them dependent on insider approval. If, as expected, the "advice" given to property funds is difficult for them to ignore, insiders will have, for all practical purposes, won the battle for the control of Russian enterprises. The press accounts expect work collectives, the managers, and officers of the industrial associations to be among the prime contestants for trusteeships of lucrative state ventures. Outside private investors are only marginally mentioned.

Finally, an important feature of Decree 721 is its treatment of industrial associations, concerns, etc. (See the subsection on industrial associations in Section 3A above.) The State Program had already previously declared that no new companies could be created on the basis of existing associations, unless such companies were brought into line with the laws of the Russian Federation (as opposed to the old *ad hoc* Soviet acts establishing the associations), and that the property funds would become the exclusive legal successors of all state organs as founders of commercial companies. Decree 721 goes further. First of all, it mandates the corporatization of all state enterprises regardless of their membership in any trusts, associations, concerns, etc., and the terms on which these enterprises are converted are the same as those in force with respect to all other enterprises. This means, among other things, that property funds will become the owners of all the stock not assigned to insiders, in accordance with the state program, and acquire corresponding rights of ownership. Furthermore, the decree requires a conversion into open joint-stock companies of all other business entities with more than 50 per cent state ownership, thus eliminating from the state sector all closed joint-stock companies and Soviet hybrid forms of business organization. Finally, the decree requires the conversion of all industrial associations themselves into bodies conforming to Russian legislation (although the associations do not have to take the form of open joint-stock companies), and eliminates their special status acquired by virtue of the plethora of special regulations. The decree set a particularly short period of time for the regularization of the status of associations, since it called on all of the heads of constituent enterprises to convene a meeting of the managerial organ of their associations by August 1, 1992, and decide which of the recognized legal forms (partnership or joint-stock company) the association should have in the future. In deciding the division of ownership rights in the new association, the enterprises' share will be determined in accordance with their accumulated contribution in the form of money and securities, while the property contributed in kind, as well as all the property conveyed to the association by administrative organs of the state, will be considered state contributions, with the appropriate shares of the new associations presumably transferred to property funds. Supervision over the whole process, and the task of issuing the appropriate regulations, have been vested in the State Property Committee. Finally, in order to break the power of the huge conglomerates characteristic of the former Soviet economy, the decree allows the transformation into separate joint-stock companies of individual divisions of enterprises or associations of enterprises, without requiring the consent of the parent organizations. The divisions, if they are of a size that would require or allow their corporatization if they had been independent enterprises, may be transformed upon the vote of their work collectives, without prior transformation into independent state enterprises.

The concrete governance arrangements common to all state-owned joint-stock companies resulting from the process of corporatization are provided in the model statutes attached to Decree 721. They basically conform to the rules set forth in the 1990 Statute on Joint-Stock Companies, with a few important special provisions made for the period during which the state holds 50 per cent or more of the shares of new companies. During that time, the Board of Directors of corporatized enterprises will be composed of representatives of (one each) the appropriate property fund (or, prior to the transfer of shares to the fund, the appropriate property committee), the work collective, and the local government. The Director General or his representative will be the *ex officio* chairman of the Board of Directors, and will have two votes. Even when the state share falls under 50 per cent, the property fund will retain a veto power over changes in the organizational and legal form of the company for as long as the state remains a shareholder.

No data on the effects of Decree 721 were available at the time of the writing of this report. According to State Property Committee officials, however, more than 6,000 privatization commissions have been established in Russian enterprises as of August 10, 1992, 2,000 of which were in enterprises for which corporatization was not mandatory. The process is said to have slowed down somewhat in August because enterprises were expecting even more preferential terms to be offered to the insiders. Officials expect some delays with respect to the very short deadlines specified in the decree, but they also expect 70 per cent of the enterprises to meet the deadlines, and the delays to involve "several weeks or months."

UKRAINE

CONTENTS

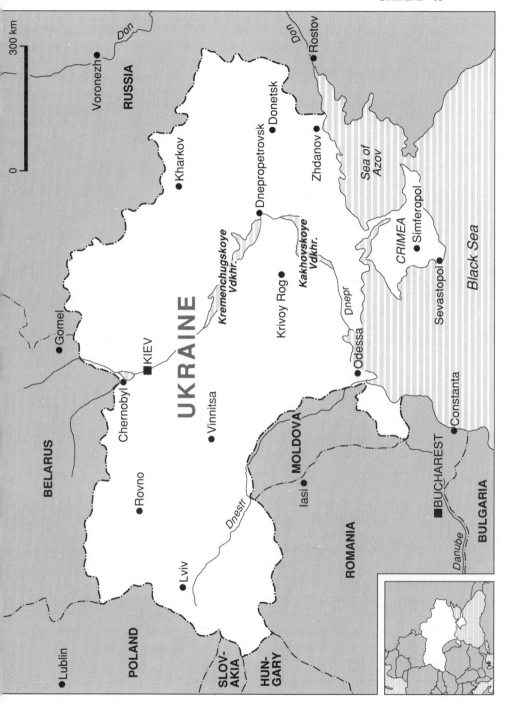

1. INTRODUCTION

Brief history of reforms

The republic of Ukraine comprises 2.6 per cent of the territory of the former Soviet Union, and 18 per cent of its population (about 52 mln persons). Ukraine proclaimed independence from the Soviet Union on August 24, 1991, immediately after the failed coup attempt. Independence was ratified by a referendum held on December 1, 1991.

Prior to independence, the economic policies of the republican administration were subordinated to the plans and policies of the union government. As a result, Ukraine began its independent life with little of the institutional and legal infrastructure necessary to formulate and implement economic policies of its own.

In the fall of 1991, Ukraine initiated the process of building its own governmental and economic institutions. A number of laws have been adopted dealing with property rights, forms of economic organizations, foreign investment activity, tax structure and other areas of economic life. The government also formulated a reform strategy which envisaged carrying out some essential de-monopolization of industry and privatization of state property before the liberalization of prices. Massive price liberalization in Russia in January 1992, however, forced a change in the sequence of Ukrainian reform measures. In early January, the Ukrainian government liberalized prices of goods and services accounting for about 60–70 per cent of the value of consumer expenditures. The authorities retained control over the prices of many key commodities.

Although the government has repeatedly stated its general commitment to a transition to a market economy, the formulation and implementation of a systematic reform strategy has become frustrated to some degree by the absence of a clear division of power and responsibility among the legislature, government ministries and the Central Bank. Moreover, Ukraine's reform efforts have been stalled by in-fighting within the government and parliament between the progressive faction, which advocates a radical transformation of the economy, and the conservatives, who prefer a much less decisive reform program. The dismissal of Deputy Prime Minister Volodymyr Lanovoi in July 1992 has been interpreted as a sign of substantial weakening of the group favoring a radical transformation of the Ukrainian economy.

2. ECONOMIC ENVIRONMENT

The structure of output

The gross domestic product (GDP) of Ukraine in current prices was Rb 166 bln[1] in 1990, and Rb 233 bln in 1991.

The share of industry in Ukrainian output has been similar to that prevailing in the former Soviet Union, while the agricultural sector has been relatively larger.

Table 2.1 The structure of net material product in 1989 (in per cent of total)

	Ukraine	Soviet Union
Industry	43	42
Agriculture	28	23
Construction	11	13
Foreign trade	6*	9
Transport and communications	5	6
Other	7	7

* Including trade with other republics of the Soviet Union.

Source: "Ukraine," and "The Economy of the Former USSR," *IMF Economic Review*, April 1992.

Output

The GNP of Ukraine in 1990 prices declined 2.4 per cent in 1990, which accelerated to 7.5 per cent decline in 1991. Net Material Product (NMP) is estimated to have fallen by at least 11 per cent in 1991, led by a 16 per cent drop in construction. The industry and transport sectors declined by about 10 per cent, while agriculture fell by about 7 per cent.

The economy continued to decline in the first quarter of 1992, with GDP falling by 20 per cent compared with the same period of 1991.

---

[1] According to *PlanEcon*, the average "commercial" ruble–dollar rate was 1.76 in 1990, 1.74 in 1991. It should be noted that these rates are distorted and thus dollar equivalents of local statistics are useful only for superficial illustrative purposes.

Industrial production fell by 15.3 per cent in the same period. However, the rate of decline in production slowed from 19.3 per cent in January to 9.2 per cent in March. According to official reports, industrial production for the first eight months of 1992 was 10.0 per cent below its level for the same period in 1991.

Investment

After a small increase of 1.9 per cent in 1990, gross investment in fixed capital fell by 11 per cent in 1991. The share of net investment in NMP also dropped from about 18 per cent in 1990 to 13 per cent in 1991.

Household savings

There is no reliable estimate of the total stock of household savings in Ukraine, since a significant proportion of savings has probably been kept outside the official banking system. According to the IMF monetary survey, the total amounts of time and demand deposits officially held by households by the end of 1991 were Rb 48.8 bln and Rb 63.9 bln, respectively.

Price liberalization

As noted earlier, Ukraine introduced price liberalization in January 1992. The measure freed prices for goods accounting for approximately 60–70 per cent of all consumer expenditures. Price increases for other goods, which remained under government control, ranged from 200 per cent for coal for household use to 12,000 per cent for electricity for rural consumers. The price of coal for industrial use was increased twenty-two times. However, since the price of oil remained low, this drastic increase in the price of coal exacerbated, rather than eliminated, existing distortions of the prices of energy inputs. The government also introduced ceilings for the prices of some basic foodstuffs, consumer goods, and industrial inputs.

The measures announced were designed to limit the number of products with regulated prices. However, in the first few days following price liberalization, prices of many goods soared five to ten times above their prior level. Under pressure from the parliament, the government reasserted control over prices of additional goods, including dairy products and sausages. Food prices were further decontrolled during the summer of 1992. While virtually all prices were increased in January 1992, prices on many goods and services remaining under government control are still far below world market levels.

Inflation

In 1990, the inflation rate in Ukraine was 4.2 per cent. Inflation accelerated considerably in 1991. Retail prices for goods and services rose 84.5 per cent for the year, while prices of food and non-food items increased by 79 per cent and 88 per cent respectively.

Prices rose by approximately 1,000 per cent during the first four months of 1992, although price increases moderated somewhat in May. However, prices are still forecast to increase by 2,000–3,000 per cent over the entire year.

Table 2.2 Quarterly retail price index (per cent change, from the same period of the previous year)

| | 1991 | | | |
	Q1	Q2	Q3	Q4
Aggregate index	13.2	90.5	99.5	120.0
including food	7.0	88.0	88.6	101.0
non-food	17.7	92.4	108.6	135.6

Source: "Ukraine," *IMF Economic Review*, April 1992.

Table 2.3 Monthly retail price index (month-to-month per cent change)

| | 1992 | | | |
	May	June	July	August
Aggregate index	26.5	22	8.3	10.5
including food			70.4*	12.7
non-food			30.2	13.2

* April 1992 is taken as a base month

Source: *Ukrainian Ministry of Finance*

Behavior of wages

The wage structure in Ukraine is based on a system of minimum wage norms set for six different occupational categories. The resulting wage structure is rather dense, with about 75 per cent of workers in industry earning approximately two to two-and-a-half times the minimum wage. In May 1992, the minimum wage was raised to Rb 900 per month.

A sliding-scale wage indexation system, which provides for differentiated compensation for price increases, depending on the relationship of a worker's actual wage to the minimum wage, was enacted in October 1991.

The average nominal monthly wage more than doubled between the fourth quarter of 1990 and the fourth quarter of 1991.

Table 2.4 Average monthly wage (excluding collective farm workers, in rubles)

| | 1991 | | | | | 1992 | |
	Q1	Q2	Q3	Q4	Jan–June	Aug	Sept
Average monthly wage	255	357	435	600	3,072	5,706	7,690

Source: "Ukraine," *IMF Economic Review*, April 1992, and the *Ukrainian Ministry of Finance*.

The authorities have tried to use direct controls to limit wage increases in state enterprises. In April 1992, the parliament adopted a resolution to freeze wages at the level of the January–April average. In response, the managers of large industrial enterprises increased the April wage levels by 100 to 700 per cent. These increases were largely financed by credits extended by state banks. The resulting average level of nominal monthly wages in industry for the first six months of 1992, Rb 3,895, was eleven times higher than the average for the first six months of 1991.

Unemployment

As in other former republics, the drop in output in Ukraine in 1991 was not accompanied by a commensurate reduction in employment. However, according to the Ministry of Finance, the number of registered unemployed persons increased drastically from about 24,000 at the end of 1991, to 300,000, or approximately 1.3 per cent of the labor force, by the end of June 1992.

State budget

After balancing revenues and expenditures in 1990, the state budget of Ukraine posted a deficit of Rb 34 bln, or 14 per cent of GDP, in 1991. In real terms, expenditures increased by about 20 per cent, while budget revenues fell by about 21 per cent. Subsidies to enterprises, reflecting the decision not to allow certain prices to increase in line with costs, increased by Rb 23 bln, or 67 per cent of the 1991 deficit. Expenditures on the social "safety net", education, and health care also increased by a total of Rb 26 bln.

The most important sources of revenue for the budget were profit and turnover taxes. In 1991, proceeds from each of these taxes accounted for over 25 per cent of total revenue collected. However, these tax revenues fell sharply in real terms relative to 1990.

The original budget for 1992 envisaged a balance of revenues and expenditures. The budget approved by parliament in June included a deficit of Rb 54 bln. However, the budget deficit for the first six months of 1992 has been reported at Rb 53 bln, or 3 per cent of GDP. The budget deficit is forecast to reach 20 per cent of GDP by the end of 1992.[2]

TAXATION
In July 1991, Ukraine introduced its own personal income tax, replacing a myriad of taxes used in the former Soviet Union. There are five marginal rates: 0, 12, 15, 20, and 30 per cent. No tax is charged on

[2] The budget deficit for the first eleven months of 1992 was 308 billion coupons. For the same period, revenues totaled 515 billion coupons. The black market buy rate for coupons per dollar was fairly stable for the first half of 1992 at about 120, but climbed precipitously in the latter half of the year, reaching 1,000 in December, according to the *Financial Times* (January 27, 1993).

incomes below the minimum wage. The 30 per cent rate levied on monthly incomes above Rb 6,000.

Turnover and sales taxes were replaced by a value-added tax (VAT) in January 1992. The rate is 22 per cent (tax inclusive) for transactions involving goods and services for which prices have been liberalized, and 28 per cent (tax exclusive) for goods and services for which prices remain controlled. A number of essential goods, representing less than 5 per cent of total net turnover, are exempt from VAT. An excise tax has also been introduced for luxury goods, tobacco products, and alcoholic beverages.

The base of the enterprise profits tax was significantly eroded in 1991. The increased independence of enterprises, coupled with the significant role in management given to employees, has resulted in a shift of a part of gross enterprise income from taxable reported profits to employee compensation. A new enterprise income tax, which brings the wage bill and profits into the tax base, was passed by parliament in February 1992. The basic tax rate on enterprise gross income has been set at 18 per cent. There are numerous deductions and exemptions. Dividends and other income from securities are taxed at 15 per cent.

Monetary policy

MONEY SUPPLY

During 1991, in an attempt to prevent purchases of Ukrainian food-stuffs by nonresidents, Ukrainian authorities introduced a payment system involving special coupons issued to Ukrainian residents and sold to nonresidents for hard currency. Purchases in state stores of basic foodstuffs and some other products could only be made with a combination of coupons and rubles.

Coupons were made legal tender in January 1992. Ukrainian workers began to receive a portion of their salary in coupons, with the remainder deposited in their ruble bank accounts. This was supposed to remedy the shortage of ruble notes, which were being printed only in Russia and supplied in insufficient quantity to Ukraine.

Initially the coupons were worth ten times their face value on the secondary market. However, the coupons declined in value, owing to continued shortages of goods in the state shops and an increasing supply of coupons. In the first quarter of 1992, the value of new coupons issued was reported to total Rb 34.8 bln. The value of the coupon relative to the ruble fell from 0.5 in January 1992 to 1.5 in

September. The authorities are considering a complete replacement of rubles with an Ukrainian currency called the "hryvnia".

The use of coupons as a substitute currency limits the utility of the usual measures of money stock in assessing the growth of "monetary aggregates during this period". Thus, the 85 per cent growth in measured M1, comprising ruble notes and demand deposits, understates the actual growth of "currency" and demand deposits in Ukraine in 1991. It is significant, however, that money emissions for the first nine months of 1992 were forty-five times greater than the emissions during the same period of 1991.[3]

As in Russia, the maturity structure of aggregate credit shortened substantially in 1991. While the nominal stock of short-term credits more than doubled, the nominal quantity of long-term credits remained unchanged.

INTEREST RATES

The National Bank of Ukraine was constituted from a branch of Gosbank in the Spring 1991. It gradually assumed the functions of the central bank on Ukrainian territory.

Most household and enterprise deposits in Ukraine are collected by the State Savings Bank. The National Bank lends these funds to the state-owned commercial banks, which in turn lend them to enterprises. These funds make up a large proportion of credit in the Ukrainian economy. Commercial loan rates are not permitted to exceed the "refinancing" charged by the National Bank by more than 3 per cent. The level of refinancing rates is thus a key determinant of lending rates in the economy as a whole.

The standard refinancing rate was 12 per cent in 1991. It was raised to 18 per cent in January 1992. However, much lower rates were charged for "preferential" refinancing, such as loans to the Agroindustrial Bank for food subsidies in 1991, or for financing of the state budget deficit.

Debt

In December 1991, Ukraine agreed to assume 16.4 per cent of the foreign debt obligations of the former Soviet Union. According to the Ukrainian National Bank, this amounted to $11.2 bln by the end of July 1992.

---

[3] On November 12th, 1992, the Ukrainian coupon became the only form of legal tender in Ukraine.

Foreign trade

In 1990, about 83 per cent of Ukrainian exports and 72 per cent of its imports were interrepublican. The machine and metalworking industrial sectors constituted the largest share of both exports and imports. Ferrous metals were the next largest export, while oil and gas ranked second among imports. The share of interrepublican exports of food products was about 5 per cent of total Ukrainian exports. Only about 20 per cent of Ukrainian exports were invoiced in convertible currencies.

In January 1991, Comecon trading arrangements among former socialist countries were replaced with hard currency trade. Although Ukrainian trade contracted sharply (transferable ruble exports were down 46 per cent, and imports were down 39 per cent), the proportion of Ukrainian exports denominated in convertible currencies increased to 50 per cent of total trade. The remaining 50 per cent was either barter trade or settled in nonconvertible currencies. The bulk of inter-republican trade is now conducted on the basis of bilateral barter agreements, with the remainder settled in rubles.

3. PRESENT FORMS OF OWNERSHIP

3A. Legal framework of economic activity

Existing and planned legislation concerning property rights

The following are the more important laws and regulations concerning property rights, the forms of business organizations, and privatization in Ukraine:

— Law on Business Enterprise (1991);
— Law of Ukraine on Economic Partnerships ("Economic Associations Law") (1991);
— Law on Enterprises in the Ukrainian SSR ("Enterprise Law") (1991);
— Law on Property (1991) (also known as Law on Ownership);
— Civil Code;
— Land Code;
— Law of Ukraine on Bankruptcy (1992);
— Law on Collective Agricultural Enterprise (1992);

— Law on Enterprises, Institutions, and Organizations under Union Subordination located within the Territory of Ukraine (1992);
— Law on Consumer Cooperatives (1992);
— Law of Ukraine on Foreign Investments (1992, superseding prior law of 1991);
— Law of Ukraine on Leasing (1992);
— Law on Privatization Certificates (1992);
— Law on Privatization of the Property of State Enterprises (1992);
— Law on Privatization of Small State Enterprises (1992) ("Small Privatization Law").
— State Program for Privatization (1992);
— Presidential Edict on the Commercialization of the State Trade and Canteen Feeding (1992, *supplemented by* Methodological Recommendations for Conducting the Commercialization of the State Retail Trade and Canteen Feeding).

Recognized forms of business organizations

STATE ENTERPRISES
Prior to the Ukrainian declaration of independence in August 1991, the respective property rights of the Soviet Union and the Ukrainian Republic in state enterprises located on Ukrainian territory were rather unclear, and the laws of the Soviet Union had widespread application. The various forms and structures of Soviet state enterprises, described in part in the chapter of this volume on Russia, were therefore equally common in Ukraine. The basic conflicts between enterprise insiders and postcommunist reformers intent on opening up the governance structure of the state sector to external control, described in the chapter on Russia, are also characteristic of the Ukrainian situation, except that the victory of the *nomenklatura* and enterprise insiders in Ukraine seems, so far, much more complete. As a result, changes in the state sector remain much less significant than those in Russia, despite the transfer of control over state enterprises to the independent Ukrainian state.

After the demise of the Soviet Union, all state and municipal enterprises in Ukraine became the property of the Ukrainian state, subject to Ukrainian legislation by virtue of a special Law on Enterprises, Institutions, and Organizations under Union Subordination Located Within the Territory of Ukraine, passed in September 1991. Even before that time, however, Ukraine had passed a series of laws regulating property relations and asserted its ownership rights to the state enterprises on its territory. Although there is no special law regulating the governance and operation of state and municipal enterprises, the general Law on Enterprises in the Ukrainian SSR ("Enterprise Law"), enacted in March 1991, subjected state enterprises to a legal regime common to all forms of Ukrainian business organization, and removed them from the control of inconsistent Soviet legal norms. Since the Enterprise Law provides only a handful of provisions that apply exclusively to state enterprises (most of which confer special rights on the employees of such enterprises), the legal regime it establishes will be discussed generally, as will other forms of business activity.

GENERAL PROPERTY RIGHTS

Ukraine passed a comprehensive Law on Property (also known as Law on Ownership) in February 1991. The set of general principles governing property relations provided by this law constitutes a clear advance over former Soviet norms, which precluded private ownership in most economically vital areas. While Ukrainian law still precludes private ownership of land, as well as of other resources termed "national wealth," it introduces equality of private, collective, and state property.

LEGAL REGIME OF BUSINESS ACTIVITY

Most commercial activity in Ukraine is governed by three separate legal norms:

* the already mentioned Enterprise Law, which provides a general framework for the operation of business associations;
* the Law on Business Enterprise of February 1991 ("Business Enterprise Law"), which regulates the activity of individual entrepreneurs;
* the Law of Ukraine on Economic Partnerships of September 1991 ("Economic Associations Law"), which specifies procedures for the governance and operation of commercial entities, such as partnerships and corporations.

Additional laws regulate the activities of consumer and agricultural cooperatives (see the subsection on cooperatives below). It will be most useful to begin by discussing the general provisions established by the Enterprise Law.

The Enterprise Law defines an enterprise as an independent organization conducting economic activity in pursuit of profit, and it identifies the following forms of enterprises:

- individual enterprise (based exclusively on the property and labor of an individual, without hired labor);
- family enterprise (based on the property and labor of a single family living together);
- private enterprise (based on individual ownership with the right to hire employees);
- collective enterprise (based on collective ownership by the workforce of a company, cooperative, or a public or religious organization);
- state-owned municipal enterprise (based on ownership by a territorial entity);
- state enterprise (based on ownership by the central authorities);
- joint enterprise (based on a mixture of ownership forms);
- mixed enterprises;
- joint ventures.

"Small businesses," which are defined on the basis of number of employees and area of activity (with maximum qualifying employment varying between fifteen persons in retail trade and 200 in industry and construction), constitute a separate category to which special legislation may apply. The law also provides for the operation of lease enterprises in Ukraine, if their creation does not conflict with legislative instruments of the Ukrainian Republic. Until recently, lease enterprises in Ukraine were governed by the Soviet legislation, in addition to the Enterprise Law.[4] But in April 1992, the parliament passed the Ukrainian Law on Leasing, which hence governs this important area. (See the subsection on lease enterprises below.)

The Enterprise Law also allows a variety of "enterprise combines," i.e. various kinds of permanent and temporary amalgamations and associations of enterprises, characteristic of the semi-corporatized state sector in the Soviet Union.[5] The creation of these combines tends to increase the monopolistic features of production and to strengthen the power of the industrial bureaucracy inherited from the communist system. The only response to these features in the Enterprise Law is to subject enterprises with a monopoly position to price controls, although the law also envisages the possibility to break up enterprises through the enforcement of antitrust legislation.

[4] For information on lease enterprises in the Soviet Union, see the appropriate subsection in the chapter on Russia.
[5] For more information, see the subsection on industrial associations in the chapter on Russia.

Enterprises are formed on the basis of a decision of the owners contributing the enterprise's property (in the case of state enterprises, the owner is the founding organ contributing the assets of the enterprise) or, under special conditions, by the workers of a state enterprise. (This last provision refers, above all, to the creation of lease enterprises.) Since land still may not be directly owned by an enterprise, the founding of an enterprise requires an authorization to use land from the appropriate soviet of people's deputies – a provision not especially conducive to the creation of an independent private sector.

All enterprises must be registered with local soviets, and must pay a registration fee. Applications may only be denied if they violate prescribed procedures (i.e., no special determination of the social utility of the proposed enterprise is necessary), and the applicant may seek damages for losses suffered due to unjustified delays.

In general, an enterprise operates on the basis of a charter approved by the owners. However, for a state enterprise, the charter approval process must involve "the participation of the workforce." The Economic Associations Law further provides that commercial enterprises[6] must maintain a reserve fund with a minimum capitalization equal to 25 per cent of their initial capital. The company must deposit at least 5 per cent of its yearly net profits until the fund reaches its minimum value.

Enterprises usually own their property (other than land), except for state enterprises, which are said to have "full economic jurisdiction" over the property assigned to them by the state. This means that state enterprises have the right to use and dispose of the property in question, though the state retains formal ownership. Enterprises also have the right to sell securities to other independent organizations and to foreign and domestic citizens, as well as the right to purchase the securities of other domestic or foreign entities. While a provision of this kind is generally desirable, its extension to state enterprises may easily lead to clouding of titles and an obfuscation of property relations characteristic of "spontaneous" or "nomenklatura" privatization.[7]

Enterprises are managed in accordance with their charters, but the law also states, among other general principles, that the workers' right to self-management must be reconciled with the rights of the owners.

---

6 The Economic Associations Law does not apply to uncorporatized state enterprises, cooperatives, or individual entrepreneurs.

7 See, for example, the chapter on Hungary in the first volume of these Reports.

The owners of an enterprise may exercise their rights directly or through a body appointed by them, and they may delegate these rights to an enterprise board. The hiring of the enterprise manager is also the prerogative of the owner or of the bodies representing the owner (which in the case of state enterprises means that the manager is appointed by the founding organ). However, the owner has no right to interfere with the manager's operational activity. (This provision is potentially of importance in connection with the management of state enterprises.)

The law grants a number of important powers to the workers of both state and private enterprises of all kinds, and contains additional provisions applicable solely to state enterprises. The general principle is that each enterprise must have a collective labor agreement, and that socio-economic decisions concerning the activity of an enterprise must be made with the participation of the workforce. The mandatory collective labor agreement is designed to regulate the "production, labor, and economic relations of the workforce and management and decide questions of labor protection, social development and the employees' participation in the use of enterprise profits, if the latter is provided for by the enterprise charter." In addition, the employees have, *inter alia*, the right to examine and ratify a draft of the collective agreement; to decide questions concerning self-management of the workforce; determine the procedure for granting employees' social benefits; and to propose candidates for state awards. The rights of the workers are exercised by the general meeting of the employees and a representative body (workers' council), composed of members elected for two- to three-year terms by a two-thirds majority of the general meeting.

Special additional provisions govern workers' rights in enterprises in which the state has an ownership interest of more than 50 per cent. The workers in these enterprises are entitled, in conjunction with the founder, to examine revisions to the enterprise charter; to determine the conditions of the hiring of the manager; to participate in the decision to split up the enterprise or create a new one; and to decide on the enterprise's entry into, and withdrawal from, an enterprise combine. The workforce of a state enterprise can also adopt a decision to lease the enterprise from the state, and to redeem it once it has been leased. Through such redemption the workers gradually acquire co-ownership of the enterprise. (See the subsection on lease enterprises below.)

Despite their professed independence, enterprises are supposed to

"harmonize" with the local soviets of people's deputies any development plans which might have environmental, social, demographic and
other consequences "affecting the interests of the population," and
are said to be responsible to the soviets for "harmful consequences of
their activity." The law also imposes on enterprises a number of rather
burdensome social obligations, including the obligation to provide
education for the workforce, to give retirees equal access to medical
care and social facilities, to provide special working conditions for
women and adolescents, and to employ specified numbers of invalids
and other types of people in need of social protection.

Enterprises are responsible for their own financial and credit relationships, and they may be declared insolvent by the lending bank if
they fail to meet their credit obligations. (See the subsection on
bankruptcy and liquidation below.)

The liquidation or reorganization of an enterprise takes place in
accordance with the charter and the decision of the owners. In the case
of enterprises in which the state maintains at least a 50 per cent
interest, liquidation and reorganization decisions occur with the
participation of the workforce.

LEASE ENTERPRISES

As mentioned above, Ukrainian legislation permitted continued operation of the lease enterprises created by the 1989 Decree of the
Presidium of the Supreme Soviet of the USSR on Lease and Lease
Relations in the USSR and the 1990 "Fundamentals of Legislation of
the USSR and the Union Republics on Lease," and introduced special
Ukrainian legislation in 1992.[8] More importantly, the legislation in
force vests the workers of state enterprises in Ukraine with full control
over the leasing process of these firms: once the majority of the work
collective votes in favor of a leasing arrangement, the state has no
right to refuse to lease the property involved, even if the enterprise in
question has already been scheduled for privatization by other means.
In fact, then, Ukrainian workers have a veto power over the privatization process of their enterprises.

The terms of these leases are also extremely favorable. To begin,
leases are not necessarily awarded on a competitive basis, since a
provision to the contrary was deleted from the 1992 State Privatization
Program. The rent amount, determined by a special regulation of the
Council of Ministers, is fixed for the duration of the lease and cannot

---

[8] See the subsection on lease enterprises in the chapter on Russia in this volume.

exceed 5 per cent of the enterprise's "income," defined as after-tax profits plus total wage payments, for the last full year preceding the lease agreement. Workers are also given the option to purchase their enterprise at any time within three years of the beginning of the lease period, and the price is fixed at the value of the enterprise at the beginning of the lease. Given the inflation rate of 25–30 per cent per month in much of 1992, the lease arrangement is likely to be a covert form of nearly-free appropriation by insiders. The real question, therefore, is whether these increasingly popular lease arrangements will replace other planned forms of ownership transformation, and what will be their effect on the governance and behavior of state enterprises. As of October 1, 1992, one out of every five state enterprises in Ukraine – altogether some 1,200 enterprises – was reportedly already leased.[9]

INDIVIDUAL ENTREPRENEURSHIP

The right of individuals, both foreign and domestic, to engage in business activity, defined as independent for-profit activity, conducted at the individual's own risk, has been established by the Business Enterprise Law. The right does not apply to military personnel or to officials of the procuracy, the courts, state security service, internal affairs departments, or state notary offices. Also excluded are administrative and government officials responsible for monitoring business activities and people found guilty of theft, bribery, or other crimes committed for gain.

Entrepreneurs can freely engage in any commercial activity, with the exception of those reserved for the state (such as the manufacture and trade in narcotics, weapons, and explosives). Licenses must be obtained before undertaking activity in other areas, such as mineral exploration, the manufacture and sale of medicines, chemicals, alcoholic beverages, and tobacco products, and medical, veterinary, and legal practice.

Individual entrepreneurs, like all other businesses, must be registered with the local soviet, and various registration fees may be levied.

THE UNLIMITED PARTNERSHIP

An unlimited or general partnership is an association in which each partner bears joint and several liability for the full extent of the

---

[9] Some doubt whether these figures are complete. Leasing arrangements are required to be reported to the State Property Fund, but registrations are said to be often delayed.

company's obligations. The founding agreement defines the value of each partner's contribution to the firm and the partners' responsibility for the management of company affairs. The Economic Associations Law defines the various forms of business activity rather rigidly, and leaves relatively little room for contractual modifications.

An unlimited partnership is managed by a joint agreement of all the partners, although day-to-day management may be delegated to one of the partners. Partners can transfer their interest only with the consent of all the other partners, but they have a unilateral right to withdraw, on three month's notice, from a partnership created for an indefinite period of time. In the case of a partnership created for a limited time, withdrawal is possible only in the case of "valid reasons," for which six month's notice must be given. Upon withdrawal, a partner is entitled to receive his share of the book value of the partnership.

PARTNERSHIP "IN COMMENDAM"
Partnerships "in commendam" are the equivalent of limited partnerships, in which the general partners bear joint, unlimited liability for the obligations of the company, and the limited partners bear liability only to the extent of their investment. General partners must contribute at least 50 per cent of the founding capital.

The rules governing partnerships in commendam are essentially the same as those governing unlimited partnerships, with the exception that only general partners are allowed to manage a partnership in commendam. However, limited partners have priority rights over general partners with respect to dividends and the proceeds of liquidation. They also have a right to inspect the company's annual reports and balance sheets.

LIMITED-LIABILITY COMPANY
The limited-liability company (LLC), referred to also as limited-liability partnership, is a familiar Eastern European economic business entity. The capital fund is divided into non-publicly tradable shares. Members are liable for the obligations of the company to the extent of their pledged contributions. LLCs are required to have a minimum capital fund of Rb 50,000, and at least 30 per cent of each member's pledged investment must be contributed by the date of registration. No maximum number of members is specified by the law.

Transferability of shares to other members is conditional on the unanimous consent of the other members. Transfers to third parties may be banned altogether, and if allowed, are subject to the members' right of preemption. An LLC may also purchase its shares, but it may not hold them for more than one year. A member is entitled to withdraw from an LLC and to receive the proportionate value of his shares within twelve months. Creditors of an insolvent member can petition for the partition of the company's property.

The highest governing body of an LLC is the general membership meeting, in which voting rights are proportional to the value of the shares held. General meetings must be held at least twice a year, and must be attended by members holding at least 60 per cent of the votes. The meetings have exclusive competence to decide on matters concerning the expulsion of members, calls for additional investments, changes in the company charter, elections and recalls of board members, and the liquidation or reorganization of the company. It is interesting to note that decisions concerning changes in the company charter or the expulsion of a member require unanimity. Most other decisions require a simple majority.

The executive governing body of an LLC is the Board of Directors, or, if the company elects to have only one executive, the chairman. The composition of the board is defined in the charter. The activity of the Board of Directors is monitored by an audit commission, elected by the membership meeting and composed of at least three members. Members of the audit commission cannot be board members.

PARTNERSHIP WITH ADDITIONAL LIABILITY

The partnership with additional liability is a rather uncommon feature in Ukrainian law. Inherited from Soviet law, this partnership[10] is a business entity identical in all respects to a limited-liability company, except for a relaxation of the limitation on liability. In companies of this kind, the members are liable for the obligations of the company to the full extent of their contributions, *plus* some expressly delineated multiple of these contributions, the maximum amount of which is specified in the charter documents.

JOINT-STOCK COMPANY

Ukrainian law allows for publicly- and privately-held joint-stock companies (JSCs), and allows for a privately-held JSC to be reorganized into a publicly-held JSC. The charter fund of a JSC must be at least Rb 100,000. In both types of companies, stockholders' liability is limited to their pledged contribution.

[10] The same arrangement is permitted in Latvian laws.

The founders of a JSC can be legal entities or citizens, and no minimum number is specified. In the case of a publicly-held JSC, the shares are sold through a public offering, which must be published and must contain specified information concerning the issue and the company (including the founders' privileges and the composition of any property they have pledged to contribute in a non-pecuniary form).

Prospective purchasers must make a 10 per cent deposit, to be increased to 30 per cent before the day of the founding meeting. The full value of the stock must be paid within one year of registration. The founders are further required to hold stocks in a sum not less than 25 per cent of the authorized capital for not less than two years. In order for the company to be constituted, 60 per cent of the stocks must be acquired by the end of the open offering period. If this threshold is not reached, the founders are required to return all monies and property to the purchasers within thirty days. If the stock offering is oversubscribed, stocks are distributed on a first-come-first-served, rather than pro-rata, basis.

The founding meeting of a JSC must be convened no later than two months after the close of the open offering period, with owners of more than 60 per cent of the offered stock comprising the necessary quorum. The founding meeting elects (by a three-fourths majority of the shares) the board of directors and the management of the company, and approves the valuation of investments, contracts entered into by the founders, and privileges granted to the founders.

A JSC can expand or reduce its initial capitalization, but an increase cannot be by more than one-third. Expansion of capitalization must be preceded by payment in full of all earlier issues. Existing stockholders have a preferential right to purchase new shares. New stock can be issued to cover operating losses.

The highest governing body of a JSC is the general meeting, for which a quorum of 60 per cent of the shares is required. The meeting is responsible for the general direction of the company, and has the authority to elect and remove members of the Board of Directors, the management, and members of the auditing commission. A 75 per cent majority is required to change the charter, terminate activities, or to create or liquidate subsidiaries of the companies. Each share has one vote, but the charter may specify a threshold number of shares required to vote, or restrict the number of votes given to any one stockholder. Proxy voting is permitted.

The law is rather vague about the rights and duties of other corporate organs. It stipulates that a JSC may have a Board of Directors exercising supervisory authority over management and performing such other tasks as may be delegated to it by the charter or the general meeting (with no specified limits on the delegation). The executive body of the company is the management, at the head of which is a director endowed with very broad residual powers. The same person cannot be a member of both the Board of Directors and the management.

A JSC must also have an audit commission, composed of stockholders elected by the general meeting. The commission must call an extraordinary general meeting of the stockholders if it discovers official abuses or threats to the vital interests of the company.

COOPERATIVES

The cooperative movement in Ukraine was governed by the appropriate Soviet laws until February 1992, when a new law on agricultural cooperatives (Law on Collective Agricultural Enterprise) was passed by the parliament. This was followed by a new law on consumer cooperatives (Law on Consumer Cooperatives), passed in April of the same year. Productive cooperatives are still governed by Soviet law.[11]

Agricultural cooperatives. The new law on agricultural cooperatives gives cooperatives title to land used by them within the rules laid down in the Land Code, and allows for free withdrawal of individuals who want to engage in individual farming. Such individuals are given the right to a grant of land from the reserve fund, and if there is no such fund, to an appropriate portion of the cooperative land. While a special provision guarantees nondiscriminatory treatment of individual farmers by the state in its procurement pricing, another provision assures cooperatives of special state support in the form of access to credit from a special fund set annually by the Council of Ministers.

The property of an agricultural cooperative is said to belong to the members collectively, and each member is entitled to a share in the "shared participation property" of the cooperative (which includes fixed and working capital, money, securities, etc., but not land) according to his or her labor contribution. This share determines the

---

[11] For a discussion of cooperatives in the Soviet Union, see the chapter on Russia.

members' right to participate in profit distributions, but individual members may also reinvest a part of the profits distributed to them, so as to increase their future shares.

The highest organ of a consumer cooperative is the general meeting or meeting of the representatives. Day-to-day operations are managed by a board elected by the meeting. The powers of the general meeting and the board are determined by the charter of the cooperative, except for the most basic decisions concerning charter amendments, liquidations, etc., which are made by the general meeting.

The decree enacting the new law requires that all existing collective farms re-register under the new regime and bring their charters into conformity with the new law.

Consumer cooperatives.   No similar provision concerning re-registration is contained in the law on consumer cooperatives, which generally stops short of significant changes to the old hierarchical structures of the Soviet cooperatives. Indeed, the law seems to presume that former cooperative "unions" will continue to exist and dominate the individual cooperatives. It does, however, depart from the traditional Soviet principle of distribution of profits according to labor contribution, and makes such distribution dependent on the share of each member's overall contributions (see below).

The property of a consumer cooperative is created by members' contributions, its profits from selling goods, services, and securities, and other activities. Each member of a cooperative society has a share in the cooperative property, the value of which is determined by the amount of his or her mandatory share contribution and other contributions, as well as accrued dividend and interest payments.

Members have the right to take part in the activities and the management of the cooperative. They are also entitled to preferential treatment in the acquisition of the cooperative's products, and to access to employment opportunities.

The highest organ of a cooperative is its general meeting of members, which adopts a charter, determines the amount of the entry fee and mandatory share contribution, and elects the society's management and monitoring organs. Each member has one vote regardless of his or her contribution, and the vote is nontransferable.

Bankruptcy and liquidation

The Law of Ukraine on Bankruptcy ("Bankruptcy Law") was adopted in May of 1992. It applies to all legal persons involved in entrepreneurial activity. However, personal insolvency or bankruptcy and bankruptcy of banks are not covered in this law.[12]

A debtor subject to bankruptcy proceedings is defined as a legal person unable to satisfy its debts within one month of a judicial order of payment or the acknowledgement of a debt. Both the debtor and its creditors can petition the Court of Arbitration for a bankruptcy declaration. The court declares the opening of the proceedings within five days of the petition, and conducts a preliminary hearing within one month of the opening of the proceedings. At that time the court appoints an administrator of the debtor's assets. The petitioner is required to publish a notice of the opening of the bankruptcy case.

The appointment of a trustee acts to end the ability of the bankrupt to manage its property. Creditors have one month from the date of publication to submit their claims to the court, as do the persons proposing a "sanation" procedure (see below). The court admits or rejects the claims based on the submitted documentation. Once the claims have been evaluated, a committee of creditors may be organized. (Such a committee must be organized if there are more than ten creditors.)

Prior to an official declaration of bankruptcy, if the creditors holding two-thirds of the total debt agree, the court may adopt a "sanation resolution," i.e., a plan by the owner or a third party for a reorganization, restructuring, or privatization of the insolvent enterprise. In cases where a state enterprise is the subject of the proceedings, the employees can request that the assets of the enterprise be leased or transferred to them, subject to the bankrupt's liabilities.

In the absence of a sanation resolution, the court declares a debtor bankrupt, and appoints a liquidation commission. The declaration terminates all the commercial activity and obligations of the enterprise, and transfers the management and ownership rights over all of its assets and debts to the liquidation commission, the interest on all debts having been suspended. The liquidation commission is responsible for the valuation and sale of the bankrupt's assets. Assets for which two or more offers are received are sold at an auction.

Money received from the sale of the bankrupt's assets is used to

---

[12] Bankruptcy of banks is regulated by the Law on Banks and Banking Activities (1991).

satisfy creditors in the following order of priority: 1) administrative costs of the bankruptcy proceeding; 2) amounts owed to employees; 3) obligations to secured creditors, as well as back-payment of local and state taxes and payments into social security programs; 4) debts to unsecured creditors; 5) refunds and interest on employee contributions to the statutory fund of the enterprise; and 6) other claims. Claims in each category must be fully satisfied before claims in the next category are reached; if the funds are insufficient to satisfy a given category, all claimants are satisfied proportionally to the size of their claims.

Regulations governing foreign investment

The Law of Ukraine on Foreign Investments took effect on April 1, 1992, superseding an earlier, incomplete law of September 1991. The current law applies to convertible-currency investors and to Ukrainian enterprises with foreign investment, but not to investments made in rubles or to most other investments from the ruble-zone republics. The law defines an enterprise with foreign investment as one in which a foreign investor controls at least 20 per cent of the authorized capital or a share worth at least $100,000.

Foreign investors are permitted to invest in the form of hard currency or convertible instruments; movable or immovable property; stocks and bonds; monetary claims and contractual rights; intellectual property; or licenses to carry out commercial activities, including the right of exploitation of natural resources. Foreign investors can purchase shares of pre-existing companies; create new enterprises jointly with Ukrainian natural or juridical persons; and establish wholly foreign-owned enterprises. Joint ventures with Ukrainian participation receive more favorable treatment than enterprises with wholly foreign capital. A special license from the Ministry of Finance is required to conduct insurance or brokerage business, and a license from the National Bank is necessary to conduct banking operations. An enterprise with foreign investment can also obtain the right to use land or concessions to exploit natural resources.

Foreign investment in Ukraine is protected against nationalization, except in emergency situations, when full compensation in foreign currency must be paid. If the legal regime for foreign investment changes, the investor may choose to have the investment governed for ten years by the laws applicable at the time when the investment was registered. Also, international agreements in effect in Ukraine take precedence over conflicting domestic legislation.

Foreign investments are valued in either foreign or Ukrainian currency. The conversion rate can be determined by an agreement among the parties involved, but the conversion rate of Ukrainian currency may not be less than its current exchange rate as determined by the National Bank. Repatriation of profits is permitted after payment of taxes, including a special 15 per cent tax on repatriated profits. With respect to profits obtained in foreign currency, the meaning of this provision is clear. But as long as the Ukrainian currency is not convertible, the ability of a foreign investor to exchange local currency into convertible currency cannot be assured.

Foreign investors are required to register their investments with the Ministry of Finance, but registration of a proper application cannot be denied, and registration fees cannot exceed the actual cost of processing. Foreign investors are required to submit monthly consolidated reports on their operations to the Ministry of Finance, the Ministry of Statistics, the Ministry of Foreign Economic Relations, and the National Bank of Ukraine.

The law provides a series of tax and import duty exemptions for enterprises with foreign investment. Duty exemptions apply to goods imported into Ukraine as part of the capital contribution of the foreign investor, raw materials or components used by an enterprise with foreign investment, and the property imported by foreign employees of such enterprises for their individual needs. With respect to taxes, most enterprises with foreign investment and the participation of Ukrainian capital are exempt from income taxation for five years after the declaration of first income, and will be taxed thereafter at 50 per cent of the rates applicable to all other enterprises in Ukraine. Such joint-venture enterprises, if they are involved in retail trade, are exempt for only three years, two years for brokerage enterprises; after the initial period of exemption each will pay taxes at a rate of 70 per cent of the established rates. By contrast, enterprises with wholly foreign capital are only entitled to reduce their taxable income by the amount of their capital investment during a given year (thus effectively enjoying the right to recoup their investment tax free), after which they have to pay taxes at normal rates. (Excess deductions may be carried forward to subsequent years.) Taxable income is to be reduced by the amount of funds reinvested in Ukraine. Finally, products, labor, and services of an enterprise with foreign investment and Ukrainian capital are exempt from VAT for five years.

3B. Structure of ownership

Statistical data on classification of property by ownership type are scarce in Ukraine, and complete information is unlikely to be available until at least 1993.

The 1992 State Program for Privatization estimated the state share of the book value of property (excluding collective farms, state farms and housing) in January 1991 at 96 per cent. The Privatization Program envisioned that the state share would fall to 92 per cent by January 1993, 81 per cent by January 1994, and 66 per cent by January 1995.[13]

Table 3B.1 Distribution of employment by ownership category (in per cent)

Per cent of total employment	1989	1990
State*	82.52	81.31
Community**	13.64	13.43
Cooperatives*	1.86	2.37
Private non-farm	0.18	0.21
Private agriculture	1.80	2.68

Notes: * Consumer cooperatives are included in "State" and excluded from "Cooperatives."
** Community includes municipal and other local government.

A further indication of the importance of the state sector in 1989 and 1990 can be gained from statistics on the distribution of employment (Table 3B.1), which show 81 per cent of the total labor force employed in state organizations (including consumer organizations), 13 per cent in community production (under municipal or other local governmental ownership), and 2 per cent in the cooperative sphere. Private non-farm business accounted for only 0.2 per cent, although private agricultural production accounted for 2.7 per cent.[14]

---

[13] Note that many of the projections appearing in the program are perhaps too optimistic, by the admission of the drafters of the program themselves.

[14] Evidence of the growth of private agriculture, or at least of its profitability, is that personal income from private plots grew from Rb 4.5 bln in 1989 to Rb 6.0 bln in 1990, representing 4.7 per cent and 5.5 per cent, respectively, of total personal income. *PlanEcon Report 42*, November 27, 1991.

Foreign ownership

Little data on the extent of foreign investment was obtained.

As of January 1, 1991, there were approximately 500 registered joint ventures.

On November 1, 1991, there were 188 joint ventures involved in industrial activity, producing goods and services valued at Rb 916.8 mln, of which the overwhelming majority were for sale on the internal market.

4. OVERVIEW OF THE PRIVATIZATION PROCESS

Introduction

The Ukrainian government, under President Leonid Kravchuk and Prime Minister Vitold Fokin, stated its commitment to change to a market economy and recognized privatization as a major feature of this transition process. It was, however, not possible to make much progress with privatization before 1992, primarily due to political circumstances within the disintegrating former USSR. Between the proclamation of Ukrainian sovereignty on June 16, 1990, and the declaration of Ukrainian independence on August 24, 1991, Ukrainian reforms were restricted to those that would be tolerated by the Soviet government.

A number of significant, if incomplete, reform measures were nevertheless undertaken in this period. President Kravchuk's Edict of October 26, 1990 liberalized foreign trade, allowed the creation of joint ventures, and established rights for foreign investors in Ukraine. Other reforms included the 1991 Law on Ownership; the simplification of the system of national economic management, which included a consolidation of certain ministries and government departments and the creation of "concerns" and other associations of enterprises in particular sectors; the strengthening of the role of local authorities; and the extension of the rights and duties of enterprises.

After the events of August 19–21, 1991 (i.e. the failed coup in Moscow) and the declaration of independence on August 24, full separation of Ukrainian from Union structures took place, from the level of individual enterprises and local authorities up to the top level of the republic's government and legislature. Some new institutions were created, including the Ministry of International Economic Affairs and the National Bank of Ukraine. It was also declared that all enterprises, organizations, and property on Ukrainian territory were henceforth exclusively the property of the Ukrainian State, thereby abolishing the abstract property of the USSR, and accomplishing a necessary step towards clarifying property rights.

The Ukrainian government's proposed series of reforms was set out in the October 1991 program, the Principal Directions of Economic Policy of Ukraine in Conditions of Independence. Under this program, partial price liberalization was implemented in January 1992, but was perceived as problematic, at least partially, because of the absence of free competition to stabilize prices. The promotion of competition, in turn, was seen to be dependent on broadening the basis of private ownership in the economy.

The Ukrainian plan is that privatization should proceed in the context of the following broader set of policies: changes in structural and investment policies directed at improving the balance of goods and services on the market; de-monopolization of industry; development of market infrastructure, involving the creation of stock markets, associations, brokers' offices, mediator-commercial enterprises, commercial banks, and a legislative and regulatory framework for their activities; agricultural reform; financial reform, with greater emphasis on economic regulatory functions (as opposed to fiscal functions) to encourage the application of science and technology and the restructuring of the economy; and reform of the state regulatory system, using an appropriate mixture of stimuli and restrictions.

The basic legislation on corporatization and privatization

The main legislation on privatization, adopted by the Supreme Council in early 1992, comprises the Law on Privatization of the Property of State Enterprises and the Law on Privatization Certificates (dealing with the distribution of vouchers to the population), both of which came into force on March 15, and the Law on Privatization of Small State Enterprises ("Small Privatization Law"), which came into force on April 15. These laws are supplemented by other legislative Acts and by Edicts of the President of Ukraine.

The Law on Privatization of the Property of the State Enterprises covers the following categories of state property: enterprises, workshops, factories, and other subdivisions of enterprises, which may be split up into independent enterprises; equipment, buildings, and other material and non-material assets; unfinished constructions; and shares in state-owned enterprises and economic associations. It excludes the following categories: property to be held by the land fund and the housing fund; the property of collective farms, consumer cooperation enterprises, arms manufacturing enterprises and the armed forces; gold and currency reserves; and national monuments and property designated for social and cultural purposes. The law stipulates that the goals, priorities, and conditions for the implementation of privatization will be determined in the annual State Program of Privatization, which is prepared by the Cabinet of Ministers and approved by the Supreme Council.

The State Program establishes recommended forms of privatization for different categories of state property; it also provides for the issuing of privatization papers (vouchers), their distribution among eligible recipients, and the extent to which property in different categories shall be reserved for voucher sales; it determines measures concerning the involvement of foreign investors; and it sets the requirements for local privatization programs. The first State Program was submitted by the government to the Supreme Council in June 1992, but, as of mid-summer 1992, it seems to have failed to win approval.

4A. Organizational structure of state regulation of privatization

The division of authority among the various governmental organs involved with privatization in Ukraine has been clearly defined neither in law nor in formal administrative procedure, nor even, in many cases, in the minds of the representatives of these bodies.

A reorganization of the government in early 1992 resulted in the emergence of a Vice Premier for Economic Reform Policy and Minister of Economy, Volodymyr Lanovoy, who was officially responsible for the economic reform as a whole, and for privatization in particular. The resignation of Mr. Lanovoy several months later left it unclear who would assume overall responsibility for the privatization program, a situation made all the more distressing in view of the complexity of the programs planned in Ukraine.

The key state organ in privatization is the State Property Fund (including its regional departments), which has taken the leading role partly because it is the only body with a clear legal mandate. Other bodies that have direct, but less well defined, roles in the process are the local privatization agencies, the enterprise privatization commissions, the National Bank, the Department of Property and Entrepreneurship, the Ministry of De-monopolization and De-statization, the State Committee on Assistance to Small Business and Entrepreneurs, and the State Privatization Fund.

The State Property Fund

The responsibilities of the State Property Fund (SPF) are set forth in the Law on Privatization of the Property of State Enterprises, the Small Privatization Law, and the Law on Privatization Certificates.

The SPF is responsible for all stages of the planning, implementation and analysis of the process of privatization for property of the Republic of Ukraine ("state" as opposed to "communal" property). This includes framing proposals for inclusion in the annual State Privatization Programs, organizing and controlling the fulfillment of these programs once they are approved, framing regulations on methods of privatization, and analyzing the implementation of privatization. Furthermore, the SPF exercises ownership rights over state enterprises and is responsible for the leasing of state property.[15]

The SPF is responsible for deciding whether or not to approve an application to initiate the privatization process for a particular enterprise. The SPF must publish its decision within one month, and, if the decision is positive, it creates a commission on privatization for each enterprise and decides whether to approve each commission's privatization plan. Preparing the enterprises for privatization and transforming them into organizational and legal forms suitable for privatization (for the corporatization process see Section 5 below) are also SPF responsibilities.

It is intended that the SPF will operate partially through regional offices, which are responsible for the privatization of state property within their jurisdictions. It may also make contracts with other entities (e.g. consulting firms) to elaborate privatization plans, conduct valuations, and grant licenses to intermediaries.

ORGANIZATION OF THE STATE PROPERTY FUND

The SPF (see Chart 4A.1) is headed by a president who is appointed by the President of the Republic, subject to confirmation by

---

[15] It does not in general, however, have the authority "to intervene in the operation of enterprises" according to the Law on Privatization of State Enterprises.

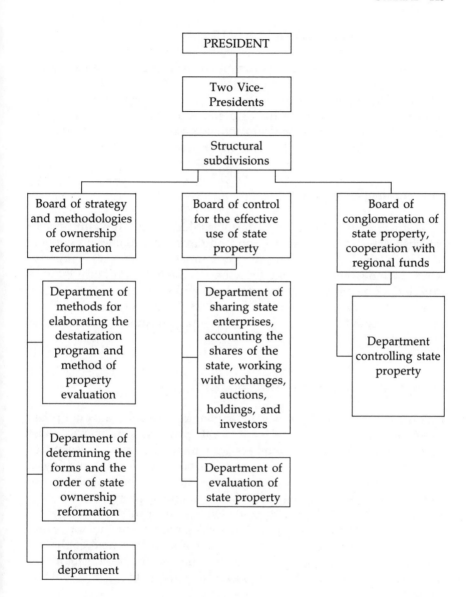

Chart 4A.1 Organizational structure of Ukraine's State Property Fund

the Supreme Council (parliament) of Ukraine. The fund is divided into three boards (each of which has its own operational departments) and includes an administrative department and a financial accounts department.

It annually submits to the Cabinet of Ministers a report that must receive final approval from the Supreme Council. The SPF is further accountable to the Supreme Council through the scrutiny of an Inspection Commission on Privatization appointed by the Council.

Local privatization agencies

Local governments (municipal and oblast-level) have the authority to establish their own procedures and administrative bodies in connection with the privatization of "communal" (municipal) property, which includes land, housing and shops. The State Property Fund is expected to develop guidelines for local authorities.

The same degree of independence has been given to the Autonomous Republic of Crimea in the privatization of republican property.

Enterprise privatization commissions

Following the initial approval of a plan to privatize an enterprise, either the SPF or the relevant local privatization agency must approve the selection of members of a privatization commission for that enterprise. The commission is responsible for formulating a privatization plan within two months on the basis of proposals from workers, prospective buyers who have submitted proposals, the local Council of People's Deputies, and the relevant privatization agency, with each of these interests being represented "equally" on every commission. "Financial institutions" are also represented, although the law does not explicitly require that their views be considered in the final plan. A commission may also choose to include outside "experts".

Where the locus of power in these commissions will lie is unclear, though this may be a significant determinant of the outcome of Ukrainian privatization. The prevailing sentiment within the State Property Fund is that the legal mandate given to the SPF implies that it should dominate these commissions. The law does state that the SPF is generally responsible for approving privatization plans, and specifically that it is to formulate regulations concerning the activity of the commissions. It remains to be seen how much influence the fund will be able to exert over enterprise insiders and local government bodies.

Intermediary institutions

The Law on Privatization of the Property of State Enterprises calls for the establishment of "commercial trust associations, investment funds, holding companies and other financial intermediaries" to "assist in the circulation of privatization certificates, create and service a primary market for securities and reduce the risks incurred by buyers . . ." At least some of these institutions would appear to be governmental bodies, but more specific plans concerning their creation and regulation have not yet been formulated.

The National Bank and the Savings Bank

Banks are involved in the process of voucher privatization in Ukraine in a role similar to that of the Federal Finance Ministry in Czechoslovak privatization. The National Bank is responsible for the issuance of privatization certificates[16] and the divisions of the state Savings Bank (*Oschadbank*) are charged with their distribution. Although the law does not so specify, presumably the establishment of individual privatization accounts (see Section 4B below) is coordinated by the Savings Bank.

Banks are also expected to act as intermediaries in the exchange of privatization certificates for shares of privatized enterprises, though the details of this procedure have yet to be worked out.

The role of other state bodies

A number of other state bodies seem likely to play some role in the privatization process. Within the Ministry of Economy there is a

---

[16] "Certificate" usually replaces "voucher" in discourse about Ukrainian privatization.

Department of Property and Entrepreneurship. There is also a Ministry of De-monopolization and De-statization as well as the State Committee on Assistance to Small Business and Entrepreneurs. The Ministry of De-monopolization and De-statization is itself divided into main boards in charge of "de-statization" and privatization, and of de-monopolization of industry. The privatization board is in turn subdivided into departments dealing respectively with the various branches of agriculture and industry, and with municipal property. The division of labor and competence among these various units is not spelled out in law or in the State Program and is still evolving.

The 1992 Program specifies that the State Property Fund create a State Privatization Fund, an extra-budgetary fund into which the proceeds of privatization are paid.

4B. Overview of privatization programs

Although much of the institutional infrastructure has been put into place, in fact little formal privatization had been accomplished in Ukraine by mid-1992. The enactment of a specific program to implement the law was still awaiting consideration by the parliament. With respect to policies, therefore, this section can only describe the draft program that was prepared in spring 1992. Since this draft failed to win the expected parliamentary approval in early summer 1992, the final version may well differ significantly.

Moreover, in describing what is only a governmental plan, we are not addressing what many observers regard as the most important type of privatization in Ukraine: spontaneous privatization. This process, whereby enterprise managers, and sometimes workers, acquire ownership rights through various quasi-legal and extra-legal means over the assets of their enterprise, is completely unregulated in Ukraine. By the very nature of these practices, there are as yet only anecdotal data concerning their extent and a more complete treatment is not yet possible.

Program for the privatization of state-owned enterprises

Assets included in the Ukrainian privatization of state enterprises are determined using a list of sectors and types of enterprises in the draft program. It is remarkable that among the groups to be privatized first are "loss-making enterprises in all branches of the economy, as long as the losses are not caused by fixed prices and tariffs regulated by the state." Sectors and types of enterprises to be privatized only with the approval of the Council of Ministers and those that are not currently scheduled for privatization are also detailed. Among the former are "enterprises trading in hard currency;" among the latter there are no particular surprises. The total adjusted book value of the enterprises in the program is estimated at 2.171 trillion rubles.

Enterprises to be privatized are further divided into six size and qualitative categories, with different goals and conditions set for each. Among the 1992 targets are, for instance, the privatization of at least 10 per cent of the smallest enterprises (value less than Rb 1.5 mln[17]) through vouchers in 1992. Of medium-sized enterprises (book value between Rb 1.5 mln and Rb 100 mln) that employees are unable to purchase with the nominal value of their vouchers, at least 10 per cent of the shares sold in 1992 are meant to be sold for vouchers.

Initiation of the privatization process comes through the submission of applications (somewhat similar to Czechoslovak "projects") from prospective buyers (the "buyers' association") to the SPF or the local privatization agency. The State Property Fund or the local privatization agencies may also initiate privatization. If approved, the application goes to a commission composed of representatives from the State Property Fund (the majority), the buyers' association, the other potential buyers, and financial institutions.

There is a required timetable for the approval of a plan containing information about the enterprise: a business plan including intentions with regard to employment; the new legal form; the methods of privatization to be used, including the price (starting price in case of an auction) and the proportion offered for vouchers; and the proposed timetable of privatization. The plan may include a proposed reorganization of the enterprise or the creation of separate legal entities on the basis of its structural subdivisions. Where enterprises have a monopolistic position, the legislation requires that limitations be placed on its market power as part of the process of privatization. The State Property Fund or local agency must give final approval for a plan to go forward; how

---

[17] According to a source inside the SPF, this level should be Rb 20 mln rather than 1.5, but the translation of the draft program says 1.5.

active they will be in initiating plans and administering the process remains to be seen.

Possible methods of sale may include buy-outs, competitive tenders, auctions of assets or of the whole enterprises, open share sales on the stock exchange, or sales of leases with buy-out options. The Privatization Law also provides for "free giveaway of special enterprises and shares in them," preferential sales to workers (see below), and, in the event of liquidation of state enterprises, for the sale of their assets at auction or through retail and wholesale channels. The initial selling price for an auction or public offering is usually determined on the basis of the book value of fixed assets, plus the real cost of current assets, and credits less debts, computed according to methods approved by the Cabinet of Ministers. There is also a provision in the Privatization Law, however, for this initial price to be altered if such a change is considered justified, in light of the earning potential of the enterprise, or, for enterprises being liquidated, in order to bring it into line with the market value of the assets.

When shares in a joint-stock company are offered for open privatization sale, subscriptions are first invited at an initial price. If there is an undersubscription, the sale goes ahead, and the State Property Fund retains ownership of the unsold shares. If there is an oversubscription by less than 20 per cent, the sale still goes ahead, but additional shares are issued to meet the subscription demand, thereby increasing the company's initial capital. In the event of oversubscription exceeding 20 per cent, the sale does not take place; a new share selling price is set, subscribers are notified, and those who do not ask for the return of their deposits within two weeks are deemed to have consented to purchase at the revised selling price.

Purchases may be made with the buyers' own or borrowed assets, and with privatization papers. The intention is to distribute through vouchers at least 40 per cent of total book value (adjusted for inflation and depreciation) of enterprises to be privatized.[18] Thus, a total value of Rb 868 bln book value will go to vouchers, implying that each of the 52 million "property privatization certificates" (one for each Ukrainian citizen) will have a "nominal value" of 17,000 rubles. The privatization commissions are supposed to be charged with "ensuring that, on average, enough property is being sold for vouchers," but given that

---

[18] A special parliamentary act, passed in September 1992, increased the portion of enterprises to be included in the voucher program from 40 to 70 per cent. All the figures in the text should thus be adjusted upwards.

each enterprise has a separate, and at least somewhat different commission, this provision seems difficult to enforce.

Vouchers in Ukraine are part of a larger system of giveaways and preferences for citizens who use their savings to purchase assets in the privatization program. The vouchers themselves are to be distributed for a small, but still undetermined, fee to all resident citizens. It seems there will also be a small fee upon redemption. Vouchers expire on January 1, 1995. Until 1993, there will be no physical certificates, but a "privatization deposit account" will be opened at the State Savings Bank for anyone wishing to use their voucher in 1992. Note that this could entail 52 million new accounts.

Beyond the type so far discussed here, vouchers for housing and vouchers for land are also planned, but these are still farther from implementation. All three types are supposed to be mutually convertible: the program explicitly states that "citizens . . . will have unrestricted options to use privatization certificates (vouchers) in different areas of privatization." Aside from this convertibility and the ability to bequeath vouchers, they are non-tradable. The program implies that this restriction will be strictly enforced. Shares purchased wholly or partially with vouchers may not be resold or transferred for two years, which may significantly impede the evolution of a new governance structure for the privatized enterprises.

The program recognizes the possibility of citizens investing their vouchers with private intermediaries "licensed by the state," but it is otherwise unclear how these still unfamiliar institutions may develop. "Holdings" of controlling stakes, investment funds limited to smaller stakes, and trust companies buying and selling shares on behalf of depositors are all envisaged.

A policy intimately related to the voucher program is the special "indexation" of savings accounts, whereby the added funds can be used only for purchasing state assets in the privatization program. These non-cash privatization funds are created by applying an "indexation" factor of ten for deposits made before January 2, 1992, and a factor of two thereafter.

Workers receive several types of preferences, both in connection with their vouchers and independently of them. The Privatization Program states that the employees and workers' collectives have priority rights to their enterprise, although only if the shares go to workers as individuals, not to the collective. That the buyers' association, a term that is not precisely defined but seems to refer to a group consisting primarily of the workers of the enterprise, is so designated is perhaps itself indicative. Buyers' associations established by the workers of state enterprises receive the added preference of a free transfer of social assets, "the objects, created at the cost of assets of social development" (recreation centers, vacation homes, day-care facilities, cafeterias) if they acquire their own enterprises, or a majority shareholding in them.

In addition to special privileges granted in the process of privatizing, the workers are the preferred buyers, everything else being equal. Workers may purchase shares at book value with their vouchers, plus cash equal to 50 per cent of the nominal value of the vouchers they use. According to the Privatization Law (Article 23), however, shares purchased on a privileged basis may not be resold for three years without the permission of the seller. When an enterprise is to be sold at open auction, the workers may form a buyers' association which then becomes the preferred buyer, all else being equal; they will also have the right to pay by installments spread over up to three years, the initial payment stipulated as 30 per cent of the purchase cost.[19]

Besides the average 40 per cent share that is supposed to go to vouchers, there are no specific targets for ownership by workers or outside domestic or foreign investors. Foreign participation is relatively unrestricted; discrimination comes in the form of special exchange rates that are used in the case of purchase of a property undergoing privatization.

Privatization proceeds are contributed to an extra-budgetary State Privatization Fund. They are used to cover expenses associated with privatization, and, "in case of emergency," to service the debts of enterprises being privatized. The proceeds may be used to offset state or local budget deficits.

The Ukrainian program is sometimes casually compared to the Czechoslovak, but it may be worthwhile to point out several significant differences. First, the Czechoslovak program has an explicit timetable requiring a large group of enterprises to go through the process simultaneously, including the submission of projects (proposals for how the privatization should be accomplished). This results in less opportunity for enterprise insiders to hesitate and delay. In Ukraine, the initiative to begin privatization rests with the buyers'

---

[19] Perhaps the most important preference for workers and other insiders of Ukrainian state enterprises is their ability to prevent the standard privatization of their enterprises by choosing to lease the enterprises on the favorable conditions described in the subsection on lease enterprises, above.

associations, which seem likely to be dominated by workers with no clear stake in the process unless they are engaged in a buy-out. Furthermore, the absence of a timetable leaves no guarantee or method of enforcing that privatization will take place within a certain period of time. A simultaneous process, compared to one that is temporally dispersed, may also impart a different dynamic to the formation of intermediaries: a "critical mass" could be necessary for individuals to decide to invest their certificates through intermediaries.

Second, the allocational mechanism in Czechoslovakia is clear: all the assets in the voucher program go through simultaneous auctions in which vouchers are the only means of payment. By contrast, in Ukraine the shares of each enterprise may be allocated using different methods. It is possible that vouchers will often be traded for fixed amounts of book value, in which case there need be no price adjustment (of the number of voucher points) to allocate especially desirable assets among many contenders. Moreover, cash can be combined with vouchers in the Ukrainian program.

Third, all Czechoslovak citizens who choose to participate do so on an equal basis. By contrast, Ukrainian workers have an important role in the process, receive significant preferences, and will probably be important in the new ownership structure, none of which are part of the Czechoslovak program.

To summarize, the Ukrainian program is a true voucher program, like the Czechoslovak but unlike the Polish or Romanian, in that Ukrainian citizens are given the choice of how to invest, or how to spend their vouchers. But the Ukrainian is not really a mass privatization program,[20] because of the lack of an overall timetable, the lack of centralization in determining methods of privatization, and the lack of equality of opportunity for all participants.

The small privatization program

The Law on Privatization of Small State Enterprises provides the framework for the privatization of units (either small enterprises or

---

[20] This should not be taken as a value judgment, as no doubt various types of privatization policies are more appropriate or are even only feasible under certain "initial" conditions determined by such factors as the history of reforms and the political situation. For an explicit analysis along these lines of privatization policies in several East European countries, see the Editors' Introduction to *Privatization in the Transition to a Market Economy*, J. Earle, R. Frydman and A. Rapaczynski (eds.), Pinter Publishers and St. Martin's Press, 1993.

subdivisions of enterprises) in trade, public food consumption, domestic consumer services, light industry (e.g., textiles, leather, foodstuffs), the processing industry, the construction material industry, construction, some types of transport, housing, and repair services. Under this law, the procedures of the small privatization program may also be used to privatize enterprises with a book value of under Rb 1.5 mln in other sectors, or units above the valuation ceiling of Rb 1.5 mln, if privatization plans are drawn up for those which elect to pursue this route.

One important provision in the law is that buildings are to be privatized as part of the relevant enterprises if the buyer wishes, unless this is explicitly prohibited by the privatizing body or the local Council of People's Deputies. By contrast, small privatization in most other countries usually involves the leasing of business premises.

The procedure for small privatization sales is set out in the second chapter of the law and is similar to that for large enterprises. It begins with the establishment of lists by the relevant Councils of People's Deputies, stating what property is to be offered for privatization by auction, by competitive tender, or by acquisition by the workers of the enterprises concerned. Prospective buyers may apply to the relevant privatizing body to add a particular enterprise or property to one of these lists, giving information about themselves, the terms they are offering for purchase and exploitation of the property, and the method of settlement. The privatizing body is required to reply to such applications within one month. The concerned state enterprise then begins to prepare for the sale, establishing a nominal price based on the standard method of valuation, publishing the relevant information on property to be privatized, and carrying out any necessary reorganization (or liquidation) of the enterprise.

If employees wish to acquire an enterprise, they can form a buyers' association, which must include at least half of the workforce, and submit their application. In this case, the price is to be determined mainly according to its book value. If the employees do not wish to acquire their enterprise, it will be offered for sale at auction or by tender, and there are regulations governing the publication of information on the terms for participation, the sale regulations, and the final outcome. In the case of an auction, sales are to the highest bidder. Competitive tenders, however, are assessed according to the terms of the business plan being proposed for the future exploitation of the property, as well as the price. This assessment is carried out by a special competition commission, created by the privatizing agency, which must determine the terms of the tender, examine the bids and associated business plans, and determine the successful tender. All other bidders are then informed about the terms offered in the successful tender, and, if no additional offers emerge, the sale then goes through.

Enterprises which remain unsold will be privatized by leasing with buy-out options, sold with deferred payment, or may be offered for direct sale to third parties on non-competitive allocations.

The law allows for sales at up to 30 per cent below the initial (nominal) price.

5. CORPORATIZATION AND COMMERCIALIZATION

The terms "corporatization" and "commercialization" are both used in Ukraine to describe the broad processes by which enterprises gain some measure of independence from supervisory state organs and by which ownership rights become more clearly defined. Under the former system of "socialized enterprises," neither ownership nor legal form were considered very important matters for precise definition, since enterprises in theory belonged to the people as a whole, and in practice operated more like administrative units of government.

"Corporatization" in Ukraine is understood as the process by which state enterprises are converted into state-owned joint-stock companies. "Commercialization" is sometimes understood as a distinct concept, implying the elimination of direct state intervention in "commercial" decisions: enterprises gain the freedom to set their own prices and choose their own input suppliers and distribution channels. However, these two processes are often combined in practice. The President's Edict on the Commercialization of State Trade and Canteen Feeding set in motion a process whereby both the legal definition of an enterprise becomes clarified and the company's behavior becomes more "commercial." Henceforth, we use "commercialization" to describe this entire process in Ukraine.

The basic legislation governing commercialization is the April 1991 Law on Enterprises and the privatization legislation itself. No limitations are set on what form of business should be adopted by former state enterprises, nor on the use of assets acquired from them. In practice, it is anticipated that the majority of enterprises which are not liquidated, but sold as going concerns, will be commercialized and privatized as commercial companies or joint-stock companies.

Commercialization of a particular state enterprise may be undertaken as part of the preparation for privatization, but commercialization itself does not necessarily involve the transfer of property from state to private ownership.

Procedures for commercialization of small enterprises

In preparation for the small privatization program, the President's Edict on the Commercialization of State Trade and Canteen Feeding was issued in late January 1992. This may be the first of a series of similar edicts on compulsory commercialization, applying progressively to all the enterprises within specified sectors of the economy. The edict was supplemented by the Methodological Recommendations for Conducting the Commercialization of the State Retail Trade and Canteen Feeding, setting out detailed procedures.

Under these procedures, commercialization is initiated by relevant state property-holding bodies, in this case the municipal property funds which are set up by executive committees of the local councils of people's deputies. A proposal for commercialization may also come from "insiders" in the enterprise concerned – management and workers – who are prepared to take on responsibility for its financial and economic management. One motive for this may be to remove the unit from the control of the conglomerate, trust, or other organization that was previously in charge of its operations, and to remove the corresponding burden of contributing to that organization's staff overhead costs. If the unit becomes a separate legal person in this way, it will also have much more control over any subsequent privatization sale. An employee "takeover" of this kind may also lead to a direct buy-out, avoiding a competitive tender or auction.

Once an entity has been commercialized, and a legal person created, it must submit its documents for registration with the executive committee of the local council of people's deputies, which must then complete the formalities of registration within one week.

Management and governance in the commercialized entities

After becoming legal persons, the new entities assume all management responsibilities themselves, including personnel decisions (hiring, dismissal, training), and have the right to conclude contracts on their own account. The original enterprise's founder represents the state's ownership rights and establishes contracts with managers to operate the business. The management must submit annual reports to the founder. Where the commercialization has been carried out by a state body, the state retains ownership rights in the first instance, but may later lease or sell (in whole or in part).

Extent of commercialization

Commercialization began on January 31, 1992, in retail trade and in catering. At the beginning of March, the Ministry of Trade inspected eighteen of the twenty-five districts of Ukraine and the Crimean Autonomous Republic to assess the extent of commercialization in this sector. It found that only one per cent, or 858 enterprises out of the total of 85,000, had been commercialized: 529 out of 45,000 in retail trade, 306 out of about 40,000 in canteen catering, and sixteen in non-trade activity. A further 3,000 working collectives had submitted applications for registration to initiate the process.

No further data on commercialization are available at this early stage. There is also no information available on the extent to which state enterprises are broken up in this process.

The government intends the changeover to be gradual, and acknowledges that it faces many obstacles, even in the initial program in the retail trade and catering sector. There is as yet no completed inventory distinguishing between property in state and in municipal ownership. The local municipal property funds, which are to implement the process, do not yet exist in all localities.

Furthermore, many of the affected enterprises may not be economically viable, especially as they lack reserves and cannot afford credit to meet short-term losses. The problems of non-viability were exacerbated by the partial price liberalization of January 1992. Costs rose rapidly, relative to revenues, when producer prices and the prices of transport and municipal services were freed, but the retail prices of about 44 per cent of food items were still regulated: shops and canteens faced a crisis with losses of more than Rb 200 mln.

ESTONIA

CONTENTS

1. INTRODUCTION

Brief history of reforms

Estonia has the smallest population of the former Soviet republics. During the interwar period, its economy was predominantly agricultural. Following its annexation by the Soviet Union in 1940 and the postwar reestablishment of Soviet control in 1944, Estonia underwent forced industrialization and collectivization. The policy of collectivization was reversed in the mid-1980s, and by the end of 1991, the agricultural sector consisted of a mixture of private and collective state farms. As in most other Soviet republics, more than half of the net material product was produced by industry, including construction.

The Supreme Soviet of the USSR adopted a decision on November 27, 1989, granted limited economic autonomy to the Baltic republics. Estonia declared complete independence in August 1991.

Estonia had begun to undertake its own reform steps even before it gained limited economic independence from the Soviet government. One of the first such steps was an initiation of price reform in December 1989. During 1990 and early 1991, prices of some consumer goods were gradually liberalized, while other prices were administratively increased. These price adjustments limited export sales and increased imports, thus helping, as intended, to relieve some of the supply shortages. Price liberalization continued in 1991, and by January 1992, most retail prices were fully decontrolled. Following the "big-bang" price liberalization in Russia in 1992, the Estonian government announced its intention to liberalize the remaining prices of consumer goods and services by early 1993.

Estonia has also undertaken pioneering reforms of its part of the Soviet banking structure. A legal framework for the development of the banking system was adopted in December 1989. It provided the basis for the establishment of a central bank, the Bank of Estonia, in March 1990. At that time the Soviet government refused to acknowledge the legitimacy of the Bank of Estonia, and the Bank coexisted with the Estonian branch of the Soviet State Bank, Gosbank. In March 1991, the Estonian government incorporated the Estonian branch of Gosbank into the Bank of Estonia. During the early part of 1992, Estonian authorities accelerated preparations for monetary reform. In June 1992, Estonia introduced the kroon, becoming the first former Soviet republic to replace the ruble with its own national currency.

Prior to 1991, Estonia's state budget was subordinate to the union budget prepared by the Soviet government. Although some initial steps toward budgetary reform took place at the end of 1989, major changes in the tax system and the budgetary process were carried out in the fall of 1990.

In 1990, Estonia also adopted its first law governing foreign trade with other republics and countries. This law replaced the previous trade regime, under which Estonian and other republican trade was regulated by the Soviet government.

2. ECONOMIC ENVIRONMENT

The structure of output

The gross domestic product of Estonia, in current 1991 prices, was Rb 16.32 bln.[1]

The structure of net material product (NMP) of Estonia has been similar to that prevailing in the former Soviet Union. As elsewhere

Table 2.1 Structure of net material product in 1989 (per cent of total)

	Estonia	Soviet Union
Industry	43	42
Agriculture	25	23
Construction	11	13
Other	21	22

Source: *PlanEcon* and "The Economy of the Former USSR," *IMF Economic Review*, April 1992

in the region, a relatively small number of large enterprises in Estonia have produced a large share of output and have employed a large proportion of the labor force.

Output

Following an increase of 6.4 per cent in 1990, Estonia's gross national product (GNP), expressed in 1990 prices, fell by 6.5 per cent in 1991. NMP also registered a drop of 8.9 per cent in 1991, after a small 1.1 per cent increase in 1990. The largest reversal was suffered by the transport and communications sectors, which, after a 20 per cent

---

[1] According to *PlanEcon*, the average "commercial" ruble–dollar exchange rate was 1.76 in 1990, 1.74 in 1991. It should be noted that these rates are distorted and thus dollar equivalents of local statistics are useful only for superficial illustrative purposes.

Table 2.2 Enterprises in 1990

	Number of enterprises	Number of employees
Enterprises by number of employees		
fewer than 4	10,555	14,159
5–9	2,680	17,461
10–19	2,056	28,444
20–49	2,197	67,845
50–99	1,093	74,225
100–199	603	84,210
200–499	616	195,765
500–999	241	163,530
more than 1,000	112	196,916
Totals	20,153	842,555

Source: Estonian State Department of Statistics

increase in output in 1990, fell by 11 per cent in 1991. NMP of industry grew by 5.4 per cent in 1990, and declined by 7.5 per cent in 1991. Agricultural output fell in both years, by 11 per cent in 1990 and 9.5 per cent in 1991.

In the first two months of 1992, industrial production fell by 36 per cent, and agricultural production declined by 46 per cent, compared with the same period in 1991. Unable to purchase on the open market many of the raw materials, previously supplied by Russia, industrial enterprises had to cut working hours. In January 1992, about one-third of all enterprises in Estonia had either completely discontinued production or were operating substantially below their standard capacity. By the end of April 1992, a great number of enterprises had completely exhausted their stocks of raw materials. According to the Estonian Department of Statistics, industrial production for the period between January and September 1992 was 36 per cent below its value for the same period in 1991.

Investment

Following a 2.7 per cent increase in 1990, gross investment in fixed capital fell by 15 per cent in 1991. The share of net investment in NMP also dropped, from about 22 per cent in 1990 to 19 per cent in 1991.

Household savings

There is no reliable estimate of the total stock of household savings in Estonia, since a significant proportion of savings has been kept outside the official banking system. According to the IMF monetary survey, the total amount of currency, time and demand deposits officially held by households was about Rb 5.5 bln by the end of 1990.

Price liberalization

As noted earlier, Estonia began the process of adjusting its price structure in December 1989. The price reform was spurred by increasing shortages, which the Estonian authorities hoped to lessen by increasing and maintaining prices at levels above those prevailing in the other republics of the union. Consequently, price controls were eliminated for a number of consumer goods, and other prices were sharply increased during the first half of 1990. After providing some compensation to the hardest hit groups of the population, in order to diffuse growing opposition to price increases, the authorities approved further increases in the prices of several food products during October 1990 and the first quarter of 1991. At the same time, state subsidies were reduced for energy, telecommunications, and transport. After a temporary price freeze during the first four months of 1991, the government continued to enlarge the scope of price liberalization throughout the remainder of 1991.

In January 1992, the breakdown of trade with Russia resulted in acute shortages in Estonia. Panic buying by the population further exacerbated the situation and the government resorted to rationing. The government's inability to stabilize the situation contributed substantially to its downfall on January 16, 1992. The new government resumed the policy of price liberalization, increasing energy prices and rents sharply in March 1992. Further increases in prices of flour, energy, and transportation were implemented in the fall of 1992. By the beginning of 1993 most relative prices in Estonia resembled relative prices typically found in world markets.

Inflation

In 1990, the cost-of-living index in Estonia rose by 80.1 per cent. In 1991 inflation accelerated considerably, as the cost-of-living index increased by 302 per cent.

Inflation accelerated from 37 per cent in the fourth quarter of 1990 to 88 per cent in January 1992, following price liberalization in Russia. Although the inflation rate dropped in February, the cumulative increase in consumer prices for the January–March period exceeded 300 per cent. After a decline to five per cent in May, inflation again accelerated in June, July and August 1992. After August 1992, the government switched from a cost-of-living index to a consumer price index. The changes in the index were 7 per cent per month in September and 8 per cent in October 1992.

Table 2.3   Cost-of-living index (month-to-month per cent change)

	Jan	Feb	Mar	Apr	May	June	July	Aug	Sept	Oct	Nov	Dec
1991	20	8	13	19	2	6	30	−.1	6	9	11	29
1992	88	74	30	11	5	11	24	18				

Source: Estonian Department of Statistics

Behavior of wages

Wages in governmental institutions are set according to fifty-five occupational classifications, the wage range in each group depending on length of service. Until February 1992, there was no systematic indexation mechanism. Wages in the government sector were adjusted at infrequent and irregular intervals and lagged behind inflation. The indexation system introduced in February stipulates monthly adjustments, with the indexation coefficient declining as the nominal wage level increases.

Wage setting in the state enterprise sector was decentralized in 1990. Enterprise insiders have been free to decide on their own compensation within parameters set by the minimum wage and a tax on "unjustifiably large" wage increases. Wages in the private sector are fully liberalized.

In 1991, the average monthly wage rose by 180 per cent. Although nominal wages more than doubled between January and May 1992, real wages dropped sharply relative to December 1991. The average nominal wage in the third quarter of 1992 was Kr 647.7 (DM 81).

Table 2.4 Average nominal monthly wage

	Rb	Kr
1991		
Jan	425	
Feb	454	
Mar	455	
Apr	578	
May	648	
June	750	
July	776	
Aug	752	
Sept	808	
Oct	961	
Nov	1,112	
Dec	1,580	
1992		
Jan	1,570	
Feb	2,200	
Mar	2,515	
Apr	3,620	
May	3,850	
June		450
July		520

Source: Estonian Ministry of Labor

Unemployment

Despite a 6.5 per cent drop in GNP in 1991, there were only approximately 900 registered unemployed persons by the end of January 1992. This represented about 0.1 per cent of a total work force of

880,000 persons employed at the end of 1990. The number of registered unemployed persons reached 8,500 by October 1992. However, the Parliamentary Commission on Social Work reported that the total number of persons out of employment, which includes registered unemployed and persons on forced holidays and looking for work, exceeded 75,000 in October 1992.

State budget

After generating a surplus of Rb 231 mln in 1990, the Estonian state budget posted an even greater surplus of Rb 898 mln (5.5 per cent of GDP) in 1991. Despite a 42 per cent drop in revenues, in real terms, the government managed to decrease real expenditures by 45 per cent. Preliminary figures for the first six months of 1992 indicate that the consolidated budgets of both the central and local governments are again expected to generate surpluses.

The 1991 tax receipts fell by 34 per cent, in real terms, about 11 per cent less than the fall in real expenditures. Current expenditures by the central government declined by Rb 228 mln in nominal terms. However, levels of both expenditures and tax receipts by local governments increased sharply, but by the same amounts, reflecting the decentralization of the budgetary process in Estonia.

TAXATION

Since 1991, personal income tax has been collected by local governments, according to uniform rates that apply throughout the country. The tax brackets were revised in January 1992, and the following marginal tax rates were introduced: incomes up to Rb 4,800 per annum – exempt; incomes between Rb 4,801 and Rb 10,800 per annum – 16 per cent; incomes between Rb 10,801 and Rb 18,000 – 24 per cent; and incomes in excess of Rb 18,000 – 33 per cent.

Corporate income tax is based on a firm's annual adjusted gross profit. The following marginal rates were introduced in January 1992: 15 per cent for annual profits up to Rb 500,000; 23 per cent for profits between Rb 500,000 and Rb 1 mln, and 30 per cent for profits greater than Rb 1 mln. In addition, all employers must contribute to the Social Security Fund. However, joint ventures with foreign participation are eligible for exemption from or reduction of the corporate income tax if they comply with certain conditions.

A value added tax is levied on most goods and services. The state rate is 7 per cent, but local governments may increase the rate to 10 per cent, and use the additional proceeds to fund local expenditures. This tax was increased to 18 per cent at the end of June 1992.

The tax structure of Estonia has recently been changed, following the introduction of the national currency in June 1992.

Monetary policy

MONEY SUPPLY

Since Estonia gained independence in August 1991, the limited supply of rubles, which traditionally had been supplied by Gosbank and used for all consumer transactions, has dominated all other monetary policy issues. In fact, the disruption caused by the cash shortage has rendered invalid the use of standard measures in the assessment of the monetary environment.

The shortage reached crisis proportions in March 1992. The authorities moved to limit the use of cash for wage payments and introduced checks as a means of payment. At the same time, the Bank of Estonia banned trade establishments from using cash in dealings with industrial enterprises and wholesale establishments. Banks were instructed to monitor all cash accounts closely. The shortage provided further impetus for the ongoing preparations for the introduction of a national currency.

In June 1992, Estonia introduced its own currency, the kroon. It is officially pegged at about Kr 8 to the D-mark. The kroon is supported by a $120 mln stabilization fund.

INTEREST RATES

Despite the impressive growth of private commercial banks, credit in Estonia continues to be provided primarily by state commercial banks. As in other former Soviet republics, these banks lend the funds "refinanced" by the Central Bank out of deposits in the state Savings Bank.

Until 1991, state banks maintained low interest rates on loans. The rapid acceleration of inflation and the conversion of the two major state banks into corporate form has led to increases in their lending rates, from about 17–20 per cent during the summer of 1991 to 35–50 per cent by the end of the year. Lending rates rose sharply in 1992. According to the Bank of Estonia, the prevailing lending rate in October 1992 was between 45 and 50 per cent.

Table 2.5 Estimated interest rates

| | 1991 | | 1992 | | |
	June	Dec	Jan	Apr–June	July–Aug
Lending rate					
"Prevailing"	17–25	35–50	60–70	100–140	40–80
Min-max	4–35	5–75	n/a–120	50–170	15–100
Deposit rate					
"Prevailing"	4–7	n/a	n/a	5–15	6–25
Min-max	2–10	2–15	2–30	2–30	2–40

Source: Based on preliminary data from the Bank of Estonia

Debt

The question of Estonia's responsibility for a portion of the external debt burden of the former Soviet Union remains to be settled. Some preliminary estimates put the total of recent loans taken directly by the Bank of Estonia at $39 mln. Estonia also expects to receive loans of $40 mln from the IMF and $30 mln from the World Bank.

Foreign trade

The first important steps toward the liberalization of foreign trade were taken in the summer of 1990. Most goods, however, remained licensed. Foreign trade transactions were significantly liberalized in the fall of 1991. Except for exports of natural resources, some raw materials, and foodstuffs, licenses are no longer required for foreign trade sales in convertible currencies. However (at the time of this writing), permits are still required for ruble exports of eighty-nine goods.

In order to establish a control system for goods crossing Estonian borders, an independent Estonian customs office was founded as an independent state organization on October 1, 1991. The Soviet customs office ceased its operations at the beginning of November 1991.

In 1990, about 94 per cent of Estonian exports and 82 per cent of its imports were interrepublican. According to the Estonian Department of Statistics, the interrepublican trade balance of Estonia moved from a Rb 335 mln deficit in 1990 to a Rb 1.2 bln surplus in 1991. The bulk of this trade was with Russia, and the 1991 surplus was almost entirely due to higher exports to Russia. This indicates that the authorities' policy of maintaining higher ruble prices in Estonia than in Russia was not effective in impeding the flow of goods to Russia. Moreover, due to various Russian export restrictions, imports from Russia remained unchanged in 1991.

Estonia's trade with the former Comecon countries collapsed in 1991, while exports and imports in convertible currencies increased by 81 per cent and 12 per cent, respectively.

An economic and trade agreement between Estonia and Russia was signed on December 28, 1991. However, due to the absence of a functioning licensing system in Russia, trade with Russia came to a virtual halt in January 1992. Moreover, a concrete agreement defining quotas for bilateral trade and the amount of state-guaranteed deliveries was signed only at the end of February 1992. With the agreement signed, imports of Russian raw materials and fuel resumed. Nominal exports to the former Soviet republics increased from Rb 5.1 bln for the whole of 1991 to Rb 7.8 bln by the end of the second quarter 1992, while nominal imports from the former Soviet republics increased from Rb 3.8 bln to Rb 5.4 bln during the same period.

Nominal trade with other countries posted a deficit of Rb 85 bln at the end of June 1992, a decrease in nominal and real terms relative to a Rb 410 bln deficit at the end of 1991.

3. PRESENT FORMS OF OWNERSHIP

3A. Legal framework of economic activity

The validity of Soviet laws in Estonia

The process by which Estonia replaced much of the old Soviet legislation with its own was gradual. Until November 1988, the principle of the validity of all legal acts was governed by the Soviet Constitution, and the Union laws prevailed over all local enactments. As of November 16, 1988, the Estonian Supreme Soviet declared the independence of Estonia and declared that new Soviet laws would be valid in Estonia only upon their registration by the Presidium of the Estonian Supreme Soviet. The declaration of independence also gave

Estonian authorities the right to suspend or restrict the validity of any old Soviet laws which conflicted with the principle of Estonian sovereignty. In practice, however, the validity of unregistered Soviet laws was rarely questioned and conflicts with Soviet laws were avoided. Moreover, in November 1989, the USSR Supreme Soviet adopted a law granting economic autonomy to the Baltic republics and restricting the validity of Soviet laws on their territory, if such laws regulated economic relations in a way that "obstructed their transition to economic autonomy." This law gave Estonia a freer hand in elaborating its own legislation, and a large number of local laws were passed concerning banking, farming, budget, taxes, joint-stock companies, collective enterprises, etc.

Estonian claims for sovereignty peaked again in March 1990, following the Estonian parliamentary elections. On March 30, 1990, the new parliament adopted a resolution "On the Political Status of Estonia," which declared that the Soviet occupation of Estonia in June 1940 did not interrupt the *de jure* existence of the Republic of Estonia. Furthermore, on May 16, 1990, the parliament adopted another law which confirmed the validity of all laws operating on the territory of Estonia at that time and made no future Soviet enactments valid in Estonia. Another law, confirming this state of affairs was passed in the aftermath of the failed Soviet *coup* in August 1991. Since then a large number of old Soviet laws have been repealed, and the validity of others seriously modified. In these cases, the old Soviet laws were not formally amended, however, but rather new Estonian legislation was passed, limiting their operation.

Existing and planned legislation concerning property rights

The following are the more important laws and regulations concerning property rights, forms of business organizations, and privatization in Estonia:

— Resolutions No. 43/1986 and No. 91/1987 of the Soviet Council of Ministers' Commission for the Improvement of Governance, Planning, and Economic Mechanism (concerning small state enterprises in Estonia);
— Law on Enterprises in the Estonian Soviet Socialist Republic (the "Enterprise Law") (1989, amended 1992);
— Law on Farms (1989);

— Government Decree on Collective (People's) Enterprises (No. 411/1989);
— Government Decree on Joint-Stock Companies (No. 385/1989);
— Law on Ownership (1990);
— Law on the Privatization of State-Owned Service, Trade,and Catering Establishments (the "Small Privatization Law") (1990);
— Government Decree on Economic Associations (No. 122/1990);
— Government Decree on the Establishment of the Department of State Property (No. 200/1990);
— Government Decree on Municipal Enterprises (No. 38/1990);
— Government Decree on State Enterprises in the Republic of Estonia ("Decree on State Enterprises") (No. 140/1990, amended on June 10, 1992);
— Government Decree on the Transformation of State-Owned Enterprises Belonging to the Republic of Estonia to New Organizational Forms ("the Transformation Decree") (No. 264/Dec. 29, 1990, amended on July 6, 1992, see infra) containing the following acts:
1. Regulations Concerning Administrative Councils of State Enterprises ("Administrative Councils Regulations");
2. Interim Regulations for the Establishment of State-Owned Joint-Stock Companies;
3. Interim Regulations Concerning the Board of Type I State-Owned Joint-Stock Companies ("Type I Regulations");
4. Interim Regulations Concerning the Board of Type II State-Owned Joint-Stock Companies ("Type II Regulations");
— Law on the Fundamentals of Ownership Reform (1991);
— Law on Land Reform (1991);
— Government Decree on Lease Relationship (No. 17/1991), including the Decree on Lease Enterprises;
— Government Decree on the Privatization of All-Union Enterprises, Institutions and Organizations Located on the Territory of the Republic of Estonia (No. 91/1991);
— Law on Agricultural Reform of the Republic of Estonia (1992);
— The Bankruptcy Law of the Republic of Estonia (1992);
— Law on Cooperatives (1992);
— Law on Making Alterations and Amendments to the Law on Privatization of State-Owned Service, Retail, and Catering Enterprises (1992);
— Government Decree on Partial Amendments to the Decree No. 264 of Dec. 29, 1990 (1992).

Recognized forms of business organizations

LEGAL REGIME OF BUSINESS ACTIVITY

The general legal basis for the development of new property relations in Estonia was established by the Law on Ownership, adopted in June 1990. The law recognized personal (private), municipal, state, and common property, and conferred equal legal status on all.[2] The law also stated that property could be confiscated only for the sake of public interest and that such confiscation must follow legal procedures.

The permissible forms of commercial activity and their regulation were, in turn, defined by the Law on Enterprises in the Estonian Soviet Socialist Republic ("Enterprise Law"), passed in November 1989 and amended in June 1992. A new Law on Entrepreneurship is reportedly in preparation.

The Enterprise Law permits commercial activity in all spheres except those prohibited by the national government. The government may also list areas of activity requiring special licenses. The law permits the foundation of commercial enterprises by state bodies (both national and local), private persons, other enterprises, and social organizations, and grants them independence from the state (except in the case of enterprises owned by the state). The law also requires, however, that a "foundation license" be obtained from an appropriate local government prior to the registration of a new enterprise. An application for such a license must be processed within thirty days, and may be denied if the enterprise's activity would be "harmful to the interests of the local territory or the environment"; if the foundation documents contain a procedural irregularity; or if the proposed activity of the enterprise is illegal. The applicant has a right to appeal a negative decision.

In addition to a foundation license, the law also requires the registration of all enterprises with the local authorities, though it specifically prohibits denials of registration based on an evaluation of the "usefulness" or "expediency" of the enterprise. All enterprises existing at the time of the enactment of the Enterprise Law were required to re-register in accordance with the new law.

THE STATE SECTOR

The state sector in Estonia comprises a remarkable variety of

---

[2] As originally enacted, the law did not allow private ownership of land, but that restriction is no longer in force.

organizational forms, some of which still have their legal basis in Soviet legislation.

- Several large enterprises formerly under the jurisdiction of the Union government still function according to the old Soviet Law on State Enterprises of 1987.
- A large number of so-called "small state enterprises" have remained in this form, originally created on the basis of special Resolutions No. 43/1986 and No. 91/1987 of the Soviet Council of Ministers' Commission for the Improvement of Governance, Planning, and Economic Mechanism, as part of an economic experiment in Estonia.
- The Estonian Government Decree (No. 140/1990) on State Enterprises in the Republic of Estonia ("Decree on State Enterprises"), together with the Regulations Concerning Administrative Councils of State Enterprises (the "Administrative Councils Regulations") and subsequent amendments, created the legal basis on which Estonian state enterprises not subject to privatization (e.g. mining establishments, railways, and power plants) are administered.
- A similar legislation, the Government Decree on Municipal Enterprises (No. 38/1990), established a legal framework for municipal enterprises in Estonia.
- Other state enterprises have been transformed into special kinds of joint-stock companies on the basis of the Government Decree on the Transformation of State-Owned Enterprises Belonging to the Republic of Estonia into New Organizational Forms (No. 264/1990) (the "Transformation Decree"). These joint-stock companies are, in turn, divided into two types, so-called Type I and Type II, the former comprising firms in which the state intends to remain a majority shareholder for the indeterminate future, the latter destined to be privatized as soon as is feasible.
- Finally, Estonia has two types of hybrid enterprises based on leasing contracts with work collectives: the first type, established by Government Decree on Collective (People's) Enterprises (No.411/1989) is referred to as a "collective enterprise"; the second type, regulated by the Government Decree on Lease Enterprises (enacted together with the Government Decree on Lease Relationships (No.17/1991)), is known under the more familiar name of a "lease enterprise."

As a result of dissatisfaction with the functioning of the state sector, extensive amendments to the Enterprise Law and the Transformation Decree were adopted on June 10, 1992 and July 6, 1992, respectively. These amendments strengthened the role of the government organs functioning as the founders of state enterprises and state-owned joint-stock companies, and tightened the rules of governance of state-owned firms. In addition, the Government Decree on Involvement of Public Servants in Business Activities (No. 164/1992) prescribed a number of rules barring directors and managers of state-owned firms from engaging in certain transactions involving their firms, as well as a number of disclosure rules concerning potential conflict of interest situations.

State enterprises under Estonian legislation. As of September 1992, there were approximately fifty state enterprises organized under the Decree on State Enterprises and the Enterprise Law, including a number of large-scale enterprises with numerous branches. (Already at this time, some 230 state enterprises had been transformed into state-owned joint-stock companies.)

State enterprises may be founded on the basis of an authorization by the government and a resolution of the parliament. Proposals for the creation of a state enterprise may be submitted by the government, individual ministries, organs of state administration, and other, already existing state enterprises. Upon the issuance of such authorization, the corresponding branch ministry or the Ministry of the Economy becomes the founder of the new enterprise.

The founder must prepare a charter for each enterprise, which defines the scope of its activities, the value and the nature of the state property contributed by its founder, the rules concerning profit distribution, and the procedure for its reorganization or liquidation.

The 1992 amendments to the Transformation Decree state that the founder is "the highest governing body" of a state enterprise, charged with pursuing the economic policy of the state. But the founder has few powers of direct intervention in the daily operation of a state enterprise; instead, except in the event of a decision to liquidate or reorganize the enterprise, the founder must act through the enterprise's Administrative Council, composed of up to seven members appointed for up to five-year terms. Half of the council members are appointed by the founder and half by the Ministry of the Economy in consultation with other interested state bodies; the members are supposed to come from the ranks of scientists, economists, financial specialists, and representatives of "social activities." (Both the founder and the Ministry of the Economy are entitled to object to each other's candidates, the government serving as an arbiter in such disputes.) Members of the council serve on the basis of a standard contract, prepared jointly by the Ministries of Labor, Finance, and Justice. A special governmental decree of September 1992 fixes their compensation at a multiple (between one and three) of the minimum wage, the multiplier being determined by the size of the enterprise's wage fund.

The Administrative Council, which must meet at least quarterly, is responsible for the appointment and removal of the director of the enterprise (whose salary, however, is fixed by the founder), the choice of the auditor of the enterprise, the approval of the annual accounts and the distribution of profits, the endorsement of next year's budget, decisions concerning transactions involving assets governed by the rules established by the Department of State Property,[3] the approval of long-term loans and investments, the establishment of subsidiaries and representative offices, and the pursuit of the economic policy of the state as defined by the branch ministry development program. The council is also charged with making proposals to the founder concerning subsidies, changes in the enterprise charter, enterprise reorganization or liquidation, and enterprise privatization of assets. The council makes decisions by a simple majority vote, except for decisions concerning charter amendments and restructuring or liquidation, which must receive the support of three-fourths of its members.

The day-to-day management of a state enterprise is in the hands of a director appointed by the council. The director prepares the enterprise budget, oversees enterprise operations, and determines salaries, bonuses, and job classifications. Enterprise directors represent enterprises in all of their official business.

State enterprises also have an Auditing Commission which monitors the annual budget and submits its own yearly report. Members of a state enterprise Auditing Commission cannot serve on the Administrative Council or be employed in the accounting department of the enterprise. Nor can they be relatives of persons in these positions.

Small state enterprises. Beginning in late 1986 and 1987, as part of the reforms associated with "perestroika," Estonian ministries, state

---

[3] For the role of the Department of State Property, see Section 4A below.

enterprises, and other bodies were given the right to establish so-called "small enterprises," employing up to fifty employees, which were governed by a special set of regulations established in the resolutions of the Soviet Council of Ministers' Commission for the Improvement of Governance, Planning, and Economic Mechanism (No. 43/1986 and No. 91/1987). The special status of these small enterprises entitled them to tax allowances and greater control over profits, prices, and salaries. By the beginning of 1991, 700 such enterprises had been established in Estonia.

The founder of a small state enterprise, which was most often an ordinary state enterprise, a cooperative, or a social organization, was responsible for the administration of the small enterprise. It could allow the small enterprise to use its equipment, rooms and other fixed assets, but nearly 20 per cent of small enterprises did not receive anything from the founder; this was in effect a disguised form of essentially private enterprises. Indeed, many of today's successful Estonian entrepreneurs first established their businesses as small state enterprises.

While many small state enterprises have been *de facto* privatized, and others are scheduled to be reorganized in accordance with Estonian laws (see Section 5 below), the process of transformation has been delayed by parliament's failure to adopt appropriate transition legislation. As a result, 627 small state enterprises are still formally listed in the Estonian Register of Enterprises and this strange hybrid still functions under Soviet legal norms.

State enterprises under Soviet legislation. The Transformation Decree of 1990 applied only to state enterprises owned by Estonia, and not to state enterprises subject to Union jurisdiction during the Soviet regime. Subsequently, Estonia has been very slow to convert former Union enterprises into entities operating under Estonian laws, although enterprises in this category were subject to corporatization pursuant to the Government Decree on the Privatization of All-Union Enterprises, Institutions and Organizations Located on the Territory of the Republic of Estonia (No. 91/1991). In fact, the process of granting Estonian legal status to former Soviet enterprises began only in September 1991, and between twenty and thirty state enterprises governed by Soviet laws were still in existence as of September 1992. Some recent proposals envisage dividing most of these enterprises during their corporatization into as many as twenty or thirty units, according to regional and technological specialization.

State-owned joint-stock companies. Large-scale reorganization of state enterprises in Estonia was mandated by the Transformation Decree. In addition to calling for the reorganization of all state enterprises owned by Estonia, in accordance with new Estonian legislation, the Interim Regulations for the Establishment of State-Owned Joint-Stock Companies, promulgated as part of the Transformation Decree, called for the conversion of most state enterprises into state-owned joint-stock companies. These new state companies were in turn divided into two types: those operating in strategic areas of the economy (Type I), in which the state intends to maintain over 50 per cent share ownership for the foreseeable future, and all others (Type II), which are intended to be privatized. The decision concerning the establishment of a state joint-stock company was to be made by the government on the motion of the Ministry of the Economy. The ministry, in turn, was supposed to consider proposals submitted by the state enterprises to be converted. The government also had the power to determine whether a Type I or Type II company would be formed.[4] The share capital of a state joint-stock company at the moment of conversion was the book value of the fixed and current assets of the former state enterprise,[5] and the new company was considered a legal successor of the old state enterprise.

Separate, but nearly identical, regulations concerning the governance structure of Type I and Type II companies were promulgated simultaneously with the Transformation Decree, and both of them were significantly amended in July 1992.[6] The regulations establish the founder of the state joint-stock company (a branch ministry or the Ministry of the Economy) as its highest organ, acting through a Board of Directors in pursuance of state economic policies. As in the case of state enterprises, however, the founder has only limited powers of direct intervention, and significantly less freedom in choosing the members of the board.

The Board of Directors of a state joint-stock company is composed of an odd number of (maximum seven) members, appointed for

---

[4] Subsequently to the conversion of most state enterprises, the July 1992 amendments to the Transformation Decree provided that in the future state joint-stock companies would be established by appropriate branch ministries or the Ministry of the Economy in coordination with the Department of State Property.

[5] The Department of State Property was required, however, to reevaluate the assets of a state joint-stock company prior to its privatization.

[6] The 1992 amendments in fact eliminated all but one of the differences between the original Type I and Type II Regulations.

three-year terms. One candidate for membership status (who cannot be the enterprise's managing director) is presented for the founding ministry's approval by the work collective of the enterprise. If the minister does not approve the work collective's candidate, a second one is forwarded, but if this person is not approved, the original candidate becomes a board member. Half of the remaining members are chosen by the branch ministry, and the other half by the Ministry of the Economy in coordination with other ministries involved, subject to the founder's approval. The members appointed by the Ministry of Economy generally include one so-called "ideologist" (usually a ministry official), one technical or financial expert (often an officer of a commercial bank) and one management consultant or business representative. The ministry seeks to ensure that board members are not senior government officials, representatives of competing firms, or members of industrial concerns or associations of which the enterprise is a part. However, since the final decision is made by the founder, which is most often the branch ministry, the balance of power under the "quota" system for appointments favors the latter and enables it to override the policies adopted by the Ministry of the Economy. A typical board in a state joint-stock company may thus ultimately comprise: a managing director of another company, a deputy minister and a general specialist from the Ministry of Industry and Energy, a chief of a department of an industry branch association, a chief of a department from the Ministry of Finance, a general director from a construction-industry commercial bank, and a professor from Tallinn Technical University. The remuneration of the members of the board is governed by the same rules as that of the members of the Administration Council of a state enterprise (see above).

The Board of Directors of a state joint-stock company has extensive powers. It can generally make all decisions within the jurisdiction of the general shareholders' meeting of an ordinary joint-stock company (see below), with the exception of determining the board members' compensation, the establishment of a procedure for the sale of shares, and the reorganization or liquidation of the company.[7] The board also appoints and dismisses the general manager of the company, selects the auditor and arranges for ordinary and extraordinary audits, approves the company's annual accounts and budgets, decides on extending long-term loans, arranges the elaboration and execution

[7] The 1992 amendments have also reserved for the government the decision concerning the payment of dividends by state joint-stock companies.

of the development program, including a program of privatization, and implements state policy drawn up by the relevant ministry. Up to the limits set by the Department of State Property, the board may also sell, lease, or write off the assets of the company, as well as invest in joint ventures and other enterprises.

The Board of Directors is presided over by a chairman, elected by a majority vote of the board members representing a state department or organization.

(For more information concerning the process of conversion of state enterprises into state joint-stock companies, see also Section 5 below.)

Municipal enterprises. In accordance with the Government Decree on Municipal Enterprises (No. 38/1990), local government authorities are permitted to establish their own municipal enterprises. (Municipal enterprises may also be created by certain other local organs, and may issue shares to their founders.) These enterprises are given the status of juridical persons governed by the executive organ of the local government, but the local authorities are responsible for the obligations of their municipal enterprises as well as for the reimbursement of any losses suffered by the enterprises as a result of their fulfillment of contracts with their founding organs. The enterprises, on the other hand, are not responsible for the obligations of the municipalities or other municipal enterprises.

The principles of governance of municipal enterprises are largely determined by their charters, with day-to-day operations being managed by a director. The director is appointed by the founding organ, and he in turn appoints his deputies and division leaders, and concludes labor agreements with employees.

LEASING ARRANGEMENTS IN ESTONIA
Estonia has two different, but very similar, types of formal enterprises based on a leasing system: the so-called "collective enterprises" and "lease enterprises." (Because of the similarity between these two types, it is expected that new legislation will subject them to a common legal regime in the future.) There also exist other, less formal arrangements, in which state property is leased to employees, but only the more formal arrangements, resulting in the establishment of a special legal form of business organization, will be discussed below.

Collective (people's) enterprises. Collective enterprises, seven of which existed in Estonia as of September 1992, are regulated by the

Government   Decree   on   Collective   (People's)   Enterprises
(No.411/1989). They use and manage state or municipal property
granted to the work collective on the basis of a signed constituent
agreement, which guarantees specified fees to the state or municipal
budget, with the remaining profits, after taxes and other required
deductions (such as contributions to the reserve fund), belonging to
the members. Collective enterprises are liable for their obligations with
their own assets, but the member-workers are also personally liable.
Up to a quarter of each member's salary may be garnished if the risk
fund proves to be insufficient to meet the obligations of the enterprise.

The initiative for the establishment of a collective enterprise comes
from the work collective of a state or municipal enterprise, which peti-
tions the central or local government which owns the enterprise that
it be converted into a collective enterprise. The request must contain
a detailed budget, a commitment that the profits of the enterprise will
not be diminished, and a draft of the bylaws. The request is supposed
to be accepted if it has the support of three-fourths of the employees.
(The application must be processed by the government within a two-
month period.) The constitutive agreement, signed between the
founder government and the representatives of the work collective,
has no prescribed term (this is one of the differences between the
collective and lease enterprises), but contains a procedure for safeguarding the governmental interest in the property of the enterprise, the
budgetary obligations of the collective, and the basis for changing the
agreement. There is no standard buy-out provision, but purchase of
the property of the enterprise may be negotiated at the time of its
liquidation. A collective enterprise can also issue non-tradable
employee shares which are sold back to the enterprise at the termination of the employee's membership.

The statutory organs of a collective enterprise are: the general
meeting of the members (or their delegates), a Council of Representatives (which is mandatory in enterprises with more than 200
employees), the Management Board (including the Director of the
enterprise) and an Auditing Commission.

The general meeting, which must be called annually, has the right to
approve any alteration of the bylaws; to hire and fire the director; to
elect the council, the Auditing Commission, and, upon the director's
proposal, the Management Board;[8] to approve labor rules and salaries,

---

[8]   The Management Board may also be elected by the council, if the bylaws so provide.

profit distributions, and long-term development programs; and to decide (by a two-thirds majority) on the liquidation of the enterprise. The council (two-thirds of which must be members of the enterprise) hires and fires deputy directors, approves the reports and instructions of the main officers, and approves the annual financial plan of the enterprise. The Management Board governs the enterprise between the sessions of the council and the general meeting. The Auditing Commission, which is responsible only to the general meeting, is authorized to examine all financial and economic activities of the enterprise.

Upon the liquidation of a collective enterprise, all property contributed by the government reverts back to the appropriate authorities and the enterprise's reserve fund is distributed among the members.

Lease enterprises. Lease enterprises, which are a common feature of the former Soviet republics,[9] are regulated by the Estonian Government Decree on Lease Relationships (No.17/1991) and the accompanying Decree on Lease Enterprises. Although the assets of a state enterprise may be leased (on an ordinary lease) to all kinds of natural and legal persons, the special legal form of "lease enterprise" can be formed only by the employees of a state enterprise, its structural unit or subdivision, municipal enterprise, cooperative, public organization, or other legal entity controlled by the state. Since the lessor is the owner of the leased assets, and a lease enterprise is, in turn, empowered to sublease its assets to other individuals, state enterprises may remove a substantial portion of their assets from direct state control and increase the power of insiders by forming a string of leased subsidiaries.

A lease relationship is established by a petition of the employees, who must approve the proposed lease and the bylaws of the enterprise by two-thirds of the votes cast at a special general meeting of full-time employees. Draft leases are examined by the Department of State Property, which can reject them if the enterprise is scheduled to be privatized, or if the lease contains improper buy-out provisions, contradicts the decentralization policy of the Estonian government (i.e., presumably makes it impossible to break up very large

---

[9] See the appropriate section of the chapter on Russia in this volume. The lease enterprises established in Estonia on the basis of prior Soviet legislation were brought into conformity with Estonian legislation, but this legislation was in part modelled on the Soviet laws of 1989.

enterprises), or fails to provide adequate guarantees for the effective use of state property.

The creation of a lease enterprise has priority over other forms of leasing of state property. Thus, neither the enterprise as a whole, nor any of its assets, may be leased to any parties (including enterprise insiders), without first giving the employees an option to form a lease enterprise. Moreover, while any other form of leasing must be initiated through an open competitive procedure, the establishment of a lease enterprise is exempted from this requirement. The amount of rent is stipulated by the lessor, taking into account foregone profits, depreciation of leased property, and the cost of services rendered to the lease enterprise. Lease enterprises are also exempt from capital requirements imposed on other lessees.

All employees who voted in favor of establishing a lease enterprise, as well as those who applied within one month of the founding meeting, become founding members, with continued membership predicated on continued employment. Non-member employees can also be hired on a contractual basis, and full-time employees at the time of the founding who do not apply for membership have priority rights to being hired as contractual laborers.

Lease enterprises are governed by a general meeting of members, a Board of Directors, the management, and an Auditing Commission.[10] The general meeting, which must be held at least semi-annually, has the right to amend the bylaws; elect the board and its chairman, the management, and the Auditing Commission; confirm the appointment and dismissal of the director; approve development plans, distribution of profits, and terms of remuneration; and make decisions concerning liquidation.

A board, which is a required feature of all enterprises with over 100 members, is composed of members of the enterprise elected at the general meeting. Its competences are established by the bylaws, and it may be given the right to make decisions in all matters not exclusively reserved for the general meeting. The rights and responsibilities of the management, elected from among the members of the enterprise, are defined in the bylaws. Day-to-day operations, as well as other tasks specified by the management, are conferred on the director, who is proposed by the board and approved by the general meeting. The

---

[10] Enterprises with fewer than twenty members may have a single auditor, instead of an auditing commission.

manager can be the head of the management, but does not have to be a member of the enterprise.

The lease enterprise has full proprietary rights over all items manufactured or produced by the enterprise, as well as all income derived from the operation of the enterprise.

In the case of a liquidation of a lease enterprise, all leased property is returned to the lessor, while the assets remaining after all creditors are satisfied are distributed among the members.

COOPERATIVES

Like all former Soviet republics, Estonia had a large pseudo-cooperative sector, primarily in agriculture and services, as well as a number of more modern, entrepreneurial cooperatives created under the Soviet Law on Cooperatives (1988, amended in 1989 and 1990).[11] As of August 1992, there were still 4,288 non-agricultural cooperatives listed in the Estonian Register of Enterprises. New legislation in place at that time, however, provided for a wholesale dismantling and reorganization of the cooperative sector in Estonia.

Non-agricultural cooperatives. A new legal regime for the cooperative sector has been established by the Law on Cooperatives, passed by the parliament in August 1992. Cooperatives existing under other legal norms were given six months to conform to the new regulations.

The law defines the cooperative as a society of three or more members which undertakes activities for the benefit of its members. It divides all cooperatives into for-profit entities, termed "commercial cooperatives," and not for-profit, termed "non-commercial cooperatives." Members, the majority of whom must be natural persons, are liable for the obligations of the cooperative to the extent of their membership contributions. They also have the right to leave the cooperative according to a prescribed procedure, involving an appropriate application and division of property.

After the satisfaction of statutory reserve requirements (20 per cent of the annual profits until the reserve fund equals at least 50 per cent of the equity of the cooperative), the profits of commercial cooperatives are to be paid out to the members. If the bylaws so provide, these payments may be in part in the form of fixed dividends, and in part in the form of payments proportional to the members' participation in the activities of the cooperative.

---

[11] See the subsection on cooperatives in the chapter on Russia in this volume.

The highest governing body of a cooperative is the general meeting of members, during which each member has one vote. (Cooperatives with over 200 members can substitute a meeting of authorized deputies for the general meeting.) The general meeting has exclusive competence over bylaw amendments and reorganization or dissolution of the cooperative. Its non-exclusive jurisdiction includes approval of the activities of the founding members, adoption of annual reports and audits, distribution of profits, definition of the conditions of service on the other governing bodies of the cooperative, and selection and dismissal of their members. Unless the bylaws provide otherwise, decisions are made by majority vote, except when decisions are made concerning the restructuring or liquidation of the cooperative (when a two-thirds majority is required).

The cooperative also has a Board of Directors which meets at least once every three months and decides on the admission and expulsion of members, hiring and dismissal of the executive director and other employees, and all other issues not reserved for the general meeting. The positions of chairman of the board and executive director cannot be held by the same person. The accounts of a cooperative are supervised by an auditing commission or, in the case of cooperatives with fewer than thirty members, a single auditor.

The reorganization of agricultural cooperatives. The reorganization and liquidation of collective farms is governed by the Law on Agricultural Reform of the Republic of Estonia, passed by the parliament in March 1992. For each collective farm, the law establishes a special Agricultural Reform Commission which is subject to local administration and composed of an equal number of representatives of the collective farm, local farmers, local government, and the state. The commission is empowered to make determinations concerning the return of expropriated land to previous owners, decide on the plots of land to be "municipalized" (i.e., turned over to local authorities), determine which persons have an ownership right in the residual collective property (see below), and approve the plan for the reorganization or liquidation of the collective farm.

Upon the resolution of all property claims put forth by original owners, municipalities, etc., the residual property of a collective farm is divided among its members and workers, with so-called "working shares" (a form of vouchers) apportioned on the basis of each individual's work contribution, measured according to both the length of service and the type of work performed. These working shares can then be reinvested with the legal successor of the collective farm, used to obtain a separate piece of the collective property, or transferred to another individual who lives in the same locality, or who has a restitutional, substitutional, or another preferential right to receive land in the same area in accordance with the Law on Land Reform (1991). (See also the subsection on vouchers in Section 4B below.)

Decisions concerning the future of the collective farm are made by the general meeting of all individuals who own working shares and other persons owning shares in the collective property, but are subject to the approval of the Agricultural Reform Commission. The general meeting can liquidate the collective farm or propose a plan for its reorganization, with priority given to new cooperative arrangements under Estonian legislation. If the commission rejects the proposals of the general meeting, the ultimate decision is made by the local government.

COMMERCIAL COMPANIES

Estonian business entities, other than joint-stock companies and individual entrepreneurs, are regulated by the Government Decree on Economic Associations (No. 122/1990), and can take the form of general or limited partnerships and limited-liability companies. A separate act, the Government Decree on Joint-Stock Companies (No. 385/1989), regulates the structure and activity of joint-stock companies. Strangely, the Estonian laws still do not provide for individual entrepreneurship, which is envisaged in the proposed new Law on Entrepreneurship.

General partnership. A general partnership is created by a written and signed deed of formation between two or more natural or juridical persons who remain jointly and severally liable for all obligations of the partnership. A partnership cannot be a partner of another partnership however. A person can be a general partner of only one general or limited partnership, and a partner's contribution can be withdrawn only with the consent of all the partners. A partnership, like all economic associations in Estonia, must have an external auditor or auditing commission, and an annual audit is required. A partner is entitled to a share of the partnership's profits corresponding to their contributions, and all partners must unanimously approve the annual balance sheets and the distribution of profits of the partnership.

The management of a partnership rests with partners to whom the partnership agreement vests managerial rights. However, these rights may be revoked by a vote of three-fourths of the partners. If more than one person has managerial rights, decisions require a simple majority, and, unless the partnership agreement stipulates otherwise, management of a partnership may be delegated to an individual manager, who does not have to be a partner. All partners are entitled to speak on behalf of the partnership, unless the deed of formation limits "representational rights" to one or several partners. Cancellation of representational rights requires a vote of three-fourths of the partners.

A partner may only leave the partnership with the consent of all the partners, and may be expelled by a vote of three-fourths of the partners (excluding the person affected). In both cases, the leaving partner's contribution (measured as a proportion of the book value attributable to his share) must be repaid to him, though this partner remains liable for partnership obligations incurred up to three years from the time of his exit from the partnership.

Limited partnership. A limited partnership consists of one or more general partners, who are jointly and severally liable for all obligations of the partnership, and one or more limited partners, who are liable only to the extent of their capital contributions. A limited partnership is governed by the same rules as a general partnership, except for a set of provisions concerning limited partners' rights and obligations.

A limited partner must pay at least 40 per cent of his contribution in cash, and may not be granted managerial or representational rights. A limited partner does have voting rights, however, on questions which do not concern the traditional fields of the partnership's activity, and at times when a transaction which was planned by a general partner with managerial rights has been suspended.

A limited partner is held responsible for the association's obligations incurred before his entry. Upon liquidation of the partnership, after creditors are paid, any residual property is distributed first to limited partners to repay their contributions.

Limited-liability company. A limited-liability company (LLC) is a familiar European form of business organization consisting of two or more partners who are liable for the association's obligations to the extent of their capital contribution. An LLC cannot be formed by a public subscription and its shares cannot be publicly traded. In addition to a deed of formation (charter), an LLC must also have bylaws. Both charter and bylaws must be signed by all the partners.

A partner (shareholder) of an LLC cannot demand repayment of his contribution, and is entitled to its repayment only at the termination or reorganization of the association. As with other associations, an LLC must have an external auditor who submits annual reports.

The shares of an LLC do not have to be of the same value, and each partner can have only one share, the value of which is proportional to his contribution. Shares are freely transferable between shareholders, but other partners have preemptive rights when a sale to a third party is proposed. Similar preemptive rights protect shareholders against dilution when an increase of the authorized capital of an LLC is proposed.

The highest organ of an LLC is the general meeting of the partners. A majority of three-fourths of the capital is required at a general meeting to change the authorized capital, approve the annual report and profit distribution, expel a member, and reorganize or liquidate the company. A simple majority is required for the election of auditors and board members, approval of contracts involving up to one-fourth of the authorized capital or agreements between the company and its shareholders, and other matters within the meeting's competences. Proxy votes are permitted, but a proxy must be another partner who is not the Chairman of the Board, the Executive Director, or the Chief Accountant. A quorum of partners representing three-fourths of the capital is required, but if the quorum is not achieved another meeting may be convened within seven to fourteen days at which no quorum is required.

The executive body of the company is the Board of Directors, elected at the general meeting. The board, in turn, elects its chairman (General Director). (Smaller companies may elect a single director in place of a board.) The board is entrusted with day-to-day management of the company, hiring and firing of employees (including the Executive Director, Treasurer, and other officers), entering into contracts on behalf of the company, etc. The board must immediately call a general meeting if the value of the authorized capital of the company has decreased by one-half as a result of business losses.

Joint-stock company. The Estonian joint-stock company (JSC) conforms roughly to the European model of a publicly traded business corporation, but the Decree on Joint-Stock Companies is sometimes rather sketchy about its governance structure and functioning.

A JSC must have a minimum capitalization of Rb 3,000 and at least three shareholders, although it may be founded by a single person. A JSC may issue different classes of shares, with different voting rights and nominal values, but all shares of the same class must have the same value, and all shares must be registered.[12]

The foundation of a JSC takes place through a share subscription, according to the rules specified in the decree.[13] In the case of over-subscription the founders have a choice of limiting the subscription on a first-come-first-served basis or presenting the matter to the foundation assembly (a constitutive meeting), which can approve an increase in the authorized capital and thus accommodate the excess demand.[14] The foundation assembly must meet within thirty days of the end of the subscription period, with the required quorum of one-half of subscribers and two-thirds of the capital. Decisions are made by a majority vote (with each person having one vote), but unanimity is required to change the company charter.[15] Among its other tasks is the confirmation of the value of non-financial deposits and the election of the Management Board and the Supervisory Council (unless the founders reserved the latter function for themselves).

The highest organ of the JSC is the general meeting of the shareholders, which must be attended by the holders of at least half of the share capital.[16] The voting at the general meeting is on the basis of one-share-one-vote, and a simple majority is required concerning most matters, including the election of the Management Board and the Supervisory Council, as well as the confirmation of their members' salaries. Decisions concerning changes in the bylaws, increases or decreases in the authorized capital, confirmation of the annual report

---

[12] The section on shareholders' rights and duties provides that each shareholder has the right "to elect and be elected to the managing and supervisory organs of the JSC." Taken literally, this would preclude non-voting shares. Similarly, no provisions are made for the issuing of debt instruments.

[13] It should be remembered that, in accordance with the Enterprise Law (see above), every business association in Estonia requires a foundation license issued by the appropriate local authorities.

[14] The bylaws of a JSC may provide for a minimum and maximum authorized capital (the former being no less than one-fourth of the latter), making it unnecessary to confine the subscription to a specific amount. All subscribers, including those who fail to become shareholders if the authorized capital is not increased, have the right to participate in the foundation assembly.

[15] Unanimity is also presumably required for the adoption of the company bylaws, and hence an increase of the authorized capital which may be required to accommodate an oversubscription.

[16] If a quorum is not achieved, the general meeting must be reconvened within fifteen days, and at the second meeting there is no quorum requirement.

and profit distribution, and the termination of the company's activities require a majority of two-thirds. Unlike the foundation assembly regulations, no explicit provision is made for proxy voting at the general meeting.

The JSC decree contains very few provisions concerning the composition and the function of the other organs of a JSC. The Management Board is said to be an executive organ of the company, with the right to direct all of its activities and to prepare the annual accounts for the general meeting. Members of the board, who need not be shareholders, elect their chairman. No provisions are made for the number of board members, and no provisions define the composition or the functions of the Supervisory Council. No reserve requirements are contained in the decree, nor are there any stipulations concerning accounting or the auditing of the accounts.

A new law on joint-stock companies is currently being prepared. It will be much more detailed and will fill many of the gaps left in the present legislation.

Bankruptcy

The Bankruptcy Law of the Republic of Estonia was enacted in June and went into effect in September 1992. It applies to all insolvent legal and natural persons located or domiciled in Estonia. Insolvency is defined expansively as inability to satisfy the claims of a creditor, where that inability is not due to a "temporary economic situation of the debtor." The law does not apply to organs of the government, and its application to banks and insurance companies is modified by special provisions of other laws.

Both debtors and unsecured creditors can petition the court for a declaration of bankruptcy. A creditor can petition the court to declare a debtor bankrupt if the debtor has performed acts intended to make him insolvent; if the creditor has obtained a legal judgement against the debtor which has been unenforceable for over three months; or if the debtor, having received notice of the creditor's intention to petition for bankruptcy, has not remitted, within ten days, payment on a debt that was over ten days overdue.

Upon the receipt of a bankruptcy petition the court appoints a temporary bankruptcy trustee to assemble and evaluate all debts and assets of the debtor. The court may also prohibit the transfer of the debtor's property, seize the debtor's property, or prohibit the debtor from leaving his domicile.

The court must rule within twenty days on a debtor's petition, and within two months on a creditor's petition. The bankruptcy judgement, which specifies the time and place of the first general meeting of the creditors, is published in a newspaper. Its effect is to transfer the property of the bankrupt to the management of a court-appointed trustee (who may or may not be the same person as the temporary trustee appointed upon the receipt of the original filing) and to bar the bankrupt, if he is an individual entrepreneur, from engaging in commercial activities until the conclusion of the bankruptcy proceedings. The announcement also serves to join all pending claims to the bankrupt's property in one proceeding, and to make all the debts of the bankrupt immediately due. At the same time, the declaration suspends the accrual of interest on the bankrupt's debts, which may be of particular significance in an inflationary economy, like that of Estonia, where debts may lose their real value during the bankruptcy proceedings.

The general meeting of creditors, whose members are required to present their claims to the trustee within two months of the bankruptcy announcement, approves the trustee, elects a bankruptcy committee, determines whether to continue the commercial activities of a legal entity bankrupt, decides on compromise proposals presented by the bankrupt and on the sale of the bankrupt's property, and defends the claims of the creditors. At the meeting, each creditor is apportioned votes in proportion to the amount of his claim. All decisions, with the exception of the approval of compromise agreements, are adopted by a simple majority of votes of the creditors attending the meeting, with no quorum requirements.

The court has the power to void certain transactions of the debtor in the process of assessing his debts and obligations. Voidable transactions include: 1) those which have occurred within the preceding year which intentionally impaired the interest of creditors; 2) those which occurred within three years of the bankruptcy if the debtor performed a criminal act in the course of the transaction and the other party knew or should have known of the transgression; and 3) those which occurred within five years if the action intentionally impaired the interests of creditors and the other party was a relative or close associate who knew or should have known of the intent of the transaction. Any transaction which occurred within ten days immediately preceding the declaration of bankruptcy, which is presumed to have intentionally impaired creditor interests, gift contracts which have been concluded within the last six months, or within the last five years if they involved relatives or close associates, can be voided regardless of the intent of the debtor or the knowledge of the other party.

All bankrupt legal persons whose assets are exceeded by the debts are to be liquidated by the end of the bankruptcy proceedings, unless a compromise agreement is approved or the debt is paid off in full. The bankrupt's property is sold at an auction or through some other method determined by the trustee. During the course of liquidation, the trustee can also terminate pre-existing labor contracts, but the state must compensate workers who are owed up to two months of wages by the bankrupt, and charge the cost of the compensation to the creditors.

The proceeds from the sale of the bankrupt's property are distributed according to the proposal of the trustee, approved by the court. The order of priorities specified in the law is the following: 1) payments needed to maintain the bankrupt and his family for up to two months; 2) satisfaction of secured creditors up to the extent of their security; 3) the costs of the bankruptcy proceedings, including the fee of the trustee; 4) wages, alimony, etc.; 4) taxes; and 5) payment of all other claims. (All claims in one category are fully satisfied before any of the claims of the next category are met.) Estonian law also contains a set of provisions concerning so-called "defense of claims," empowering the creditors' meeting to decide the acknowledgement and satisfaction of all unsecured claims against the bankrupt, to the extent that such claims exceed the bankrupts' assets. All claims are first examined by the trustee, with the trustee and the bankrupt having the right to submit their objections. The general meeting then examines each claim in the order of its submission and determines how much of each claim to acknowledge, and what proportion to satisfy.

At any point in the bankruptcy proceedings, the debtor may propose a "compromise" agreement for debt reduction or rescheduling. The proposed compromise is then presented to the meeting of the creditors, and is deemed to have been accepted if it receives the support of two-thirds of the present creditors holding at least two-thirds of the non-secured debt, as long as the debt reduction is less than 50 per cent. If the debt reduction sought is over 50 per cent, the compromise must be supported by three-fourths of the creditors present holding at least three-fourths of the non-secured debt. The court can reject the compromise in the event of procedural irregularities, or when the compromise is discriminatory with respect to some creditors, or harms the interests of secured creditors. A judicially confirmed compromise returns to the debtor rights to his property.

Regulations governing foreign ownership

The legal framework for foreign investment in Estonia is provided by the Estonian Republic's Law on Foreign Investment (Sept. 17, 1991) (the "Foreign Investment Law"). The law establishes the principle of equality, by virtue of which foreign investors in Estonia have the same rights and obligations as domestic persons in an analogous situation. The law specifies, however, a number of privileges and guarantees extended to foreign investors, and affirms the supremacy over domestic law (including the Foreign Investment Law) of all international treaties and agreements to which Estonia is a party. Excluded from the law's coverage are also certain specific sub-categories of foreign investment, such as those in free-trade zones and concession contracts, which are left for separate legislation.

The Foreign Investment Law provides a broad definition of a foreign investor, including all natural or juridical persons (even Estonian citizens residing abroad). But since foreign investment is defined as investments made in convertible currency (or out of profits of a convertible currency investment), the law in effect does not apply to ruble zone investments. On the other hand, the parliamentary order putting into effect the Foreign Investment Law conferred the status of "businesses with foreign capital" on all joint ventures already established under Soviet decrees, with the proviso that the Estonian law will apply to those joint ventures to the extent that it does not worsen the terms of their business activities.

The law contains no formal restrictions on the type or structure of foreign investment, whether it be a greenfield project or a partial or total acquisition of an existing business. It permits wholly-owned subsidiaries and branches of foreign corporations, as well as local agencies designed to represent and protect the interests of a foreign legal entity. Indeed, "any business established under Estonian law whose assets are partly or entirely owned by one or several foreign investors" qualifies as "a business with foreign capital." However, to qualify for certain privileges granted to foreign investments, such as tax holidays and a release from certain import and export restrictions, a business with foreign capital must have more than 30 per cent foreign participation.

Foreign investment may also be restricted from operating in certain sectors, and the government may impose special licensing requirements for certain activities. Such licensing requirements apply to air, sea, and rail transportation; international trucking; mining and geological works; trade in precious metals and production of goods involving such materials; production and sale of alcoholic beverages, narcotic, toxic, and radioactive substances; provision of medical care and production of pharmaceuticals; security services; insurance; some areas of construction; radio and television transmission; and some educational activities, among others. One area in which the law itself imposes a licensing requirement is that of banking. It identifies the Bank of Estonia as the only licensing body empowered to deny permission to operate to an investor who is judged "unreliable" or is seen as "seeking to gain a monopoly power over the Estonian banking system." Foreign investment licenses are sometimes required in addition to the "foundation licenses" required of all business associations in Estonia (see the subsection on legal regime of business activity in Section 3A, above).

A business with foreign capital is permitted to acquire real estate necessary to carry out the activities determined in its charter. No custom duties are charged on assets brought into Estonia as part of a foreign investment, and foreign investors can, without any restrictions, repatriate after-tax profits or proceeds from the sale of their investment. The significance of some of these privileges is temporarily mitigated, however, by the nonconvertibility of the Estonian currency. Given existing currency restrictions and inflation, it is of some significance that businesses with foreign capital may keep foreign currency accounts in Estonian banks and receive payments for their goods and services outside Estonia. A business with foreign capital may pay for goods with either foreign currency or the official currency of Estonia.

Together with the Foreign Investment Law, the Law on Tax Allowances to Enterprises with Foreign Capital granted special tax concessions to businesses with foreign participation. The same tax concessions were later incorporated into the Law on Corporate Income Tax, which took effect as of January 1992. According to these provisions, new businesses with at least 30 per cent foreign participation receive a two-year exemption from corporate taxation (beginning with the year in which profits are realized), followed by a 50 per cent reduction for the next two years. For businesses satisfying the same requirements and active in special "preferential fields" determined by the government, the initial exemption is extended to three years. Finally, businesses with at least 50 per cent foreign participation amounting to more than $1 mln receive a three-year exemption, followed by a 50 per cent reduction for the subsequent five years. In addition, up to 25 per cent of the profits of a business with foreign capital may be tax-free if these profits are paid into a fund for fixed capital formation and spent during the subsequent fiscal year. It should be noted, however, that the value of the tax concessions granted to foreign businesses in Estonia may be diminished by a combination of inflation and the accounting procedures used in the countries of the former Soviet Union. Since the Estonian Foreign Investment Law provides that a foreign investor's convertible currency contribution to the capital of an Estonian enterprise must be recalculated in local currency on the books of the enterprise, rapid inflation is apt to reduce its book value to a fraction of its original worth and result in generation of purely paper profits, which are then exempted from taxation before any real gains are realized.

3B. Structure of ownership

As discussed in more detail in Section 5, most socialized enterprises in Estonia have been transformed into joint-stock companies. In addition to these newly formed state-owned companies, the state sector in Estonia also includes non-profit organizations, and municipal, collective, cooperative, and leased enterprises.

The other ownership categories are joint ventures and the private sector. The latter includes joint-stock companies, farms, partnerships, and sole proprietorships as well as the so-called "new" cooperatives formed from 1987 onwards by entrepreneurs who were previously sole private operators in personal services, catering, trade, and some other areas within the private sector. This group also includes a number of collective farms and other formally cooperative enterprises which have recently reorganized themselves semi-legally, most often into limited-liability companies.

It is evident from Table 3B.1 that the number of privately-owned economic units had grown dramatically, even before the collapse of the

Table 3B.1 Number of economic units by ownership category (excluding non-profit organizations)

| | Number of units | |
	Jan. 1, 1990	July 1 1991
Total	6,774	17,824
State sector	3,310	4,211
Municipal enterprises	159	407
State-cooperative sector	1,426	1,570
Joint-ventures	115	290
Private sector	3,349	13,323
"New" cooperatives	2,454	3,623
Joint-stock and limited-		
liability companies	61	4,231
Sole proprietorships	6	168
Farms	828	5,301

Source: Estonian Ministry of the Economy

Table 3B.2 Classification of economic units by ownership category (excluding state non-profit organizations; as per cent of total) as of November 1991

	Number of enterprises	Book value	Employment
State sector	18.80	71.50	66.32
Municipal enterprises	1.70	2.31	1.89
State-cooperative sector	2.87	16.60	16.93
Joint ventures	1.88	1.04	0.71
Private sector	78.46	10.86	16.04
"New" cooperatives	23.52	1.02	4.03
Joint-stock and limited-			
liability companies	41.48	9.81	11.75

Source: Register of Enterprises*

* The Register of Enterprises is not complete, and thus the figures in Tables 3B.1 and 3B.2 are based on different sets of enterprises.

Soviet Union in August 1991. The state sector, however, continues to dominate the Estonian economy.

Foreign investment

The first joint ventures were established in Estonia in 1987. This form of mixed ownership between a domestic state enterprise or a cooperative and a foreign company has grown rapidly since the enactment in December of 1988 of the Soviet Law governing joint ventures. The cumulative number of newly established joint ventures increased from eleven in 1988 to 313 by the end of September 1991. However, the majority of joint ventures are small, with founding capital not exceeding Rb 500,000 ($1,430). Only 9.9 per cent of joint ventures had founding capital over Rb 1 mln, while 48.7 per cent had a founding capital under Rb 100,000. As of the end of September 1991, about 50 per cent of the aggregate capital invested in joint ventures had been contributed by Estonian enterprises, about 10 per cent by enterprises from the other republics, and about 40 per cent by foreign investors. Swedish and Finnish investors had been the only significant partners among the Western investors.

Table 3B.3 Joint venture capital in 1991

	Jan. 1 1991	July 1, 1991	October 1, 1991
Number of joint ventures	229	290	313
Amount of capital (Rb mln)	113.1	159.8	212.0
Domestic capital (Rb mln)	56.4	79.7	102.2
Capital from other republics and the Soviet Union (Rb mln)	12.1	15.3	16.3
Other foreign capital (Rb mln)	44.7	64.9	93.4

Source: Computed on the basis of the data provided by the Estonian Department of Foreign Economic Relations

Foreign physical or legal persons can also invest in Estonia by contributing capital to the establishment of a joint-stock company. The first joint-stock companies with foreign participation were founded during the summer of 1990. By the end of March 1991, the number of newly-founded joint-stock companies exceeded the number of joint ventures. As has been the case with joint ventures, joint-stock companies have involved modest capital investment, the foreign capital having come mainly from Finland and Sweden.

Table 3B.4 Joint-stock companies with foreign participation

	Jan. 1, 1991	Oct. 1, 1991
Number of companies	184	803
Total capital (Rb mln)	54.7	192.5
Domestic capital (Rb mln)	45.1	112.4
Capital from the other republics and the Soviet Union (Rb mln)	6.1	27.1
Other foreign capital (Rb mln)	3.5	53.0

Source: The Estonian Department of Foreign Economic Relations

4. THE PRIVATIZATION PROCESS

Introduction: the development of Estonian privatization policy

Between 1990 and 1992 Estonia witnessed an evolution in prevailing views about the appropriate goals and pace of privatization. Previously, during much of the period of the "reform of socialism" within the Soviet system, it was believed that a market economy could at least begin to be created if enterprises were freed from the chains of central planning. Concepts such as "multiplicity of property forms", "equal treatment of different property rights", and "legality of private ownership" were widely used during the Soviet period.[17]

---

[17] A first step in decentralization, starting even as early as 1988, was to break up large enterprises by spinning-off some of their subsidiaries located in remote places, and granting them full economic and legal independence. This type of decentralization was especially successful in construction and transportation. Once the Enterprise Law was passed in November 1989, the process extended to other sectors as well, but ultimately did not yield the desired results (see Section 5 below).

Sudden and extreme interest in an active privatization program, however, came simultaneously with the beginning of Estonia's transition to independence in March 1990, when the new Supreme Soviet was elected and the government of Edgar Savisaar came to power. An important step of the new government was the Law on Ownership, approved in June 1990. From this period date the disputes about the extent of property restitution and the use of vouchers, and popular pressure to prevent the acquisition of Estonian property with "external rubles" (i.e. from other republics of the former USSR).

In September 1990, the government formulated a stage-by-stage approach to privatization in a document called "Conception of the Estonian Government of General Principles of Privatization." The document treated privatization as an essential part of economic reform, with the goal of "establishing ownership relationships adequate to a market environment, and, to this end, increasing economic efficiency." This document explicitly rejected the earlier notion that corporatization alone, with the state retaining 100 per cent ownership, could lead to improved incentives and enhanced competition. Privatization was supposed to start as "an emergency-dictated process to be implemented within a certain time frame," a period of five to six years being considered necessary to privatize about half of all state property. Although the document states that "in case of uncertainty as to the need to restore ownership, no property should be privatized until the final decision concerning every particular case [restitution claim] has been passed," the Savisaar government accepted restitution largely as a political compromise.

According to this document, the privatization process should include three main stages. The first is preparatory, settling issues related to reprivatization, developing the legal framework for privatization, and starting an "experimental privatization" of a few large state-owned enterprises; this stage also includes small privatization in trade, services, and catering; privatization of housing; and intermediate forms of privatization, such as leasing. The second stage expands privatization, especially of small and medium sized enterprises, to other sectors, using domestic capital. The third stage is mass privatization of large enterprises relying on a variety of means for acquiring property, such as personal savings, advantageous credits, and vouchers.

The Conception was neither accepted nor rejected by parliament, and the Law on the Privatization of State-Owned Service, Trade, and Catering Establishments (small privatization), designed on the

Conception's basis, was passed by a one-vote majority in December 1990, and took effect on January 1, 1991. The government also adopted decrees that allowed for leasing and commercialization of state enterprises. The first state-owned joint-stock companies were founded (corporatized) in February 1991, and the first auction of small units took place in March. In mid-1991, seven large enterprises were selected for pilot privatization. In the second half of the year, the "municipalization" of state property began.[18]

Decisions of still greater importance were made by the parliament in December, 1990, through the adoption of two Resolutions concerning the "restoration of the continuity of ownership rights" and land reform, setting the reprivatization agenda. Citizens began submitting applications for restitution later in 1991, coinciding with growing dissatisfaction in parliament over the route which the government's privatization program was taking. Reflecting this dissatisfaction, the "Law on the Fundamentals of the Ownership Reform", adopted in June 1991,[19] placed priority on an immediate program of direct restitution and the use of vouchers, both for compensation and as a more general tool for privatization. Motivations for this policy were the perceived need to rectify past injustices; fear that Estonian property might fall into the control of foreigners or those who had accumulated money through "speculation" and "mafia-related" means; and a strong reaction against the continuing spontaneous "nomenklatura privatization." The nationalist parties were the chief supporters of this stress on restitution.

The Savisaar government, however, placed less emphasis on these so-called "political" considerations that dominated the parliament, and more on creating active, entrepreneurial private ownership and on keeping the problems of restitution as separate as possible from the privatization process. Sales were the preferred method of privatization, and the domestic capital shortage was to be addressed mainly by installment payment and credit arrangements, as mass distribution by means of vouchers was thought to create undesirable diffusion of ownership. The proceeds of privatization were to be an important budget resource supporting the introduction of the national currency, the restructuring of production, the creation of a market economy infrastructure, and the easing of social tensions during the transition

---

[18] For all these programs see Section 4B below.
[19] See Section 4B below.

period. It was decided that the logical sequence for privatization should be corporatization, followed by privatization of housing and small-scale units, and experimental (pilot) privatization, then partial sales of the shares of state-owned joint-stock companies, and only thereafter the mass privatization of large units.

The conflict of approach between the parliament and the Savisaar government created an impasse in the reform process, with the parliament rejecting government proposals for partial sales of shares of state-owned joint-stock companies, a program to privatize small state-owned enterprises, housing privatization, and other programs. Together with disputes over the status of non-Estonians, this disagreement over privatization was one of the factors leading to the fall of the government in January 1992.

Relations between the parliament and the temporary government of Tiit Vähi, which held power from late January 1992 to the end of September, 1992, began more positively, the government expressing intentions of implementing programs that reflect the decisions of the parliament. In fact, the housing and agricultural privatization legislation formerly proposed by the Savisaar government was adopted with only a few amendments, and small privatization was extended to medium enterprises and to all branches of the economy, while insider preferences were considerably reduced. But only in June did the government acquire a clear direction in large privatization policy, with the appointment of Olari Taal as Minister of Economy: emphasis shifted back towards sales, especially to foreign investors in the hope that the proceeds could be used to redress the balance of payments deficit. Although the government declared its agreement with the parliament's view on restitution, in practice little progress was made. It does seem likely, however, that a voucher plan will be used for compensation, as well as for housing privatization and possibly for a mass privatization of state-owned enterprises.

Macroeconomic conditions affecting the Estonian reform program have been drastically altered by the reform policies initiated in Russia at the beginning of 1992. Hyperinflation, a cash crisis, shortages of energy and basic raw materials, and a sharp decline in production and living standards made Estonia's previous steps toward introducing a market economy, which at the time had been felt to be truly radical, seem like a mere curtain-raiser compared with the subsequent onslaught of "shock-therapy." Nonetheless, unlike in some other countries, these macroeconomic problems have not yet led to a political backlash against reforms.

It is difficult to predict the implications of the recent parliamentary elections (September 20, 1992). The "Fatherland" block of parties, which campaigned for restitution but seems to be moderating its views, is the strongest group in a diverse coalition with a variety of views on the best means for privatization.

4A. Organizational structure of state regulation of privatization

The current organizational structure of property reform in Estonia is shown in Chart 4A.1. Six levels of state apparatus are involved: parliament, government together with its commissions, branch ministries, state departments, county governments, and parish authorities.[20] The structure is still considered provisional, and the division of rights and responsibilities among the various levels is not always completely clear. It remains to be resolved, for instance, which level of government has land ownership rights. The extent of transfer of much other state property to the municipalities is still undecided and incomplete (see Section 4B on privatization programs). This section describes what seem to be the current roles and tasks of the bodies within each organizational level, but this structure may undergo modifications.

Organizational levels

PARLIAMENTARY SUPERVISION
The importance of the bodies at the parliamentary and governmental levels was particularly pronounced during the period of acrimonious disagreement between the parliament and the Savisaar Government in 1991.

Prior to its abolition in July 1992, in April and June 1991, the *Presidium of the Supreme Council* approved the list of large enterprises

---

[20]   The Estonian administrative structure comprises three levels: the republic itself, the fifteen counties (and six towns with similar status), and the primary administrative units, which include parishes, boroughs and small country towns, all within the counties.

The government at the overall republican level, as of fall 1992, consisted of seventeen ministries and thirty-eight "state departments," independent executive bodies of the government. The new government reform draft calls for a radical reduction in the number of ministries (to twelve) and of state departments.

An administrative reform, under way since 1991 and largely complete by fall 1992, gives greater powers and a stronger revenue base to local governments.

to be privatized "by way of experiment." In July 1992, it selected the enterprises and assets that will remain indefinitely in state hands.

Prior to the recent election, the *Temporary Property and Agrarian Reform Commission* was the key parliamentary body for ownership reform. This role has now been assumed by the *Commission of Economy and Agriculture* in the new parliament.

GOVERNMENTAL LEVEL

Within the government, which, as discussed above, has often played a role quite distinct from that of the parliament, there are a number of committees and commissions involved in privatization policy. Despite its high formal status and ministerial composition, the *Property Reform Committee* has not been very important in practice, and never even met under the Vähi Government. The *Agrarian Property Reform Preparation and Execution Commission* was charged with examining basic issues relating to property reform in agriculture, including property relations in state and collective farms, privatization procedures, and foreign rights to buy land. The commission is headed by the Minister of Agriculture, with ten other members including department heads and representatives of farmers and producers' associations. The activity of the commission, however, has thus far proven more passive than expected, with the Ministry of Agriculture retaining the lead role in agricultural reform.

A *Central Commission of Compensation for and Restitution of Unlawfully Expropriated Property*, established under Government Decree No. 202 of October 2, 1991,[21] has responsibility for setting the entire framework for restitution, coordinating and monitoring the activities of local Restitution Commissions, and deciding cases appealed from local bodies. One of its statutory functions is preparing draft resolutions on issues arising in the restitution process. The Central Commission is chaired by the Minister of Justice, its deputy chairman is the General Director of the Department of State Property, and there are twelve other members, including three deputy ministers and four department heads.

A separate *Interinstitutional Commission on Privatization of State and Municipal Housing* has also existed since the summer 1992.

---

[21] An earlier version of this commission existed between November 1990 and October 1991 to handle legal aspects of restitution of and compensation for property in the rehabilitation and denationalization process.

1. *Parliamentary level*

Supreme Council of the Republic of Estonia

Presidium of the Supreme Council

Budget and Economic Commission

Temporary Property and Agrarian Reform Commission

2. *Governmental level*

Government of Republic of Estonia		
Interinstitutional Property Reform Commission (until June 1992)	Interinstitutional Commission on Privatization of State and Municipal Housing (since June 1992)	Central Commission of Compensation for and Restitution of Unlawfully Expropriated Property

3. *Ministerial level*

Ministry of the Economy	Branch ministries (Industry; Construction; Commerce)	Ministry of Agriculture	Ministry of Justice	Ministry of Finance	Bank of Estonia

4. *State departmental level*

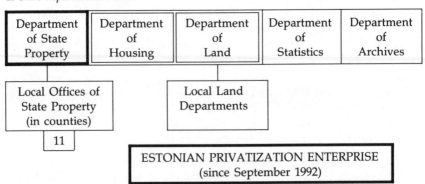

Department of State Property	Department of Housing	Department of Land	Department of Statistics	Department of Archives

Local Offices of State Property (in counties)	Local Land Departments

11

ESTONIAN PRIVATIZATION ENTERPRISE (since September 1992)

5. *County or republican town level*

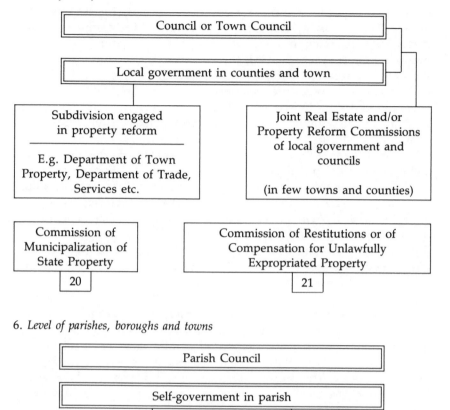

6. *Level of parishes, boroughs and towns*

Chart 4A.1 Organizational structure of the property reform during the Vahi Government (January 1992–October 1992)

MINISTRIES

At the ministerial level, property reform is currently the responsibility of the *Ministry of the Economy*. Its work includes "forecasting economic results of privatization and ownership changes and working out proposals for counterbalancing the economic disturbances created by the property reform." Under the Savisaar government, privatization and restitution were the responsibilities of the Ministry of the Economy and the Ministry of Justice, respectively, but since then the Ministry of the Economy has become responsible for all components of property reform.

The *Ministry of Finance* has the task of "working out the methods for determining the value of property and providing solutions to problems concerning the application of the voucher concept." It must also adjust the budget system to the needs of the property reform, as well as create a credit system for large-scale privatization. The ministry has not so far influenced the conceptual framework of property reform. The new government resurrected an old proposal of the Savisaar government to merge the Ministries of Economy and Finance into one Ministry of Finance.

Branch ministries are involved in the property reform process in that they currently control the state-owned enterprises that may be subject to privatization or restitution. Furthermore, they are involved in implementing corporatization (appointing the Boards of Directors) and leasing (as the lessor), although usually less in the actual privatization of their property. The *Ministry of Agriculture*, however, has been active in planning as well implementing property reform involving agricultural enterprises.

Branch ministries may also play a political role through the promotion of certain interests; for instance, the *Ministry of Industry* under the Savisaar government was associated with efforts to encourage a privatization policy favorable to industrial associations, company management, and enterprise directors. The ministry favored the rapid transfer of enterprise assets on favorable leasing terms to joint-stock companies formed by insiders.[22] The new government may merge the Ministries of Industry, Commerce, and Construction into a new Ministry of the Economy.

The primary role of the *Ministry of Justice* in the area of privatization is in restitution issues.

The *Bank of Estonia* was involved in property reform in 1990 because

---

[22] See Section 4B on privatization programs below.

of its interest in generating sufficient income to support for the convertibility of the Estonian kroon. Lately it has also dealt with problems concerning the conversion into vouchers of savings deposits which are not exchanged in the currency reform.

STATE DEPARTMENT LEVEL
The Department of State Property (DSP) was established in autumn 1990 and placed under the Ministry of the Economy, although the relationship is one more of cooperation than subordination. Although created as an executive body, the DSP has also been involved in elaborating normative acts concerning the privatization of enterprises; under the Vahi government, however, it fulfilled strictly executive functions. The department's provisional statute, as approved by the government, defines its basic responsibilities within two categories: management of state property, and control over its transfer to new owners.

Included in the first category are tasks such as supervision of possession, use and disposal of state property, and analysis of economic efficiency and purpose of use of property. The second category of responsibilities includes coordinating and implementing privatization, municipalization, and leasing of state property; registering leasing arrangements and other transfers of ownership rights; confirming lists of enterprises and structural units to be privatized; and submitting to the Estonian government proposals concerning privatization, leasing, or municipalization of property. Among its more specific duties, the DSP is also required to set forth proposals for carrying out reprivatization, to provide guidance on "compiling a register of former owners and their inheritors," as well as to regulate the activity of DSP territorial branches and of the local Commissions of Municipalization of State Property (see subsection on the local authority level below).

The DSP may give an order or authority to carry out privatization to the governing body of local authorities, ministries, state departments, enterprises or other organizations. Prices are set and sale-purchase contracts signed by the General Director of the Department of State Property. Property privatized by authorized bodies in this way accounted for slightly less than one-half (254 out of 558) of all units sold as of the beginning of 1992, and slightly more than one-half (487 out of 855) of those whose privatization had begun.

The DSP, together with the Ministry of the Economy, also organizes the hiring of foreign experts for the execution of individual stages of privatization (assessment of properties, arrangements of auctions, etc.). So far these experts have mostly been Estonians living abroad, but now agreements have been concluded with Western consulting firms, as well, to advise on privatization.

The main governing body of the DSP is a ten-member *Board of the Department of State Property*. Day-to-day management of the DSP is carried out by a General Director appointed by the Prime Minister and assisted by a staff of forty-two, including twenty-two people stationed in regional offices. The board includes five members appointed by the government and five appointed by the Board of the Bank of Estonia (in practice, as an initiative of the government, the bank's appointments have been members of opposition parties and outsiders), and it elects a Chairman and a Deputy Chairman from its members.

The board's duties are to:

a) report to the Estonian government the initiative the DSP has taken in accordance with its competence;

b) review the lists of enterprises to be privatized and of property to be transferred into municipal possession prior to their endorsement by the Estonian government;

c) submit to the Estonian government proposals concerning the terms of property municipalization;

d) endorse the methodology for the administration of privatization;

e) stipulate the procedure of privatization and determine the initial sale price in case the residual value in the balance sheet exceeds Rb 500,000, or 600,000 kroons since June 1992 (starting prices for smaller enterprises are determined by the General Director);[23]

f) determine the preferential rights for different categories of purchasers of privatized property;

g) determine the types of shares of enterprises that are privatized, as well as the nominal and selling price of shares;

h) review other issues concerning the activities of the Department of State Property upon the request of the General Director of the DSP, the Chairman of the Board, or his/her deputy, or when at least four members of the board request it.

According to its provisional statute, the board is supposed to meet at least once a month. However, the recent volume of activity has been

---

[23] In the case of the list of enterprises to be privatized by the Estonian Privatization Enterprise (EPE), the board must still approve the composition of the list, but the starting price, the preferential rights, and the types of shares are determined by the EPE.

in examining lists of enterprises to be privatized or municipalized and determining the procedures to be followed in privatization has necessitated bimonthly meetings. If the Estonian Privatization Enterprise becomes more important in the implementation of large privatization, as planned, the board of the DSP may become more concerned with longer term economic policy.

The *Estonian Privatization Enterprise* (EPE) was established on September 15, 1992, on the initiative of the government by Parliamentary Resolution (passed August 13, 1992). The EPE may become the leading institution for privatization in Estonia, taking over large sales from the DSP. To an as yet undetermined degree, the establishment of the EPE may also signal a radical shift in Estonian privatization policy: toward individual foreign sales, and away from domestic mass privatization. It is expected that the EPE will function like the German *Treuhandanstalt*, and a certain amount of cooperation with the German privatization agency has already been agreed upon. Under the authority of the Minister of Economy, the EPE should be independent of the state budget, and will only receive some (still undetermined) percentage of the revenue from the properties it sells.

The main tasks of the EPE are as follows:

1. To prepare enterprises for privatization, including restructuring;
2. To inform buyers about sale conditions;
3. To determine the initial price of the property;
4. To sell the assets, shares, and stocks of state enterprises;
5. To submit proposals about privatization;
6. To submit proposals to liquidate enterprises.

Other state departments are also involved in property reform, especially in the commercialization of enterprises and in leasing arrangements. The *Department of Land* is charged with the preparation and subsequent implementation of land reform. Its duties include compiling a land register with the assistance of its regional offices. The *Department of Utilities* (now renamed Department of Housing) is involved in preparing the privatization of state-owned housing, while the *Department of Statistics* is helping with the design of the real estate register, and the *Department of Archives* processes applications for restitution.

LOCAL AUTHORITY LEVEL

Commissions of Restitutions or of Compensation for Unlawfully Expropriated Property were set up by local governments under the October 1991 regulations in every county and almost every parish. They handle the registration of restitution claims, settle complaints lodged against officials, examine the applications, and make rulings on them. Two members of each local commission are nominated by the Central Commission, but otherwise they act quite independently.

Local Agrarian Reform Commissions were set up under the Law on Agricultural Reform of February 1992, with the purpose of examining applications submitted by former owners of land, compiling lists of property to be transferred into municipal ownership, and supervising any disposal of assets by state and collective farms. According to the law, these Local Commissions are responsible for agricultural reform. They are established at the parish (lowest) level, and are composed of representatives of collective farms, local private farms, the local government, and the state.

In order to carry out its activity throughout the entire territory of Estonia, regional offices of the DSP, referred to as *Local Offices of State Property*, were set up in eleven counties out of the total of twenty-one (as of November 1992). The Local Offices of the DSP organize on their territories the privatization, municipalization, and leasing of state property processes. The Local Offices' main tasks are to identify the property located on their territory; to ensure maintenance and efficient use of state property; to present complete lists of enterprises subject to privatization, leasing or municipalization; and to settle issues concerning property restitution.

In order to assist with the implementation of the municipalization[24] process, local commissions referred to as *Commissions of Municipalization of State Property* have been established in each republican town or county under DSP Regulation No. 72 on the Establishment of Commissions of Municipalization of State Property. They began operating in late September 1991 and have the following tasks:

a)   to evaluate the applications of local governments, most of which come from parishes (although county governments also

---

[24]   ''Municipalization'' (*sic*) is a common term in Eastern Europe for the acquisition by municipalities of certain assets, the ownership rights to which are thereby clarified.

have this right), concerning municipalization of state property;[25]
b) to provide guidance to local governments in the course of the municipalization process;
c) to forward complete lists of enterprises to be municipalized to the Department of State Property;
d) to coordinate and monitor the transfer of property into municipal possession on their territory;
e) to organize the privatization of municipalized property adhering to the stated requirement for further privatization, while supervising the conditions under which the process is carried out.

The structure of the commissions is regulated by the Department of State Property, but, according to DSP Regulation No. 72, must include at least one representative from the Department of State Property, one from the respective county and one from the local government.

Regional Offices of the Department of Land were being established at the county level at the end of 1991. According to a recent (February 1992) government resolution, Department of Land offices are being established at the level of towns of republican importance as well.

4B. Overview of privatization programs

Major privatization programs in Estonia include small and large privatization and special programs for agriculture, housing, and cooperatives. Currently being implemented are small privatization and the "experimental" privatization of seven large enterprises. The legislative basis for both programs is the Small Privatization Law (the Law on the Privatization of State-Owned Service, Trade and Catering Establishments, passed on December 13, 1990 and effective from January 1, 1991). Important changes were introduced in the small privatization program by the Law on Making Alterations and Amendments to the Law on Privatization of State-Owned Service, Retail, and Catering Enterprises, passed on May 21, 1992. Peasant farms are currently being established in place of the collective farms, and leasing contracts have been concluded both for whole enterprises and for

---

[25] Since municipalization began again on September 4, 1992, the parishes have submitted their applications directly to the DSP. The main task of the Local Commissions remains the settling of disagreements.

separate assets. This section contains brief descriptions of some of these programs plus descriptions of some of those planned; more detailed analyses will appear in future *CEU Privatization Reports*.

The small privatization program

According to the Small Privatization Law, property in this program may be a whole or any self-contained part of an enterprise with a book value not exceeding Rb 500,000.[26] Land, natural resources, and properties to be reprivatized, may not be sold under this program. Selection of particular units for inclusion is made on the basis of proposals coming from the relevant branch ministry, local authority, or the Department of State Property (DSP). Since May 1991, the General Director approves the list of state-owned enterprises to be privatized.

The total number of units to be privatized under small privatization is estimated at about three thousand: roughly 1,200 service facilities, 500 shops, 350 booths, and 800 catering facilities. The government's initial intention was to privatize 25 per cent of these in 1991 and the rest by the end of 1992. However, most experts expect the process to continue into 1993.

Eligibility to purchase property in this program was restricted to adults who have lived in Estonia at least ten years. Since the May 1992 Amendment, immigrants and foreigners are also eligible to purchase property. In the past, the DSP could grant preferential treatment, in the form of "preemptive rights," to several categories of participants: employees, local residents, leaseholders, and holders of compensation securities (vouchers, described below). Employees receive further preferences in the form of reduced prices on the purchase of up to one-third of the shares and in the possibility of postponing 60 per cent of the payment for up to a year. The exercise of the preemptive right carries with it the obligation to continue the "designated-purpose usage" of the property for a period of five years.[27] Except when there

---

[26] For the purposes of accounting for the effects of inflation and of broadening the coverage of the program, the maximum book value has been increased to 6 mln rubles, as of May 1992.

[27] This requirement was rationalized as a deterrence to speculative acquisitions using rubles originating from "eastern" criminal or otherwise suspicious sources.

were multiple claimants, the preemptive right allowed the purchase of the property at its "initial price," superseding the normal requirement for a competitive auction or tender.[28]

Calculation of this initial price is regulated by the Department of State Property, which is revising the rules for property evaluations in the "Methodical Recommendations for Determination of the Initial Price of the Property to be Privatized or Leased." Valuations must be conducted by experts certified by the DSP; more valuable assets undergo multiple valuations. Methods used include simple adjustment of book values for inflation and depreciation, and more complex attempts to derive measures of profitability and future income.

In the first auctions, which began in March 1991, the initial prices were on average a multiple of three to four times the book value, but due to hyperinflation, the multiple has risen to ten or twenty. Since most sales are to employees, final selling prices have not been that much different from initial prices: on average 1.5–2.5 times greater. Particular controversy has arisen over two issues in the setting of initial prices: whether they should be denominated in convertible currency or in rubles, and whether they are too low and thus provide too strong a preference for insiders, who have successfully exercised their preemptive rights in about two-thirds of the sales thus far.[29]

In an attempt to accelerate the process, it was decided in August 1991 to transfer smaller units and those of local importance to municipalities, who were then required to privatize them under the DSP Decision "Methodical Recommendations for the Privatization of Municipal Property." The transfer began in late 1991, and by September 1, 1992, the Department of State Property had already received 3,339 proposals from local governments, of which the government had approved the transfer of 1,307 properties to municipal ownership.

These transfers began in early 1992, but were halted by a Resolution of the Board of the Department of State Property on March 9, 1992. The temporary Commission of the Ownership Reform of the parliament had successfully objected that the existing municipalization process was unlawful (under Section 21 of the Law on the Fundamentals of the

---

[28] However, the May 1992 Amendment withdrew these insider preferences and certain of the restrictions on property usage.

[29] This controversy, over the denomination of prices, has disappeared since the introduction of the Estonian Kroon (EEK) in June 1992. All prices are now denominated in EEK (which is pegged to the DM). Controversy over insider preferences remains, however.

Ownership Reform), since no register had been completed of the properties which were to remain in state ownership.[30]

The program began slowly, however, and only 205 properties were entered in the government privatization registers by July 1, 1991, of which forty-four had been sold. The process accelerated somewhat in the second half of 1991, and by January 15, 1992, 763 units were registered, of which 208 had been sold, seventy-six were ready for sale, and initial prices for 143 were being set. The proceeds had reached Rb 18.23 mln. By September 1, 1992, 855 units were registered, of which 558 had been sold, 124 were ready for sale and 144 were having initial prices set. Revenue had reached Rbs 114.8 mln (EEK 14.7 mln).

Small privatization has been more successful in services, which had 454 units registered, and 330 sold by September 1, 1992, but much slower than expected in retail trade, with 408 units registered, but only 228 sold. The overwhelmingly predominant method of privatization under this program, approximately 80–90 per cent of the total number of units, has been sale at the initial price to employees; less than 10 per cent of the units have been sold by tender; less than 5 per cent were sold by public auction; while the sale of shares has been used in only four cases. About ten properties designated for privatization (mostly unprofitable services such as saunas) have remained unsold. They have been, as a rule, transferred to municipal ownership.

The process of small-scale privatization has been criticized because of the slowness of the process, the danger of corruption, the possibility that purchasers are acting as fronts for "eastern" interests, and the predominance of sales to employees at lower than "market value" initial prices, and the perceived exclusion of buyers other than employees'; the result of insider preferences. Employee ownership is increasingly viewed as obstructing the necessary restructuring, and fiscal difficulties have increased pressure to obtain higher revenue from privatization. Consequently, the general trend seems to be more towards public auctions, and restrictions limiting preemptive rights have been imposed since May 21, 1992. One indication of the changing official attitudes is the new procedures in Tartu (the second largest town in Estonia) that permit preemptive sales to employees and sales by tender only in exceptional cases and have eliminated tender as a possible means of privatization (in favor of auctions and share

---

[30] On September 4, 1992 a new procedure for municipalization was approved by the government. Since then the process has resumed.

subscriptions). Important changes were introduced in the small privatization program by the Amendment passed on May 21, 1992.

EXPERIMENTAL PRIVATIZATION

The program to privatize "by way of experiment" was aimed at gaining experience and assessing the suitability of different forms and procedures of privatization, before launching large-scale privatization. Its legal basis was Section 2 of the Parliamentary Decision "on the Enactment and Application of the Law on the Privatization of Service, Trade and Catering Establishments," allowing the privatization of a small number of enterprises with book value above the former 500,000 ruble ceiling. The Presidium of the Supreme Council gave permission for the experimental privatization of four enterprises in April 1991 and for three more in June 1991.

The enterprises were chosen from different branches (clothing, automobiles, transport, repair) and locations, with a range of sizes (book values from Rb 170,271 to Rb 20,255,800). Various techniques were used: sale at the initial price to a joint-stock company established by the employees on the basis of the enterprise's assets, with an obligation to increase the capital stock; sale in separate self-contained units by auction; sale by tender; formation of a state-owned joint-stock company, and then sale of the majority of voting stock by open competitive bidding; sale of shares to employees either with deferred payment or using preemptive right on preferential terms; and sale of shares by auction. In the sale of shares, different types of shares were used: government stock, preference stock for current and former workers, shares carrying multiple voting rights, and different payment terms. In most cases 20 per cent of the capital stock was reserved for the state, to be sold later for compensation and national capital vouchers.

By April 1992, all enterprises had completed the privatization process, with proceeds of EEK 5.8 mln to the Department of State Property as of the end of January. However, two of these had serious conflicts. In the privatization of the Tallinn Taxi Fleet, the managers wanted to buy the fleet as a whole themselves, whereas drivers wanted the taxis sold separately at low prices, and other private firms requested a public auction. In the case of Association Talleks, two factions formed joint-stock companies, mainly involving rival groups of employees. Although the tender was won by the group of younger professionals, it has been contested by the group backing the former Director General, who for several months refused to transfer the assets.

Experimental privatization was criticized by the former Minister of the Economy, Heido Vitsur on the grounds that a program of such small scale cannot produce an adequate market, which requires many buyers and many objects of sale. The program has nonetheless yielded some experience with different procedures and their suitability in different situations. It has also indicated the interests of different social groups and how they may behave in the privatization process.

Plans for large privatization

The Savisaar government proposed a program in May 1991 "On Starting the Selling of the Shares of State-Owned Joint-Stock Companies," to begin simultaneously with corporatization. The newly formed joint-stock companies are divided into two categories: Type I, planned to remain under majority state ownership, and Type II, planned for immediate privatization. The proposal stipulated that 5 per cent of the shares of Type I and 20 per cent of the shares of Type II firms are to be sold; more than 20 per cent, up to a maximum of 49 per cent, of the Type II shares may also be sold "by way of experiment." Preemptive rights are granted to employees for up to 100 per cent of the shares sold of Type I and up to 50 per cent of the shares of Type II, but there is supposed to be no discount on the price: the "real market price" is determined by a prior auction of at least 100 shares.

The draft legislation for this program was blocked in connection with the disputes between the parliament and the Savisaar government over restitution and the use of vouchers. However, it was revived in March 1992 by the new government and received parliamentary approval on August 13, 1992.

The new government planned three stages of large privatization. In the first stage, not clearly distinguished from the foregoing partial sale of shares program, 10 to 20 per cent of the shares of state-owned joint-stock companies are to be sold. This stage was supposed to begin in April 1992. Revenue from the sale of shares is supposed to be used to support the currency reform. In the second stage, after the introduction of the kroon, the extensive privatization of large enterprises starts, with up to 20 per cent of the shares sold for vouchers. In the third stage of large privatization, supposed to begin in 1993, the share of privatization vouchers may be increased.

It was also planned that some enterprises will be sold wholly or in part to foreigners. The previous government had proposed a concrete program as part of a draft law "On Continuing and Speeding Up the Ownership Reform." Although the new government withdrew the draft, new regulations are being prepared, including the stipulation that the board of the DSP must approve all sales to foreign investors.

These plans, however, have not yet been realized, and may have been superseded by the founding of the Estonian Privatization Enterprise and the decision to sell shares in state enterprises before vouchers are available.

Agriculture

Under the Estonian SSR Law on Farms of December 1989 and various pieces of subsequent legislation, a total of 6,500 *peasant farms* had been established as of October 10, 1991. Another 2,700 were awaiting approval by the Land Department, and 8,000 by communes. Most of these are new peasant farms, but there has also been some restitution to the heirs of former farm owners. By mid-January 1992, there were 7,227 registered peasant farms; including individual household plots, there was a total area of 184,753 ha, representing 15.3 per cent of the grain fields in Estonia, 59.7 per cent of the area under potatoes, and 74.1 per cent of the area under vegetables. The government forecasts that there should eventually be 40–60,000 peasant farms, with 50–80 ha each to be economically viable; compared with the January 1992 average of 25.6, this implies significant growth in the size of the average farm. The Law on Land Reform of October 1991 has slowed the establishment of new peasant farms, pending the resolution of restitution issues, although land will not be restored to previous owners if it has already been granted to a peasant farmer in perpetuity under the Law on Farms.

The *"privatization of enterprises processing agricultural products,"* which covers about twenty large monopolies in meat and milk processing, is anticipated following the creation of peasant farms. Current plans entail the initial formation of state-owned enterprises (already under way in December 1991), with a board made up of representatives of the Farmers' Central Union, the Agricultural Producers' Central Union (representing state and collective farms), the county government, the enterprise, and the Ministries of Agriculture, Trade and the Economy. The board will spin off some units of the enterprises, returning some subsidiaries and structural units to farmers' associations as restitution, and leasing others either to them or to other interested parties. Central plants and other remaining facilities will probably be run as joint-stock companies, and the government has stated its intention to privatize them mainly through vouchers. Target dates for completion were originally set for mid-1992, but have been postponed by four to five months.

Spontaneous privatization

The methods of spontaneous privatization in Estonia are similar to those in all the East European countries. Managers of enterprises, frequently members of the former "nomenklatura," profit by taking ownership of state property at nominal prices during the reorganization and privatization processes. There are also transfer pricing schemes where enterprise managers or others establish private joint-stock companies whose sole activity is to purchase the output of their state enterprises at low state prices and simply selling it off at a considerable profit, to the detriment of the consumer. These phenomena are inherently difficult to measure, but they have been sufficiently widespread in the perception of the public to cause dissatisfaction and disillusionment with privatization more generally.

Privatization of leased property

Leasing of state assets to employees of state enterprises in Estonia is described in Section 3A above. In addition, other forms of leasing of state assets to private entities, an intermediate form of privatization, will be discussed in a future *CEU Privatization Project Report*. A program to sell the assets to the lessees is under elaboration. The quick method for this would be for the lessee to make regular buy-out payments in addition to the rent; the slower route would be for assets to become the property of the lessee as they are amortized.

Vouchers

The use of vouchers in Estonia was originally, and is perhaps still most strongly, motivated by the desire to compensate those who had lost property through nationalization during the Soviet period, although it was also recognized that vouchers could alleviate the shortage of domestic capital and involve more citizens in the privatization process. Restitution in kind is also being used, but is often inappropriate or impossible, for instance when the expropriated asset is non-physical. Public opinion favored compensation both for lost financial assets and for the "injustice from the higher exploitation of employees under the Soviet rule."

Three types of vouchers are currently planned. First are "compensation vouchers," given in proportion to their losses of property to those who either are permanent residents of Estonia or were citizens on June 16, 1940. Second, "national capital or work contribution vouchers" will be issued to all permanent residents in proportion to their "work contribution," defined as the number of years of employment between January 1, 1945 and January 1, 1992. Provisions are made to include credit for maternity leave (each mother receives a credit of five years' work for each child), and time spent in higher education and military service also counts, as well as years in prison or exile. Third, "agricultural work contribution vouchers" will be distributed to current and former workers on collective farms in relation to work time, as in the national contribution vouchers, except that work days instead of years are calculated, and mothers receive only 250 days for each child. Agricultural workers have the right to exchange their agricultural vouchers for national capital vouchers (but only in the event that the value of the capital vouchers to which they are entitled is greater than that of their agricultural vouchers). (See also the subsection on cooperatives in Section 3A above.)

The type of property to be supplied in exchange for the vouchers thus far includes housing and former collective farm property, although the program will probably be expanded to include small shops, large enterprises, and/or land. The approach to privatization of these latter categories has been controversial politically, with successive governments taking very different points of view, but it is likely that there will also be significant voucher privatization in these groups. For the categories of housing and farm property, however, it seems clear that vouchers will represent the dominant form of privatization.

But how the program will be organized is still unresolved. The national capital vouchers have a longevity of four years and can be given to family members; families can thus pool their vouchers, but otherwise vouchers seem to be non-tradable. In purchasing housing they can be combined with compensation vouchers and cash. The value of a national capital voucher corresponding to one year of employment is expected to be one square meter of floor space in a standard panel building. Where cash is the (partial) means of payment, the (corresponding fraction of the) price is calculated somehow according to the market. The cost of participation has been the subject of debate, and would perhaps vary with the type of voucher: compensation vouchers would be free, but the cost of national capital vouchers may be equal to zero, to the expense of printing the certificates, or to an average monthly wage.

It is expected that in the next two to three years, about 65–75 per cent of the housing floorspace will be privatized, of which 80–85 per cent will be purchased with vouchers. This would imply that about 60–70 per cent of all national capital vouchers will be expended on housing and, because the value of the vouchers is supposed to be the same in all alternative uses, this would leave enough to obtain about 10–15 per cent of the rest of the property to be privatized in Estonia.

With regard to farm property, the amount available in exchange for vouchers will be determined as a residual after reprivatization, reimbursement to the central and municipal governments for investments, and all debts and other obligations have been satisfied. This makes it difficult to forecast the value of these vouchers, but it has been estimated that about 10–15 per cent of the property of the former collective farms will go to vouchers.

The precise future of vouchers in Estonia is therefore rather unclear. It may be noteworthy that in the experimental privatization, five of the seven large enterprises reserved 20 to 40 per cent of their shares for later voucher privatization.

5. CORPORATIZATION

In general, corporatization in Estonia aims to clarify legal ownership rights, particularly vis-à-vis the claims of enterprise insiders, and is considered to be a prelude to privatization. However, despite their common goals, two separate processes can be distinguished: one concerning the reorganization of small, the other of large state-owned enterprises. These processes are distinct, first of all because of the different nature of ownership relations prior to corporatization (which, in turn, determined the adoption of separate legislation and procedures) and second, because of the different time period in which they occur. Both corporatization programs are discussed below.

Corporatization of small state-owned enterprises

The origin of the so-called "small enterprises" in Estonia was described in Section 3A above. The need for a change in their legal status became clear in light of the increasingly muddled ownership relations and rights in these enterprises, the fact that business forms of this kind are still not covered in Estonian legislation, and the wish of small state enterprise employees to privatize.

Draft legislation designed to convert small state enterprises into Estonian legal forms was presented to parliament as early as June 1991, but it was rejected in October of that year, and had still not been passed as of November 1992. The draft provides that ownership of the small enterprises should be assigned to their original founders, to the extent of the value of any assets which they had given the enterprises at their foundation, with the remainder, corresponding to the increase in the value of their assets since that time, going to the employees. According to the proposed procedure, small state enterprises could be reorganized through transformation into a joint-stock company or partnerships involving the founder and the employees, or by leasing assets to employees. In the latter case, the assets would be leased only when neither the founder nor the employees are interested in becoming shareholders or partners in the business. The draft leaves to the employees the initiative in choosing the form of reorganization, with the ultimate decision to be arrived at in negotiations between the founders and employee representatives. The draft would also require that the reorganization be completed within two months from the date of enactment of the law.

In practice, however, the majority of small state enterprises (all except about 200) have already been effectively privatized, as founders from mid-1991 onwards began reorganizing them into joint-stock companies through agreements with the enterprise managers, without changing the formal registrations of these enterprises. Conflicts are therefore likely to arise in the future between the founders and employees of small state enterprises.

Corporatization of large state-owned enterprises

The process of transforming large state-owned enterprises into joint-stock or limited-liability companies began at the end of 1990 under the Transformation Decree (Government Decree on the Transformation of

State Enterprises Belonging to the Republic of Estonia into New Organizational Forms). Enterprises which under the Soviet regime had been run from Moscow may also be subject to corporatization, pursuant to the Government Decree on the Privatization of All-Union Enterprises, Institutions and Organizations Located on the Territory of the Republic of Estonia, although this process has been significantly delayed (see the subsection on state enterprises in Section 3A above). Municipal enterprises are also subject to corporatization.

According to the Transformation Decree, state enterprises under Estonian government control were required to set forth, prior to May 1, 1991, proposals concerning their conversion into new organizational forms. In fact, their choice was limited. In effect, enterprise insiders had to choose between recommending a form of leasing of the whole enterprise (to a work collective, a private joint-stock company, or an outside lessee) or its conversion into a collective (people's) enterprise (which amounts to much the same as the creation of a lease enterprise; see the subsection on leasing arrangements in Section 3A above), and proposing the conversion of the enterprise into a state-owned joint-stock company. (For the governance structure of state joint-stock companies, see the subsection on state enterprises in Section 3A above.)

Initially, most enterprises proposed forming joint-stock companies, especially Type II companies, insiders hoping to profit from future privatization involving favorable terms for the sale of shares to employees and to attract foreign investment when the state's share was further reduced. (See Section 4B above.) With time, however, there has been a gradual change in favor of leasing, since it has become evident that the privatization legislation was designed to promote competition rather than preferential treatment for the insiders. In the case of leasing agreements, on the other hand, a greater decision-making role is played by the branch ministries (as opposed to the Ministry of the Economy and the Department of State Property, which are more involved in privatization), and enterprise insiders may be better able to secure a favorable leasing deal from a sympathetic branch ministry, and preclude the involvement of prospective competitors. They may then be in a stronger starting position for a later privatization, perhaps through a favorable buy-out option.

The procedure originally established for the conversion of state enterprises into state joint-stock companies involved a preliminary examination of the proposals coming from the enterprises by relevant branch ministries, some of which formed special commissions for this purpose. A joint recommendation of the branch minister and the enterprise director was then submitted to the Department of Entrepreneurship within the Ministry of the Economy, the final approval being reserved for the government (which also decided whether the enterprise would be converted into a Type I or Type II company). Recently, however, the 1992 amendments to the Transformation Decree left the whole matter to the branch ministries and the Ministry of the Economy, in coordination with the Department of State Property, which might make the process more congenial to insiders.

In general, the corporatization process in itself has not led to major changes in the organizational structure of the enterprises included in the program. Indeed, the need for the recent amendments to the Transformation Decree was a direct result of the state's loss of control over much of the state sector and its inability to effect more significant changes in their operation. At most, the process simply divided some large units into somewhat smaller units.

As of September 1992 there were some 230 state joint-stock companies in Estonia, of which thirty-six were Type I and 194 Type II companies.

LATVIA

CONTENTS

1. INTRODUCTION

Brief history of reforms

Following the Soviet invasion in 1940, Latvia was constituted as one of the Soviet republics. Over the next fifty years, Soviet authorities imposed typical Soviet economic structure on the Latvian economy. By the end of the 1980s, the economy was dominated by overgrown industrial enterprises, agricultural collectives, and state farms. The Soviet government formally granted limited economic autonomy to the Baltic states in January 1990. Latvia gained complete independence concurrently with other Baltic republics in August 1991.

In 1989, Latvia introduced legislation that permitted the creation of industrial cooperatives and private farms. These laws began the transformation of the economic structure of the country. Mirroring the changes in the other Baltic republics, further institutional reforms were introduced in 1990 and 1991. These included the establishment of the Bank of Latvia in July 1990, and the first independent budget, accompanied by the introduction of a new tax system, in January 1991. In the fall of 1991, Latvia assumed control over the last union enterprises situated on its territory.

Although some prices were freed in 1990, more substantial price liberalization took place in 1991. Some prices were decontrolled, while others were fixed by the authorities, or subject to ceilings. Prices of most consumer and producer goods were further liberalized in January 1992. However, the profit margins of state wholesalers continued to be regulated.

2. ECONOMIC ENVIRONMENT

The structure of output

According to the IMF, the gross domestic product (GDP) of Latvia in current prices was Rb 11.9 bln[1] in 1990, and Rb 22.3 bln in 1991.

---

[1] According to *PlanEcon*, the average "commercial" ruble–dollar exchange rate was 1.76 in 1990 and 1.74 in 1991. It should be noted that these rates are distorted and thus dollar equivalents of local statistics are useful only for superficial illustrative purposes.

The structure of net material product (NMP) in Latvia was the same as that prevailing in the Soviet Union.

Table 2.1   The structure of net material product in 1989 (per cent of total)

	Latvia	Soviet Union
Industry	45	42
Agriculture	24	23
Construction	10	13
Other	21	22

Source: "Latvia," *IMF Economic Review*, April 1992

Output

Following a 3.1 per cent drop in 1990, the net material product of Latvia, expressed in 1990 prices, fell by an additional 6.0 per cent in 1991. The largest decline (15 per cent) was registered by the construction sector, which had grown in 1990. Industrial output also fell by 2 per cent in 1991, following a 9.8 per cent increase in 1990. Transport and communications posted a decline of 4 per cent in 1991. After a 15.3 per cent drop in 1990, agricultural NMP fell by another 12.9 per cent in 1991.

Overall GDP registered a decline of 32 per cent for the first six months of 1992, relative to the first half of 1991. All sectors of the economy fell sharply, the largest declines having been in the construction and manufacturing sectors, which suffered decreases of 44 per cent and 36 per cent, respectively.

Investment

After a decline of 8.2 per cent in 1990, gross investment in fixed capital fell by another 11 per cent in 1991. However, the share of net investment in the net material product remained unchanged at about 20 per cent.

Household savings

There is no reliable estimate of the total stock of household savings in Latvia, since a significant proportion of savings has been kept outside the official banking system. According to the IMF monetary survey, the total amount of ruble deposits officially held by households was Rb 5.80 bln, by the end of 1991. In addition, households reportedly held $1 mln in official foreign currency accounts.

Price liberalization

Substantial price liberalization began in January 1991, with the removal of controls on a number of consumer and producer prices. According to some local estimates, prices of goods comprising about 60 per cent of total expenditures and 90 per cent of non-food expenditures were freed by June 1991. The prices of other goods were either fixed centrally on the basis of the costs of production and allowable profit margins, or were subject to centrally-set ceilings. These prices were adjusted a number of times during 1991.

Prices of foodstuffs and of related goods were increased by two to four times in January 1991. In April, the controlled prices of many producer and consumer durable goods were raised by the Latvian authorities, concurrently with similar price increases in Russia. Prices of energy and fuels were increased by five to six times in November 1991.

In January 1992, prices were further decontrolled. Many of these formerly fixed prices were permitted to exceed their upper limits, while the prices of a large number of goods previously subject to ceilings, including many foodstuffs and consumer products, were freed of government control. Prices of fuels, oil, coal, and energy products for industrial use were liberalized in late 1992. Controls, however, remained in effect for transportation tariffs and rents.

Inflation

During the first half of 1991, the largest increase in the consumer price index (CPI) occurred in April, following a major increase in controlled prices. After subsiding between May and November, the CPI increased by 55 per cent in December. This sharp increase was primarily due to panic buying in anticipation of the January 1992 price liberalization, and the decontrol of most farm and retail food prices. For the whole year, the CPI of goods and services rose by about 300 per cent.

Mirroring price developments in the other Baltic states, the CPI in Latvia continued to rise in 1992.

Table 2.2 Consumer price index (month-to-month per cent change)

	Jan	Feb	Mar	Apr	May	June	July	Aug	Sept	Oct	Nov	Dec
1991	29	13.6	4.2	20.6	4.1	−2.2	5.4	0.7	17.8	7.6	7.0	55
1992	64.1	48.6	33.8	11.0	13.2	15.2	19.6	16.3	12.1	25.1		

Source: The Committee for Statistics of the Latvian Council of Ministers

Behavior of wages

The government sets both the minimum wage and overall pay scales, linked to the minimum wage, for organizations funded directly from the state budget. The minimum wage increased from Rb 460 in February 1991 to Rb 1,500 in June 1992. Other enterprises, in both the state and private sectors, set their wages autonomously.

The average nominal wage increased from Rb 600 in 1991 to Rb 5,960 in September 1992.

Table 2.3 Average nominal wages (in rubles)

1991				1992					
Q1	Q2	Q3	Q4	Jan	Feb	Mar	Apr	May	June
480	562	504	600	1,385	1,850	2,550	2,790	3,590	4,675

Source: The Committee for Statistics of the Latvian Council of Ministers, and *Baltic Independent*, August 14–20, 1992

Unemployment

Latvia began registering its unemployed in February 1992. The number of registered unemployed persons reached 32,600 in September 1992. This represented about 2 per cent of the labor force. However, the time lost due to forced vacations and temporary closures is estimated to have totaled 2.6 mln working days between January and September 1992. The effect of these closures is equivalent to an average of about 13,400 additional unemployed persons during every month of this period.

State budget

The Latvian budget process is decentralized. Central and local governments share tax revenues and prepare their own budgets. All budgets, and the financing of any budget deficit through borrowing from the Bank of Latvia, must be approved by parliament. For the first time, the 1991 state budget did not include flows between the Latvian and union budgets.

The price liberalization of 1991 boosted central and local receipts from turnover and profit taxes. The government also implemented other, ad hoc, revenue enhancing measures. As a result, the 1991 budget posted a surplus, reported by the Latvian Department of Statistics at Rb 942 mln. Preliminary estimates show a balanced budget for the first six months of 1992.

TAXATION

Parliament determines the coverage of central and local taxes, the rates of central government taxes, and the maximum rates for local taxes. Local governments are allowed to grant tax exemptions up to the local share of any tax.

Personal income tax is progressive, with marginal rates ranging from 15 per cent on incomes equal to three times the minimum wage, to 35 per cent on incomes equal to twenty-five times the minimum wage. Employees also pay one per cent of their wages as social security tax.

The profit tax rates range from 15 per cent to 45 per cent. They depend on the ownership form of the enterprise, with higher rates for state enterprises than for private enterprises, and on its line of activity. In addition, enterprises pay 37 per cent of total wages, salaries, and other labor compensation to the Social Security Budget.

The main tax levied on transactions involving goods and services is a turnover tax. The basic rate is 12 per cent, with a 6 per cent surcharge for certain food products. There are also excise taxes ranging from 10 to 91 per cent, depending on the goods involved.

Monetary policy

CREDIT AND INTEREST RATES

In 1991, lending by the former branches of Gosbank and other specialized state banks accounted for about 84 per cent of lending to Latvian enterprises. In December 1991, these financial institutions were merged with the Bank of Latvia. In contrast to other countries in the region, the Bank of Latvia has become the dominant commercial lender in the country, with additional credit provided by newly created commercial banks, usually founded by state enterprises.

Loans to enterprises represented about 98 per cent of total credit in 1991, while the volume of nominal credit increased by about 140 per cent relative to 1990. This implies a sharp drop in the volume of credit in real terms.

Since January 1991, branches of the Bank of Latvia have been free to set their deposit and lending rates independently, though they are required to charge preferential rates on lending to enterprises in some sectors, such as agriculture. In 1991, lending rates were extremely low, following the rate of 8 per cent charged by the Bank of Latvia on its refinancing credits. Following an acceleration of inflation, the average lending rate reached 106 per cent in August 1992.

Debt

The question of Latvia's responsibility for a portion of the external debt burden of the former Soviet Union remains to be settled.

Foreign trade

By August 1991, the number of organizations permitted to engage in foreign trade had grown to 1,700. However, involvement in foreign trade activities still requires a license.

Exports of goods to the other former Soviet republics are governed by bilateral agreements, while exports to other countries are subject to quotas. Exports of certain goods, including gasoline and petroleum products, are prohibited.

Import tariffs are imposed on convertible currency imports. No special import licenses are required.

In 1990, about 97 per cent of Latvian exports and 87 per cent of imports involved trade with other former republics. According to estimates by the Latvian authorities, the interrepublican current account posted a surplus in both 1990 and 1991 (Rb 208 mln and Rb 1,721 mln, respectively). In 1991, imports increased by about 11 per cent, while exports were up by 41 per cent.

During the first quarter of 1992, the trade account posted a surplus of Rb 2.9 bln, mostly due to an interrepublican trade surplus. Trade with Russia comprised about 25 per cent of total imports, and about 50 per cent of exports.

3. PRESENT FORMS OF OWNERSHIP

3A. Legal framework of economic activity

Existing and planned legislation concerning property rights

The following are the most important laws concerning property rights, business organizations, and privatization in Latvia:

— Civil Code (1990);
— Labor Code (1990);
— Law on Agricultural Reform (1990);
— Law on Entrepreneurial Activity ("Enterprise Law") (1990, amended in 1991 and 1992);
— Joint-Stock Companies Law of the Republic of Latvia (1990, amended in 1991 and 1992);
— Law on Land Reform in Rural Areas (1990);
— Law on Local Government Enterprises (1990);
— Law on State Enterprises (1990, amended 1991);
— Law on Cooperative Companies (1991);
— Law on Foreign Investment of the Republic of Latvia ("Foreign Investment Law") (1991);
— Law on Limited-Liability Companies (1991, amended 1992);
— Law on Partnerships (1991);
— Law on Privatization of Municipally-Owned Small Objects of Trade and Commerce, Restaurants, Cafes, and the Service Sector (1991, amended 1992);
— Law Reforming the Ownership of Land Located in the Towns of Latvia (1991);
— Law on Reprivatization of Buildings (1991);

— Law on Return of Buildings to their Legal Owners (1991);
— Council of Ministers' Resolution on the Creation and Operation of Foreign Business Offices in the Republic of Latvia (1991);
— Decree on the Establishment of Institutions for the Conversion of State Property (1991);
— Supreme Council Decree on State Property and the Basic Principles of its Conversion (1991);
— Law on Certificates (1992);
— Law of the Republic of Latvia on Insolvency and Bankruptcy of Enterprises (1992);
— Law on the Order of Evaluation of Objects of State and Municipal Property to be Privatized (1992);
— Law on the Order of Privatization of Objects of State and Municipal Property (1992);
— Law on Privatization Commissions of State and Municipal Property (1992);
— Supreme Council Decree on the Concepts and Preparation Program of Privatization of State and Municipal Property (1992).

Recognized forms of business organizations

THE LEGAL REGIME OF BUSINESS ACTIVITY
In accordance with a pattern common to the former republics of the Soviet Union, Latvia has passed one act, the Law on Entrepreneurial Activity (1990, amended in 1991 and 1992) ("Enterprise Law"), establishing a single legal framework for all business activity, including private, state, and municipal enterprises. The law defines an entrepreneur as a physical or juridical person, family, "an entrepreneurial association,"[2] local government, or social or religious organization allocating a portion of its property for entrepreneurial activity. The portion of the property so allocated is defined as the enterprise, and the law guarantees equal treatment to all forms of business activity.

All enterprises and entrepreneurial associations must be registered with the Enterprise Registry of the Republic. They must also be audited annually by an audit committee or an outside auditor, and disclose information required for tax and statistical purposes. They are

[2] Defined as a registered association of property owners or entrepreneurs.

also required to purchase mandatory insurance. Labor relations are governed by mandatory collective labor agreements. The law further provides that the state will conduct an industrial policy through taxation and a procurement program.

The Enterprise Law reserves some areas of economic activity for the state (the production and sale of narcotics, weapons, and explosives, and the printing of securities, money, and postage stamps), and requires a license for the conduct of others, such as mining, the manufacture of pharmaceutical and tobacco products, the production and sale of alcoholic beverages, and air, shipping, and rail transportation services. Additional areas of activity may be subject to restrictions approved by the parliament.

The Enterprise Law makes distinctions between a number of different forms of business organizations specified below, some of which are also the subject of special, additional legislation.

STATE AND MUNICIPAL ENTERPRISES

State enterprises in Latvia are formed by a decision of the Council of Ministers, while local government enterprises are formed by decrees of the relevant local authorities. Although the Latvian privatization program envisions a large-scale transformation of state enterprises into joint-stock and limited-liability companies (see Section 5 on corporatization below), it is not envisaged that all of these enterprises will be transformed or liquidated in the near future.

In addition to the provisions of the Enterprise Law, the legal framework for the operation of state and municipal enterprises is provided by the Law on State Enterprises (1990, amended 1991), the pertinent provisions of the Civil Code and the Labor Code, the Law on Local Government Enterprises (1990), and by the charters of individual enterprises.

The Law on State Enterprises defines a state enterprise as a legal person and an independent, self-governing economic unit utilizing property allotted to it by the state. State enterprises must have their own charters with provisions concerning their management and control, reorganization and liquidation, distribution of profits, and accounting procedures for the use of state-owned capital.

The law contains a number of provisions guaranteeing the autonomy of state enterprises, including their right to dispose of assets allotted to them by the state. Nonetheless, the state retains very considerable powers. The most important of these is the right of the Council of Ministers to appoint the director of the enterprise and determine his remuneration and conditions of employment. At the same time, however, the director is employed on the basis of a written contract, so that there is a possibility that his partial independence may be secured. The Council of Ministers can also decide on the reorganization, lease, or liquidation of parts or of the whole of a state enterprise.

The director of a state enterprise is the sole organ of its management. He acts on behalf of the company in awarding contracts, managing the assets of the enterprise, establishing and dissolving affiliate offices, setting up and managing bank accounts, hiring and discharging employees, and making all other necessary decisions. Enterprises are regularly audited on behalf of the Council of Ministers, but may not be audited more than twice a year.

INDIVIDUAL ENTERPRISES AND FAMILY FARMS
Individual enterprises and family farms are unincorporated businesses owned by one person or by a single family. They must be registered with the Enterprise Registry, and their names must contain the surname of the owner or the name of the house (in the case of the farm). Their owners are personally liable for all enterprise obligations.

GENERAL AND LIMITED PARTNERSHIPS
Latvian partnerships are governed by the Enterprise Law and a special Law on Partnerships (1991). A partnership is not a legal entity and does not have a right to issue securities. The law recognizes both general and limited partnerships: the former are composed exclusively of general partners, who bear full personal liability for the obligations of the enterprise, while the latter include limited partners, whose liability is limited to the extent of their contribution. General partners leaving the partnership remain fully liable for three years after their departure, while new general partners assume liability for obligations incurred prior to their assumption of partnership status. The names of limited partners cannot appear in the name of the partnership without rendering their liability unlimited.

General partners are responsible for the management of the enterprise, and, unless the partnership agreement provides otherwise, each general partner has one vote (regardless of contribution) in partnership affairs. A general partner cannot own an individual enterprise without the consent of the other partners, nor can he be a general partner in another enterprise. Limited partners, on the other hand, are essentially passive investors; they have a right to obtain information about partnership affairs but do not normally participate in management and decision making (although the partnership agreement may give them the right to vote on certain matters).

The distribution of profits and the allocation of losses may be specified by the partnership agreement, but in the absence of such a provision, both profits and losses are distributed in accordance with the capital contribution of each partner, with partners providing services in lieu of capital receiving a share equal to the smallest of the other shares. The law also prohibits the allocation of all gains and losses to one partner.

LIMITED-LIABILITY COMPANY

Limited-liability companies (LLCs) are governed by the Law on Limited-Liability Companies (1991, amended in 1992), in addition to the Enterprise Law. They are familiar European forms of small and medium-size corporate organizations. Latvian law allows LLCs to be formed by one or more persons (either domestic or foreign), and limits the number of shareholders to fifty; if the number of shareholders increases above fifty, the enterprise must be transformed into a joint-stock company within two years. The minimum capitalization of an LLC is fixed at Rb 20,000. The company must also accumulate a reserve fund, equal to no less than one-third of its authorized capital, in order to cover unexpected expenses.

In the absence of contrary provisions in the charter, the transferability of the shares of an LLC is restricted by the right of preemption of the other shareholders. Even if no shareholder wishes to buy the offered shares, the executive body of the LLC has the right to buy them from the owner at a price determined in accordance with stipulations contained in the charter, and to re-sell them to a party of its choice. Only if the executive body is unable to find another buyer within one month of the offer are the shares returned to the original participant, who is then authorized to sell at his discretion. The marketability of shares may be restricted even further, since the law also allows the charter of an LLC to provide that a sale of shares requires the unanimous consent of all shareholders. Likewise, existing shareholders are protected against any dilution by having the right to increase the value of their shares before any offering is made to outside investors. Both increases and reductions in the authorized capital of an LLC must be approved by the meeting of the shareholders and reported to the Enterprise Registry.

The highest organ of an LLC is the shareholders' meeting. The meeting has exclusive authority to decide on charter amendments, share issues and transfers, and the appointment of auditors and members of the executive body, as well as on restructuring and reorganization. The meeting can also hire and fire the managers of the enterprise or delegate that function to the executive body of the enterprise. Voting can be in person or by written proxy, but members of the executive body cannot function as proxies. Each share or multiple of one share has one vote, but the charter may restrict the voting power of large shareholders. A quorum of at least half of the shareholders is required for most decisions, increasing to three-quarters if decisions concerning charter amendments or liquidation are to be considered. If a quorum is lacking, the meeting can be reconvened within fifteen days and the number of shareholders attending will be construed to constitute the quorum for ordinary decisions.

An LLC also has an executive body (a board, directorate, or administration) composed of between one and twelve persons elected at the shareholders' meeting. The rights and obligations of the executive body are determined in the charter, and the charter may also stipulate that one or more managers be elected from among the members of the executive body to perform the duties determined by the shareholders' meeting. An LLC must also have an auditing commission, elected for three-year terms by the shareholders' meeting. The commissioners are personally liable for "losses incurred by erroneous or illegal actions they have taken."

ASSOCIATION WITH ADDITIONAL LIABILITY

This is a rather unusual form of business organization permitted by the Enterprise Law.[3] It corresponds to a limited-liability company in which investors are liable for the enterprise obligations in an amount greater than their contributions. While the law is not clear on the ultimate limitation of their liability, it presumably extends to some multiple of the shareholders' contribution to the authorized capital, and not to all of their personal assets.

JOINT-STOCK COMPANY

In addition to the Enterprise Law, the Joint-Stock Companies Law of the Republic of Latvia (1990, amended in 1991 and 1992) regulates the structure and operation of Latvian joint-stock companies (JSCs).

A JSC may be formed either as a new enterprise or through the

---

[3] The laws of Ukraine permit the creation of a similar business entity.

transformation of an existing one (in particular a state or municipal enterprise). The minimum capitalization of a JSC is Rb 100,000; Rb 5 mln for banking enterprises, and Rb 3 mln for insurance companies. The founding of a JSC requires three promoters (founders), who may be domestic or foreign, unless the JSC is incorporated by the government, in which case a "one-person" JSC is formed. The founders, who must subscribe to at least 25 per cent of the authorized capital, must prepare an agreement governing operations until the JSC is properly constituted, the charter of the proposed company, and the prospectus. Prospective shareholders must pay 10 per cent of the price of the shares at the time of purchase and 25 per cent by the time of the constitutive meeting. The constitutive meeting must be called within six months of the publication of the prospectus. The quorum requirement is three-fifths of the total number of shareholders, representing three-quarters of the company's capital, and most decisions are made by a simple majority of the shares (decisions concerning founders' privileges and revaluation of property need unanimity).

A JSC may issue different classes of shares and bonds; employee stock may also be issued at a discount or free of charge for up to 10 per cent of the authorized capital (employee shares must be issued out of the excess of the company property over its authorized capital). Employee shares carry full voting rights and their value must be paid in full upon the employee's departure from the company. Preferred shares cannot exceed 25 per cent of the authorized capital, and their issue requires approval of at least four-fifths of a general meeting of shareholders, attended by shareholders representing at least 75 per cent of the capital. Bonds may not exceed 20 per cent of the capital; but they may be exchanged for stocks, if authorized by the shareholders' meeting. While the transferability of shares is presumed, the charter may grant the existing shareholders the right of preemption. The JSC's purchase of its own stock is only authorized in special circumstances (in which case the stock is retired). A reserve fund equal to one-third of the authorized capital must be accumulated from profits.

The highest organ of a JSC is the general meeting of the shareholders. This annual meeting can review the company's budget, elect the members of other corporate bodies, determine the distribution of profits, and decide on charter amendments or liquidation. A JSC also has a Supervisory Council, charged with oversight functions; and a Management Board, charged with day-to-day operations, as well as an auditing commission composed of three persons chosen for staggered terms. Finally, the activities of a JSC are subject to the supervision of the Minister of Finance, who has the right to order an independent audit of the enterprise at any time.

The council, which officially governs the company between shareholders' meetings, consists of at least three members and two to seven candidates, not all of whom are necessarily shareholders. The maximum number of members may vary depending on the size of the company; it may be as high as twenty-one. The Management Board is composed of three to twelve members, who need not be shareholders. At least one-third of the members of the council and at least one-half of the Management Board must be Latvian citizens or persons who have resided in Latvia for twenty-five years.

Finally, the law contains a number of provisions limiting the concentration of corporate power through mergers and acquisitions. It distinguishes between regular and holding companies, and imposes a number of restrictions on the latter.

COOPERATIVES

Until October 1991, Latvian cooperatives were governed by Soviet laws (see the chapter on Russia). Latvia enacted its own Law on Cooperative Companies in August 1991, and the decree putting it into effect required that all existing cooperatives had either to restructure themselves in conformity with the new law and re-register before March 1, 1992, or to dissolve in accordance with the law's provisions. Moreover, since the new law severely restricts the areas in which cooperatives may be active in Latvia, it effectively forced the dissolution of a significant portion of the old cooperatives.

The new law defines the cooperative company as a self-financed group of natural persons dedicated to mutual aid in their daily needs and to the material well-being and cultural advancement of the members. The permissible areas of cooperative activity listed in the law include savings and insurance associations, credit unions, retail trade, agricultural and fishing production and processing, housing, medical care, information services (including newspapers), and sports and recreational activities. All other types of cooperatives may be founded only with the approval of the Council of Ministers. Moreover, cooperative companies are precluded from becoming closed organizations, and must accept new members unless the cooperative's goals cannot be met by serving the interests of a larger group of members.

Five founding members are necessary for the foundation of a cooperative company. Each member is required to make a contribution to the company, either in kind (including labor) or in money, depending on the statutes of the cooperative. In exchange, each member is entitled to use all the facilities of the cooperative, receive membership discounts and dividends (which are distributed in proportion to the members' contributions), and participate in the governance of the company. The statutory organs of a cooperative are the general membership meeting, the management, and an auditing committee elected by the meeting.

Bankruptcy

The Law of the Republic of Latvia on Insolvency and Bankruptcy of Enterprises took effect on January 1, 1992. It is characterized by a heavy emphasis on attempts to restructure and reorganize, rather than liquidate, insolvent enterprises, and it is relatively harsh on creditors. It applies to all enterprises, including individual entrepreneurs, but not to personal bankruptcies in noncommercial contexts.

The law defines insolvency as the debtor's inability to pay its debts, if such debts are acknowledged by the enterprise or determined by the courts. Bankruptcy is defined as the forced sale or dissolution of an insolvent enterprise in order to obtain funds to settle the claims of its creditors. An enterprise is to be declared bankrupt if it is unable to make payments equal to or exceeding 50 per cent of "the investment earmarked for operations" and no further credit or revenue from the sale or mortgaging of real property is available, or if insolvency has become "apparent." Insolvency is "apparent" if the debtor admits, and the court recognizes, that the debtor's assets are insufficient to satisfy creditors' claims, or if the debtor takes steps (such as selling large amounts of enterprise property or disappearing without notification) which signal the debtor's unwillingness or inability to honor its obligations.

Insolvency proceedings can be initiated by the creditors or the debtor itself, and the court investigates insolvency claims exceeding Rb 1,000 for an individual enterprise or Rb 10,000 in the case of a company. If the petition is deemed "reasonable," the court commences an insolvency proceeding by: warning the debtor of its duty to report changes in residence and to respond to requests for information; notifying all creditors; appointing an auditor to inventory the debtor's property; and suspending the collection of judgments issued against the debtor within the preceding three months. If the court determines during this inquiry that none of the prescribed schemes for bringing the debtor back to solvency (see below) can be effective, it will declare the enterprise bankrupt and order the sale of its assets at an auction.

If the court determines that a return to solvency is possible, it declares the debtor insolvent, publishing its decision in the official and local press and notifying the official Enterprise Registry and the municipality in which the enterprise was registered. Creditors have three months from the date of publication to file their claims, and the court appoints an administrator to manage the enterprise prior to the first meeting of the creditors. The administrator is charged with ascertaining the identity of the enterprise's creditors and organizing a creditors' meeting, and is authorized to sell enterprise property if such action is in the interest of creditors.

The creditors' meeting, which occurs prior to any further decisions concerning the insolvent enterprise, has the right to review the conduct of the administrator and can petition the court for his removal. The meeting also appoints a Board of Trustees, sets the compensation of the administrator and the board, and makes decisions concerning the course of management. There are no quorum requirements for the creditors' meeting, provided that each creditor has received ten days' notice. Decisions are passed by a simple majority, each creditor receiving a number of votes proportionate to the monetary value of his claims.

The Board of Trustees assists the administrator in the performance of his duties and registers all creditors' claims. A meeting of the creditors is then called to pass on each claim, and uncontested claims are accepted for payment. Contested claims may be reviewed by the court within two weeks of their rejection by the meeting.

Following the declaration of insolvency and the creditors' meeting, the court considers the possibility of the following means of returning the debtor to solvency:

- peaceful settlement;
- administration by creditors;
- a "scheme of arrangement."

Peaceful settlement is an agreement between the creditors and the debtor, which can occur at any time prior to the sale or distribution of the debtors' property. It requires the consent of at least two-thirds of the creditors holding at least three-quarters of the value of all claims. Peaceful settlement is not permitted, however, in the event of "malicious bankruptcy," i.e. a situation in which the debtor failed to notify the court of its insolvency, obstructed judicial inquiries, or wilfully caused the insolvency of the enterprise to avoid paying its debts.

Administration by creditors is an arrangement by which the creditors take charge of the insolvent enterprise in order to avoid liquidation and bring the debtor back to financial health. It is established pursuant to a court order and a petition of the creditors representing no less than three-quarters of the value of all outstanding claims, and it may offer the debtor an opportunity to participate in the reorganization process. The objectives of the administration by creditors are set by the court, but an administrator is appointed by the creditors' meeting, which also determines the scope of his responsibilities and those of the debtor. The duration of the administration by creditors is one year, with the possibility of renewal for another year, subject to the creditors' approval. After that time, bankruptcy must be declared if the claims of the creditors remain unsettled.

If neither a peaceful settlement nor an administration by creditors have been arranged, the court solicits proposals from the debtor for the firm's reorganization, termed a "scheme of arrangements." (In the case of a state or municipal enterprise, the scheme of arrangements is the responsibility of the Council of Ministers or the municipality involved.) Such a scheme may involve a detailed restructuring program prepared by the debtor or a competition during which restructuring plans may be proposed by the owner, the employees, creditors, or other businesses and individuals.[4] A scheme of arrangements must be accepted by the court, and its operation cannot exceed eighteen months (two years in the case of agricultural enterprises), with a possibility of a six-month extension adopted with the creditors' approval. The scheme must not be less advantageous to the creditors than outright dissolution, and at least 40 per cent of all creditors' claims must be satisfied within one year of its initiation.

In the event of a declaration of bankruptcy, the Board of Trustees takes over the administration of the enterprise and supervises the liquidation of the enterprise's property. Strangely enough, the law is very cryptic on the subject of creditors' priorities. It specifies that the costs of administration are covered first and that the rest "is

---

[4] This strange arrangement, in which the owner may call for competitive proposals in which it participates itself, becomes more understandable in the case of state and municipal enterprises, when the Council of Ministers or the municipality forces the management or other state institutions to compete with third parties for control over the restructuring process.

distributed among the creditors in accordance with the law and the decision of the Board of Trustees, as approved by the meeting of the creditors.'' Some further information may be obtained from the provisions of the Enterprise Law concerning liquidation, which specify creditors' priority. The law puts taxes and other payments to the state in the first category, followed by social insurance payments for future medical costs of persons tortiously injured by the enterprise, followed by debts to the budget,[5] environmental liabilities, debts to creditors who declared their claims within the prescribed term, and debts to other creditors. Presumably the priority of secured over unsecured creditors follows from their legal status, but the Enterprise Law contains no explicit provisions to this effect. The rights of employees are treated separately in the Labor Code.

Regulations governing foreign ownership

Foreign investment in Latvia is governed mainly by the 1991 Law on Foreign Investment of the Republic of Latvia (''Foreign Investment Law''), and the establishment of foreign offices is regulated by the Council of Ministers' Resolution on the Creation and Operation of Foreign Business Offices in the Republic of Latvia (1991).

The Foreign Investment Law defines foreign investment as convertible currency earmarked for entrepreneurial activity and property of foreign investors imported from abroad, thus excluding ruble investment. But the definition of a ''foreign investor'' (foreign persons investing in entrepreneurial activity in Latvia) does not exclude ruble zone investors. Foreign investors can establish limited-liability or joint-stock companies, with or without a local partner, participate in existing businesses, establish branches, and open agency offices not authorized to undertake business activities in Latvia.

Enterprises with foreign investment are, in principle, guaranteed equal treatment with domestic companies under the national laws, except for the special provisions of the Foreign Investment Law.[6] In fact the Foreign Investment Law does contain a number of important

---

[5] In contradistinction to the first category, these are presumably contractual obligations (or other obligations peculiar to state enterprises), rather than obligations arising out of the operation of law, such as taxes, excise or custom duties, etc.

[6] An interesting question is whether any future laws discriminating against enterprises with foreign investment would be invalid on the basis of this provision.

exceptions. Foreign investors are not permitted to gain (voting or other) control of enterprises in certain sectors of the economy, including defense, mass media, national education, mining, fishing, hunting, and port management, unless specifically licensed by the Council of Ministers. Violators of these restrictions must sell their share of the illegally controlled enterprise within three months, or face a forced sale, with 25 per cent of the proceeds going to the state. Moreover, a special agency authorized by the Council of Ministers must be notified about any planned investment exceeding $1 mln. Prior authorization must be obtained for such an investment, as well as any investment in a state enterprise, or an acquisition of a controlling interest in a Latvian enterprise with capital exceeding $1 mln. The authorities issue licenses based on six broadly defined criteria, relating to the impact of the foreign investment on the Latvian economy (including job creation, the use of local services and resources, and exports), raising productivity and developing new products and technologies, as well as on competition within the industry, foreign domination of Latvia's economy, the competitiveness of Latvian products abroad, and the environment.

Foreign investors are protected against arbitrary expropriation, and guaranteed full compensation within three months from the day of the expropriation. In principle, the law also provides guarantees against future, less favorable regulation of foreign investment, but the exceptions to this principle (for laws "necessitated by national security, social order, taxation system other than the tax concessions stipulated by this law, environmental protection, morals, the health of the population as well as anti-monopoly laws") seem to negate the rule.

Foreign investors are generally subject to Latvian tax laws, but are also granted a number of exceptions. Enterprises with over 30 per cent foreign investment are granted two-year tax holidays (beginning with the first year in which profits are generated) and a 50 per cent reduction for two subsequent years. If, in addition, the enterprise is engaged in one of seventeen broadly defined activities to which a preferred economic status is granted by the Council of Ministers, the initial tax holiday is extended to three years. Finally, enterprises in which foreign investment exceeds 50 per cent and $1 mln are granted tax holidays for three years and a 50 per cent reduction in taxes for the subsequent five years. Further tax reductions may be granted after the initial period for enterprises producing "goods of high importance for Latvia," but any enterprise with foreign investment ceasing operation within three years of its registration is liable for full taxes on all profits earned during its operational life. Foreign investors may repatriate after-tax profits,[7] and imports used for investment purposes are exempt from customs duties.

3B. Structure of ownership

Traditional state enterprises in Latvia still employ a large fraction of the labor force and produce most of the country's output. As noted in Section 5 below, the transformation of state enterprises into shareholding companies or limited-liability companies only began, on an experimental basis, in 1991, involving twenty-seven enterprises, which together represented 9.2 per cent of total output and 9.5 per cent of the industrial workforce.

Other ownership forms are also beginning to emerge. In 1989, the Soviet Union permitted the establishment of cooperatives as part of state enterprises. By the end of 1991, these cooperatives and individual private businesses employed about 10 per cent of the labor force.

Collective farms continue to dominate the agricultural sector. By the end of 1991, however, individual farms accounted for about 22 per cent of agricultural employment.

Table 3B.1 Employment in state and private sectors (in thousands)

	1990	1991
Total	1,408.7	1,404.7
State enterprises	1,139.3	1,088.8
Cooperatives and individual business	88.3	133
Collective farms	152.1	146.9
Individual farms	25.9	32.9
Self-employed	3.1	3.1

Source: The Committee for Statistics of the Latvian Council of Ministers

---

[7] No provisions are made, however, for the conversion of local currency into convertible currency.

4. THE PRIVATIZATION PROCESS

Introduction

Latvia began to reform its centrally planned economic system while still under the rule of the USSR. Changes in the agricultural sector began in the late 1980s, marking a movement away from the centralized system of state farms and collectives imposed under Soviet rule. Growth in the number of small privately-run farms was particularly rapid in 1989.

The first decentralizing reforms in the industry and services sectors began in 1989. The Soviet Law on Cooperatives permitted employees to establish cooperatives in order to lease the assets of their enterprises. Although they bought raw materials at controlled prices through the state system, these cooperatives were allowed to set the prices for their own output and to divide the profit among their members. The intention of the law may have been to create better incentives for the improvement of efficiency and productivity, but instead the effect was a form of "spontaneous privatization," whereby enterprise insiders achieved effective ownership of state assets.[8] The Latvian government suspended these actions through a decree in October 1990, taking effect on December 31, 1990.

More important changes were initiated only after January 1, 1990, when Latvia declared itself economically independent within the USSR, seeking the freedom to proceed with a more comprehensive program of economic liberalization. The introduction of legislation to create the structure for a market economic system began at this time.

The legislative reform process further accelerated after the declaration on May 4, 1990 that the independent Republic of Latvia, as recognized internationally in the interwar period, legally still existed. This declaration asserted the sovereignty of Latvian over Soviet law, although the break with the USSR was not made complete until the declaration of full independence on August 21, 1991. The transfer to Latvian jurisdiction of the all-union enterprises on Latvian territory took place in October–November 1991, Union institutional structures having by then collapsed.

---

[8] See the subsection on lease enterprises in Section 3A of the chapter on Russia.

Independent Latvia's first step towards privatization and reprivatization was taken on November 20, 1990, when the Council of Ministers submitted a proposal on The Conversion of State Property (Basic Concepts and Program). Based on this, the Supreme Council (Parliament) passed a Decree on March 20, 1991 on State Property and the Basic Principles of its Conversion. The basic principles enunciated in this decree had important implications for the development of Latvian privatization policy. They included, first, individual treatment of sectors (branches), which was later reflected in the power given to branch ministries in the privatization process. Second, eligibility for reprivatization was made independent of citizenship. Third, the means of payment in privatization was declared to be "the currency currently in use in Latvia," which led to fears that many Latvian assets would be acquired by foreigners with Russian rubles; this was arguably a prominent factor in the slow pace of Latvian privatization prior to the introduction of the Latvian Ruble on July 20, 1992. Finally, the use of vouchers (certificates) was proposed, although the Law on Certificates was passed only a year and a half later, on November 4, 1992.

An "experimental" small privatization program was launched in the middle of 1991, when five of the largest municipalities were each allowed to privatize up to three small trade, catering, or service establishments each. But the small privatization program really started with the Law on Privatization of Municipally-Owned Small Objects of Trade and Commerce, Restaurants, Cafes and the Service Sector, passed on November 5, 1991. An "experimental" large privatization program also began in 1991, with the establishment of twenty-six joint-stock companies and twenty-two limited-liability companies on the basis of enterprise assets.

Progress, however, was slow, and the government submitted to parliament the "Further Directions of Development of the Privatization Process" in February 1992, on the basis of which the Supreme Council passed a Decree on March 3, 1992 on the Concepts and Preparation Program of Privatization of State and Municipal Property. The main practical provisions of this decree included continuation of the transfer of state property to municipalities, restrictions on the means of payment for privatization purchases, encouragement of small privatization, and more detailed proposals on privatization of large state enterprises. The government was also requested to submit fifteen draft laws on various aspects of the process. Although the intent of the decree may have been to accelerate the process, it is also argued that this extensive legislative agenda may have had a contrary effect.[9]

Further legal building blocks for the large privatization program were put in place with the passage of the Law on Privatization Commissions of State and Municipal Property (March 17, 1992), the Law on the Order of Evaluation of Objects of State and Municipal Property to be Privatized (June 10, 1992), and the Law on the Order of Privatization of Objects of State and Municipal Property (June 16, 1992).

The largest Latvian brewery was privatized through the formation of a joint venture with a Swedish firm and a Finnish firm in May 1992, and small privatization greatly accelerated in the summer and fall of 1992. On August 18, 1992, the Council of Ministers passed a "List of Objects to be Privatized," including 637 large enterprises and assets in a mass privatization program. Projects were supposed to be submitted by November 18, 1992, three months after the official publication date of this list.

4A. Organizational structure of state regulation of privatization

There is no single institution for overall control and implementation of the privatization process in Latvia. Four levels of state administration play important roles: parliament (Supreme Council), government (Council of Ministers), ministries (including the Ministry for Economic Reforms), and local governments. The process is rather decentralized, with branch ministries being the dominant institutions in large privatization, and local authorities playing the largest role in reprivatization and small privatization. A proposal to initiate a small privatization can be submitted by essentially any party, while branch ministries are the prime initiators in large privatization. Competition of "privatization projects" is supposed to be a feature of both large and small privatization, although it is unclear how well this competition works in practice. No formal provisions grant preferences to enterprise insiders, although in practice insiders seem to have a significant advantage in small privatization.

At the top level of state regulation, the *Supreme Council* has a number of commissions that are supposed to play significant roles in

---

[9] It is often said that the delays in implementing a large privatization program in Latvia have led to extensive spontaneous privatization, but no estimates of the precise magnitudes or character of the process are available.

privatization. The most important of these could have been the special *Commission for the Safeguarding and Conversion of State Property*, created with the March 1991 Decree on the Establishment of Institutions for the Conversion of State Property. Despite its mandate, however, this commission has never really functioned, and privatization legislation is instead reviewed in the *Economics Commission* before being submitted to the Supreme Council.

Among others, the *Land Commission* of the Supreme Council was established; pursuant to the Law on Agricultural Reform of June 1990 and the Law on Land Reform in Rural Areas of November 1990. It is meant to "coordinate the land reform work and assure its legality," as well as draft a series of regulations concerning the implementation of agricultural reform. After passing the Law Reforming the Ownership of Land Located in the Towns of Latvia (November 1991), the Supreme Council created the *Urban Land Commission*. Finally, a *Special Commission for Food* was established in June 1992 to ensure the supply of food and promote the privatization of food shops and warehouses.

At the second level of authority, the *Council of Ministers* must approve the lists of enterprises to be privatized and individual privatization projects (proposals for the method of privatization of a particular enterprise) where convertible currency or objects of cultural importance are involved. The council adjudicates disputes between the Ministry of Economic Reforms and branch ministries, appointing a commission to review the projects concerned, and can overrule municipal approval of a project within three weeks of the submission of a project. Together with the Bank of Latvia, it was made responsible for developing a "mechanism to protect the interests of the Republic of Latvia," which would restrict the use of rubles in the privatization process to permanent residents of the Republic. The council was also charged with deciding on the publication of information on privatized units, and with the implementation of agricultural reform and its integration in the overall reform process, which included a legislative initiative to change existing regulations that are relevant to agriculture. Authority for privatization matters within the council centers on the *Commission on Economic Reform*.

Prior to November 1991, the council played a more important role, primarily through its directly subordinated *Department for Conversion of State Property* (DCSP), created in May 1991 as a successor to the previous Privatization Department (which existed until January 1991). The DCSP cooperated with relevant branch ministries in the implementation of privatization policies, and was responsible to the Commission on Economic Reform. Sections within the department worked on various aspects of privatization: evaluation of assets, methodology, and the small and large privatization programs. In November 1991, however, the DCSP was dissolved simultaneously with the reorganization of the Council of Ministers. Its functions were divided among the Ministry of Economic Reforms, branch ministries, and municipalities.

As a result of these changes the role of the third level, that of the ministries, was strengthened. The Privatization Division of the newly created *Ministry of Economic Reforms* (MER) is the single most important of these institutions and has five sections:

1. Privatization methodology and business operations legislation;
2. Establishment of conditions for the development of the private sector;
3. Privatization of small objects;
4. Privatization of large enterprises;
5. Management of state property improvement.

The duties of the MER include the monitoring of the privatization process, in cooperation with the Ministries of Justice and Finance. The MER compiles lists of enterprises to be privatized, after reviewing the proposals prepared by branch ministries. It also reviews all the projects submitted (including competing projects) and may halt branch ministry approval of a project. On the recommendation of the branch ministries, the MER approves the composition of the privatization commissions, which implement the approved project (one per enterprise). Finally, the MER is responsible for providing analysis and information about privatization of state and municipal property.

The reorganization of the government also gave a leading role to branch ministries. In addition to their tasks in cooperation with the MER, they prepare lists of enterprises to be privatized, including the technique to be used. When the project approval process begins (originally scheduled for late November 1992, but probably postponed), it seems to have been planned that branch ministries will submit their approval of a privatization project within a three-day period, although this is obviously an extremely short time to evaluate projects. Although the branch ministries also appoint the members of the privatization commissions, subject to the approval of the MER, the relationship between them is not entirely clear. For instance, whether the commissions may in practice mechanically implement the decisions of the branch ministry, or whether the commission is involved in project selection and price determination is unclear. In general, however, it is agreed that the reorganization has placed much of the responsibility for privatization in the hands of these ministries.

Finally, at the local level of authority, the main bodies, playing a role analogous to that of the branch ministries with respect to local property, are the regional, urban, and rural *Councils of Deputies*. The councils determine which assets to privatize and organize the process of project submission. According to the Law on Privatization Commissions for State and Municipal Property, they appoint *Local Privatization Commissions*, which regulate the privatization of all property under the jurisdiction of this municipality. Composed of members of the councils, representatives of organizations such as trade unions, and "experts," these commissions have a great deal of freedom in choosing which projects to approve and in deciding the method, price, and additional conditions for sale.

Local Land Commissions have been established under the Law on Agricultural Reform to perform the duties of the Land Commission throughout the country's territory. *Special Denationalization Commissions* evaluate applications for restitution.

For the management of the state's share in state-owned enterprises and other businesses, the creation of a state property fund is under consideration, but no decision on this matter has yet been made. Rather, ownership rights in transformed state enterprises are still vested in founding organs.[10]

4B. Overview of privatization programs

Small privatization

The small privatization program in Latvia is conducted at the local level. The transfer of properties to the jurisdiction of local governments began with a Supreme Council Decree in July 1991 and lasted until early fall 1992. The process of transfer was slow because of reluctance on the part of both the local governments and the Commerce Ministry. The former were reluctant to take on the responsibility of

---

[10] A state enterprise exercises ownership rights when it holds shares in another company.

privatization, and the latter, their founder, was loath to lose control over them. The Commerce Ministry has recently been liquidated, and distribution networks are now under the jurisdiction of the Foreign Trade Ministry.

The legal basis for small privatization is the Law on Privatization of Municipally-Owned Small Objects of Trade and Commerce, Restaurants, Cafes and the Service Sector passed on November 5, 1991. The law pertained to units below certain size limits: a maximum of 100 square meters for shops, thirty seats for restaurants, and ten employees for small service industry enterprises. However, the size restriction was removed in an amendment to the Law on February 25, 1992; thus, the program now covers all units in these branches. Property nationalized or otherwise confiscated without payment after June 17, 1940 is excluded from this program. (Reprivatization is handled under a separate program, described below.)

The Local Councils of Deputies (or their boards) draw up lists of units to be privatized on the basis of the enterprise's own initiative, or that of its employees, or of any physical or legal person. After the publication of a list, anyone can submit a project proposing a particular method of privatization (most likely a sale to him- or herself) within a three-month period. The Local Privatization Commissions then decide on the method and conditions of sale.

The law permits the following techniques of privatization: sale or auction to employees, sale or open auction to physical and legal persons (except state legal entities), including foreign investors, and auction to selected participants (tenders). The organization of small privatization auctions is regulated by a Decree of November 5, 1991 (as amended September 10, 1992), which also stipulates that they are to be organized by the Local Privatization Commissions. These Privatization Commissions form "Inventory Commissions" that determine the book value of the assets being privatized. On this basis, and according to their judgment of market value, the Privatization Commissions set the initial price, which must not be lower than the book value.

In the cases of direct sales and closed auctions, the Privatization Commissions have a large amount of freedom in setting the conditions of sale and the requirements for participation, respectively. The law explicitly requires that "guarantees by the purchaser to continue the operation of the object, thus ensuring continued service to the public" be considered, and a three-year period of maintained use is mandatory for food stores. In these cases, the variety of goods offered for sale must also be maintained.

The law stipulates that "length and place of residence in the Republic" is a criterion for participating in an auction,[11] but the commissions often set further conditions, for instance that the purchaser speak Latvian. In some cases, the Commissions have required the performance of a particular service, such as obtaining a specific quantity of fuel from Russia for municipal use. Formally there are no employee preferences (the "first right of refusal" of employees in the original law was removed by the Amendment to the Law on February 25, 1992), but the commissions seem nonetheless to grant them in practice. The commissions may also set the conditions for installment payments.

As is typical of small privatization policies throughout the region, premises are never sold under this program in Latvia. What is sold is rather the equipment, inventory, "good will," and the right to lease the space for five years.[12] The law (paragraph 37) requires either that the lease term be a minimum of five years or that the new owner of the business be given the first right of refusal in the event that the premises are sold, but it is expected that most buildings will be reprivatized.

By October 1, 1992, 136 units had been privatized in this program, representing about two per cent of all objects scheduled to eventually undergo privatization. Auctions were used as the method of privatization in only 17 per cent of all cases; final sale price was generally three to four times higher (although sometimes much higher still) than the starting price. Legal persons were the successful buyers in 56 per cent of all sales; of the physical persons, nearly all were employees. Roughly 60 per cent were sold outright, while the initial deposit was about 25 per cent of the price, and the term was usually two years, in the cases of delayed payment.

Prices for hairdressers were between 2,100 and 20,000 rubles (about $7 to $56 at an exchange rate of 300 rubles to the dollar), approximately

---

[11] The law is actually somewhat vague on the question of who can participate: citizens and permanent residents who have lived in Latvia for at least sixteen years are listed along with foreign physical persons and legal entities (Chapter V, Paragraph 11).

[12] As is also true elsewhere in the region, there are a variety of leasing arrangements other than those under the rubric of the "small privatization program." For instance, when enterprises lease premises in their buildings to private entrepreneurs, this is generally not covered by the Law on Privatization of Municipally Owned Objects. It is said that the complicated requirements of the law are burdensome, raising the attractiveness of other legal routes. But such alternative leasing arrangements need not be significantly different in economic terms from those in the program. A future CEU *Privatization Report* will address this issue in greater detail.

uniformly distributed over this range. Photographic shops sold for between 4,000 and 16,000, a tailor shop with two employees for 2,700, and a fashion design shop with sixty-three employees for 116,500 rubles. Table 4B.1 shows the total starting prices, selling prices, and extent of delayed payment for retail trade units, restaurants, and services. It is interesting to note that final prices increased over the initial price most for restaurants, then trade, though they rose hardly at all for services. Nearly all delayed payments were for units in the services sector, while trade and restaurant sales were characterized almost exclusively by outright payment.

Table 4B.1 Small privatization as of August 1992 (thousand rubles)

Sector	Total starting prices	Total book value of basic assets	Total sales revenue	Total immediate payments	Total delayed payments
Trade	1,568.3	431.8	5,179.7	5,144.2	35.5
Restaurants	345.2	178.1	1,758.5	1,758.5	0
Services	2,257.4	1,058.5	2,269.0	490.8	1,778.2
Total	4,170.9	1,668.4	9,207.2	7,393.5	1,813.7

Source: The Committee for Statistics of the Latvian Council of Ministers

Large-scale privatization

Large privatization, at least that which is reported or is part of an official program, has made still less progress in Latvia. The first partial privatization of large enterprises came in the form of sales of shares to employees of state enterprises, as decribed above.

The Supreme Council Decree of March 3, 1992 on the Concepts and Preparation Program of Privatization of State and Municipal Property provides that, once the Council of Ministers has approved the transformation of a state enterprise into a "statute" company (i.e. corporatizing it prior to privatization – see Section 5 below), one or more of the following techniques for privatization may be chosen:

(a) open subscriptions for shares, organized by an authorized state commission, with initial offer prices based on a valuation of the company which relates to its anticipated profitability;

(b) sale of reserved shares to the employees equal in value up to 20 per cent of the company's basic capital, to be exercised within the first year after a subscription sale is announced (further described in Section 5 below);

(c) auction sale of whole enterprises, or subunits thereof, to a single Latvian buyer (natural or legal person);

(d) auction sales to foreign investors (individuals or companies) for convertible currency. Assets sold to foreign investors must be approved by the Council of Ministers. Enterprises with a monopoly position in the market, or those essential for national interests (such as energy suppliers) are excluded;

(e) leasing of enterprises or subunits with an option to buy at the termination of the leasing contract. An enterprise's assets may be leased by insiders (new companies formed by employees pooling their savings), or to other companies.

In early April 1992, the Guidelines for the Privatization of State and Municipal Enterprises were passed by the Latvian parliament, followed by the June 1992 Law on the Order for Privatization of Objects of State and Municipal Property. They stipulate that payment for the purchase of property may be made over an extended period, allowing time for the introduction of the national currency (the Lat), and thereby ensuring that state property would be sold for Lats or convertible currency rather than for rubles. Large enterprises are scheduled to be sold mostly for hard currency until the Lat is introduced, after which the local currency may be used.

The question of the appropriate, allowable means of payment has continued to be controversial, entangled as it is with questions of citizenship and nationhood. The use of the Russian ruble created fears of massive Russian purchases. For a time, it seemed that only convertible currency would be used (except for 10 per cent of the price, which could be paid with the "currency currently in use in Latvia") until Lats and vouchers were introduced. This drastically slowed the politically possible rate of privatization, due to the fear of a sell-out to foreigners. The problem seemed to have been solved by the introduction of the Latvian ruble in July 1992, and the intention to reverse this policy was announced by the Prime Minister in September, making Latvian rubles an acceptable means of payment.[13] The use of Latvian

13 However, the degree to which other currencies can be converted into Latvian rubles for privatization purchases, and thus why the introduction of the Latvian ruble should alleviate the fear of foreign investors, is not clear. It was also uncertain, as of November 1992, when the Lat would be introduced, or even under what conditions.

rubles was confirmed by a Parliamentary Decision in early November, which also confirmed the use of vouchers (see the next subsection).

On August 18, 1992, the Council of Ministers published a list of state enterprises to be privatized by various means, on the basis of proposals from branch ministries. The further procedure is not entirely clear. Enterprise managers and other interested parties were to submit "privatization projects," proposals for the method of privatization of an enterprise (similar to the Czechoslovak large privatization program), within three months. It was expected, however, that the period would be extended (as also happened in Czechoslovakia), due to an initially sluggish response. After projects are approved, Privatization Commissions are then to be established for each enterprise (unlike the centralized process in Czechoslovakia) to implement the privatization.[14]

Vouchers[15]

Although the use of vouchers was enunciated as one of the basic principles of Latvian privatization in the March 20, 1991 Supreme Council decree, both the overall concept and its detailed elaboration were quite controversial. The Law on Certificates was finally passed only on November 4, 1992. Even so, the law leaves open many questions about how the program will actually work, and about how important vouchers will ultimately be in Latvian privatization.

Starting from the supply side, the law provides that essentially all types of assets may be privatized through vouchers. Vouchers will be the only means of payment for housing and for both rural and urban land. They will also be used, combined with cash, both in auctions for small units and share sales for large enterprises. There may also be some special privileges associated with vouchers, for instance, advantages for buyers who are able to pay the full price with vouchers alone. A list of enterprises that are to be privatized without the use of any vouchers (on the grounds that new investment is necessary and will be a condition of sale) has been assembled and currently contains about twenty-five enterprises.

---

[14] The precise division of labor and relative weights of authority of the Commissions, the Branch Ministries, and the Ministry of Economic Reforms are also unclear.

[15] Much of the information in this section was obtained from Mr. Aivars Bernans, Head of the Department of the Ministry of Economic Reforms in charge of the voucher program.

Vouchers are actually not material, but accounts at the Savings Bank. These accounts are scheduled to be established by March 1993, but there is little confidence that the process will move forward so quickly. Vouchers are tradable, but not to foreigners and only through the accounts in the Bank. Moreover, voucher sales are supposed to be taxed, at a rate still to be determined by the National Bank but only if the total sales price in a given month exceeds the monthly minimum wage. This unusual feature is intended to discourage widespread voucher sales while avoiding penalizing poor individuals excessively.

The number of vouchers received by any individual depends on several factors. First, one voucher is received for each year of residency in Latvia. Second, the number of vouchers received is reduced by five for non-citizens (still not precisely defined). Third, citizens receive fifteen extra vouchers. Fourth, years of work in high Communist Party posts do not count towards residency. Fifth, exiled and politically repressed individuals (identified by a special commission) receive two to five times the number of vouchers for their years of oppression. Altogether, it is expected that the program will issue about 110 mln vouchers.

Aside from the restrictions mentioned above, vouchers are used just like cash in privatization purchases: there is no special allocational mechanism, as in Czechoslovakia. The value of each voucher is meant to be set at the cost of building one half of a square meter of housing in a standard panel building. It is unclear whether and how often the initial nominal value will be indexed for inflation. According to some estimates, these various provisions imply that vouchers may account for approximately 40 per cent of all privatization in Latvia.

Reprivatization

The main principle of the reprivatization program is that property expropriated under the Soviet regime will be returned to previous owners if they present a valid ownership claim (as of June 17, 1940), if the property still exists, and if its return does not conflict with national interests. In all other cases, compensation is to be achieved by issuing special compensation certificates for use in privatization sales. These compensation certificates may be used to obtain property of equal value to that lost; in the case of a previous (part) owner of a factory, to obtain shares in the new "statute" company established on the basis of his former business, or shares in another statute company;

to purchase apartments and land owned by the state or municipalities; and to pay for newly built housing or establish individual farms.

One problem in Latvian reprivatization is that deadlines for applying to have property returned have been repeatedly extended. For land, the deadline was June 1992, postponed to the end of 1992. For real estate and enterprises, the current deadline is December 31, 1994. The problem, of course, is that property rights remain muddled in the meantime, retarding the entire privatization process.

The most important reprivatization programs are being implemented in land and housing. They are briefly described in the following subsections.

Land reform

The issue of reorganization of agriculture was raised in Latvia for the first time in June 1990 when the Law on Agricultural Reform was passed. This was supplemented by the Law of November 1990 on Land Reform in Agricultural Regions. Privatization issues were explicitly raised in the Law on the Privatization of Land in Rural Areas (July 10, 1992).

These laws provide that the land reform, which includes all agricultural land, is to be carried out in two stages. In the first stage, land will be allocated for use by natural and legal persons, without changing the ownership structure. The second stage involves the renewal of ownership rights of the former owners, or the new establishment of such rights for natural persons (with or without payment) after a valuation of the land is effected.

According to the Law on Agricultural Reform, the "former land owners or their inheritors, current users of land, as well as new claimants to land" were required to submit, no later than June 1991, an application to the district or village National Deputy Council which allocated land. In exceptional cases ("urgent, socially important cases, as well as for farmers' farmsteads") the National Deputy Council was permitted to allocate land prior to the expiration of the application period, but only if all possible claimants to the land had surrendered their rights.

Restitution of land in urban areas is covered by a different law, on Land Reforms in Towns and Cities, passed in November 1991. Three "phases" of this reprivatization process may be distinguished. First, applications for restitution were to be submitted by previous owners, present users, and other applicants, to the appropriate municipality, no later than June 20, 1992. Pending completion of the restitution program, municipalities were to stop allocating land for use unless it is needed for construction considered essential for the community. However, rights of usage of real estate may be granted, without ownership title, under the Law on the Use and Organization of Land. Second, applications are processed, ownership rights are renewed, and municipalities draw up social and economic development programs. During the third phase, land is transferred to approved claimants; this is planned to begin in most of Latvia no later than January 1, 1994, but in Riga not later than January 1, 1996.

Housing

Reprivatization of housing is covered by the laws passed on October 30, 1991: On Reprivatization of Buildings, and On Return of Buildings to Their Legal Owners. Claims are required to be filed within three years from the date on which these laws come into effect (i.e., December 31, 1994). According to these laws, even when ownership has been restored to former owners, tenants may not be evicted for the next seven years, unless equivalent accommodation can be provided for them.

As of October 1, 1992, a total of 14,135 claims by previous owners or their heirs had been filed. Some 1,779 buildings with a total area of 382 thousand square meters had been returned to former owners. These recipients were mostly Latvian residents (82 per cent), with the remainder residents of the United States (9 per cent), Australia (2 per cent), and Canada (1 per cent).

5. CORPORATIZATION

Corporatization in Latvia, considered an interim stage in the privatization of state-owned enterprises, is carried out under the Laws on Joint-Stock Companies of December 1990, and on Limited-Liability Companies of January 1991. Rather than the two processes occurring simultaneously, as in some countries, corporatization in Latvia has usually occurred prior to privatization. Corporatization has generally been initiated by insiders (employees and management),[16] who submitted a proposal on transformation of the enterprise to the responsible branch ministry, which examined the feasibility of the plans, as well as their conformity with legal requirements. The review of corporatization proposals was originally conducted by the Privatization Department, then by the Department for Conversion of State Property, and currently by the Ministry of Economic Reforms. Proposals are then submitted to the Council of Ministers. The decision to transform a specific state enterprise into a shareholding (statute) or a limited-liability company was then enforced by a Decree of the Council.

The state retained a certain share of the authorized capital[17] of each company, and exercises its ownership rights by appointing its representatives in the general meeting of the shareholders. The new government's view on privatization is that the state's share in the shareholding companies may be subsequently privatized through a public offering, once adequate governance systems are put into place and the "government considers it essential to privatize an enterprise." Furthermore, a block of shares amounting to up to 20 per cent of the authorized capital is supposed to be reserved for the employees, who may subscribe within one year from the announcement of the public offering.

A new corporate governance structure was introduced for the "statute" companies. The shareholders' interests are expressed at their general meeting. They elect a Board of Trustees which operates as the supervisory body, a Board of Directors which elects among its members a President and a Vice President, and an auditing commission.

As of June 1992, corporatization had been carried out "experimentally," and has included the conversion of twenty-two large state

---

[16] They were motivated by the opportunity to acquire ownership stakes in the enterprise at a reduced price before privatization had been worked out in detail. From the point of view of the operation of the enterprise, corporatization was expected to bring about improvements in terms of increased productivity, because employees had an interest in the profitability of the enterprise. As far as the government administration was concerned, experimental corporatization provided useful experience and tested the use of different techniques.

[17] The basic capital (the "statute fund") of the company is determined by a valuation, based on the book value of assets, carried out by expert auditing firms, and is equal to the total nominal value of the company's shares.

enterprises into shareholding ("statute") companies, i.e. joint-stock companies, and the conversion of twenty-six more into limited-liability companies. Simultaneous with their corporatization was partial privatization through sale of shares to their employees. These companies represent together 9.2 per cent of total output and 9.5 per cent of the industrial workforce.

LITHUANIA

CONTENTS

1. INTRODUCTION

Brief history of reforms

In the interwar period, most of the land in Lithuania was owned by private farmers, and a large fraction of the population was employed in agriculture. Following the Soviet takeover in 1944, Lithuania underwent forced industrialization and collectivization. By the end of the 1980s, about one half of net material product was produced by industry, including construction. The Soviet government formally granted limited economic autonomy to the Baltic states in January 1990. After an unsuccessful attempt to secede in March 1990, Lithuania gained complete independence from the Soviet Union in August 1991.

Lithuania began its reform process by enacting a series of laws in 1990 and 1991. These laws dealt with a wide range of economic activities, including the creation of joint-stock companies and banks, wage and price setting, the initial privatization of state property, and the governmental budget process.

During 1991, the authorities pursued gradual price liberalization. In February, price setting in the emerging private sector was freed of governmental control, while prices set by state firms were subject to indirect controls based on the costs of production and "fair" profit margins. In June, price subsidies for basic foodstuffs were cut, and prices increased substantially. Finally, during the fall of 1991 and the first two months of 1992, almost all retail and wholesale prices were liberalized.

Lithuania founded its own central bank, the Bank of Lithuania, concurrently with its bid to secede in March 1990. However, the Bank only began to take over the functions of Soviet banks in January 1991. By December 1991, all of the Gosbank's assets in Lithuania had been absorbed by the Bank of Lithuania. Preparations for the introduction of a national currency are currently underway.

Following the adoption of laws regulating the state budget process in 1990, Lithuania accelerated its move toward budgetary independence. In 1991, Lithuania adopted its own budget, discontinuing flows to and from the centralized union budget.

2. ECONOMIC ENVIRONMENT

The structure of output

According to *PlanEcon*, the gross national product (GNP) of Lithuania in current prices was Rb 13.7 bln[1] in 1990. The gross domestic product of Lithuania, in 1991 prices, was Rb 27.7 bln.

The share of agriculture in the net material product of Lithuania was larger than that prevailing in the former Soviet Union, while the share of industry was smaller.

Table 2.1 The structure of net material product in 1989 (per cent of total)

	Lithuania	Soviet Union
Industry	36	42
Agriculture	31	23
Construction	14	13
Other	19	22

Source: *PlanEcon*, and "The Economy of the Former USSR," *IMF Economic Review*, April 1992

Output

Following a 6.1 per cent drop in 1990, the GNP of Lithuania in 1990 fell by an additional 4.3 per cent in 1991. NMP also fell by 10 per cent in 1990 and 6.4 per cent in 1991. In 1991, the largest drop (18 per cent) was registered for the NMP of the construction sector, which had been the only sector still growing in 1990. Transport and communications posted a decline of 8.5 per cent, and the NMP of agriculture and industry fell by 6.1 per cent and 2.5 per cent, respectively.

---

[1] According to *PlanEcon*, the average "commercial" ruble–dollar exchange rate was 1.76 in 1990, 1.74 in 1991. It should be noted that these rates are distorted and thus dollar equivalents of local statistics are useful only for superficial illustrative purposes.

Investment

After a decline of 10.3 per cent in 1990, gross investment in fixed capital plummeted by 36.6 per cent in 1991. The share of net investment in NMP also fell from about 21 per cent in 1990 to 16 per cent in 1991.

Household savings

There is no reliable estimate of the total stock of household savings in Lithuania, since a significant proportion of savings has been kept outside the official banking system. According to the IMF monetary survey, the total amount of deposits officially held by households and "other private sectors" was Rb 6.96 bln by the end of 1990.

Price liberalization

As noted earlier, price reform was gradually carried out between February 1991 and February 1992. Most retail prices (except for those of some basic foodstuffs) and wholesale prices were fully free from controls by the end of 1991. Most of the remaining controlled prices, including those of milk and dairy products, were liberalized in January 1992.

Inflation

Until 1991, the consumer price index comprised only goods. It rose by 6.5 per cent in 1990. The 1991 index, now including services, increased by roughly 300 per cent in 1991. Inflation accelerated further at the beginning of 1992, with the consumer price index rising by 336 per cent between December 1991 and July 1992. By July 1992 the price index reached twenty-one times its value in December 1990 (see Table 2.2).

Behavior of wages

The authorities set both the minimum wage and overall pay scales for organizations funded directly by the state budget. Other enterprises,

Table 2.2 Consumer price index (month-to-month per cent change)

	Jan	Feb	Mar	Apr	May	June	July	Aug	Sept	Oct	Nov	Dec
1991	7	5	18	33	13	25	17	−6	2	5	10	50
1992	54	42	18	10	7	11	29					

Source: Lithuanian Ministry of Economics

in both the state and private sectors, set their wages autonomously.

1991's gradual price liberalization was accompanied by compensatory wage adjustments recommended by the state at that time. The adjustments were linked to changes in the minimum wage, which was indexed to changes in the price of the basic consumption basket. Since this price increased faster than the overall consumer price index, nominal wages also rose faster than consumer prices. As a result the average real wage increased by about 11 per cent between the last quarter of 1990 and October 1991.

Table 2.3 Average nominal wages (in rubles)

1991				1992					
Q1	Q2	Q3	Oct	Jan	Feb	Mar	Apr	May	June
321	505	665	1,029	2,279	2,798	3,240	4,118	4,978	5,768

Source: Lithuanian Department of Statistics, and *Baltic Independent*, August 14–20, 1992

Unemployment

Despite a 4.3 per cent drop in GNP in 1991, there were only approximately 4,200 registered unemployed persons by the end of January 1992. This represented about 0.2 per cent of a total workforce of 1.86 mln persons employed in 1990. The number of registered unemployed persons reached 7,600 in July 1992.

Unemployment benefits are payable from the eighth day of registration for a maximum of six months in any twelve-month period. Initial benefits are equal to 70 per cent of the person's previous average wage over the last three months of employment. Benefits decline to 60 per cent of the base wage for the next two months, and 50 per cent for the fifth and sixth month. However, in no circumstances can unemployment benefit be lower than the minimum wage.

State budget

Lithuania's first independent state budget posted a surplus of Rb 499 mln, or 1.8 per cent of GDP, in 1991. Total revenues, led by tax receipts, more than doubled, while subsidies increased by only 16 per cent in nominal terms. Especially significant was the dicountinuance of Lithuania's net transfer to the union budget, which amounted to Rb 500 mln in 1990.

TAXATION

There are five main taxes in Lithuania: personal income, corporate income and social insurance, and value added and excise.

Personal income taxes have not yet been unified in Lithuania. Rates depend on the source of income, with top marginal rates of 33 per cent on income from one's principal job, and 35 per cent for secondary jobs. A reform of the personal tax system is planned for 1993.

Legal entities pay a 29 per cent tax on their income, with lower preferential rates granted for certain activities. In addition, enterprises contribute 30 per cent of their total wage bill to the Social Security Fund, to which employees also contribute 1 per cent of their wages.

Value added and excise taxes replaced turnover taxes in December 1991. The VAT rate has been set at 25 per cent, while excise taxes range from 2.5 per cent to 45 per cent, depending on the item purchased.

Monetary policy

MONEY SUPPLY AND INTEREST RATES

According to the IMF monetary survey, Lithuania's M2, including foreign currency deposits, increased by 161 per cent in 1991. This was largely due to a revaluation of foreign deposits. However, standard monetary measures do not adequately capture the degree of liquidity in Lithuania in 1991, since a portion of all wages was paid with special coupons. These coupons were used as means of payment for certain goods, in a fixed proportion with rubles. According to Western press reports, rubles were withdrawn from circulation on October 1, 1992, and were replaced by coupons, the *talonas*, pending introduction of the national currency, the *litas*, at some future date.

The Bank of Lithuania sets the ceilings for interest rates charged on loans and paid on deposits by the country's commercial and savings banks. In December 1991, lending rates ranged between 2 and 7 per cent, while the average deposit rate was 6.8 per cent. Interest rates rose significantly in 1992. By July, lending rates ranged between 20.5 and 65 per cent, and the average deposit rate was 33.8 per cent.

Debt

Lithuania has accepted responsibility for the part of the Soviet debt associated with enterprises on its territory. However, Lithuania has not assumed any formal responsibility for any part of the general Soviet debt, and it has not been making any debt service payments.

Foreign trade

There are no quantitative restrictions or licensing requirements on imports to Lithuania. However, the export of goods covered by bilateral agreements with other republics, and of those in short domestic supply, is under direct state control. Export licenses are issued by the designated ministries on the basis of quotas. In effect, this system applies to a large number of goods.

In 1990, about 94 per cent of Lithuanian exports and 86 per cent of imports involved trade with other former Soviet republics. According to the IMF estimates, the Lithuanian interrepublican trade balance moved from a Rb 490 mln deficit in 1990 to a Rb 2.3 bln surplus in 1991. A substantial net increase in agricultural exports accounted for most of the reversal in the trade balance.

As reported by the Lithuanian Ministry of Economics, interrepublican trade represented 85 per cent and 91 per cent of total exports and imports, respectively, during the first six months of 1992. The interrepublican trade surplus during that period amounted to about Rb 3.1 bln, out of a total trade surplus of Rb 4.8 bln.

3. PRESENT FORMS OF OWNERSHIP

3A. Legal framework of economic activity

Existing and planned legislation concerning property rights

The following are the more important laws and regulations concerning property rights, forms of business organizations, and privatization in Lithuania:

— Law on the Accumulation of Private Capital of Employees in State Enterprises (1990);
— Civil Code (1990);
— Law on Enterprises (1990), and accompanying Implementation Decree;
— Law on Foreign Investment (1990, amended 1992);
— Law on Joint-Stock Companies (1990);
— Law on Partnerships (1990);
— Law on the Register of Enterprises (1990);
— Law on State Enterprises (1990);
— Law on Agricultural Partnerships (1991);
— Law on Agricultural Reform (1991);
— Law on the Initial Privatization of State Property (1991); modified by: On the Changes of Some Articles of the Law on Initial Privatization (1991), and Decree (N30) of January 21, 1992 implementing these amendments, and changed by Resolution N1-2444 of March 26, 1992; and Law on Amendments and Changes to the Law on Initial Privatization (1992);
— Law on the Legal Status of Foreigners (1991);
— Law on Privatization of Flats (1991);
— Law on Privatization of Insolvent State Enterprises (1991);
— Law on Privatization of the Property of Agricultural Enterprises (1991);
— Law on Procedure and Terms of Restitution of Ownership Rights of Citizens to Their Real Estate (1991, supplemented and modified in 1992);
— Law on Procedure for Using One-Time Investment Vouchers and Other Supplementary Compensations for Credits on Construction of Cooperative and Individual Houses (1991);
— Law on Reprivatization (1991);

— Law on Spheres of Business Activity Wherein Foreign Investment is Prohibited or Restricted (1991) ("Law Restricting Foreign Business Activity");
— Law on Bankruptcy of Enterprises in the Republic of Lithuania (1992);
— Law on Priority for Employees in Buying the Shares of Privatized Enterprises (1992);
— Resolution N520 on the Procedure for Privatization of State Property for Freely Convertible Currency (1992).

Recognized forms of business organizations

THE LEGAL REGIME OF BUSINESS ACTIVITY
In a pattern common to the former republics of the Soviet Union, Lithuania passed, in 1990, a Law on Enterprises, regulating in general terms all forms of business organizations. Precise details missing from the Law on Enterprises were filled in by subsequently enacted special laws and regulations.

The Law on Enterprises establishes the right of physical and juridical persons to engage in economic activity. All business entities in Lithuania (including individual entrepreneurs) must be registered with the local authorities, but registration cannot be refused, except when there are procedural defects in the application. Additional authorizations are needed for enterprises funded by the state budget, which must obtain permission to operate from the Ministry of the Economy, and for enterprises engaging in certain specified activities, including the exploitation of natural resources, and manufacturing and sale of medical substances and certain alcoholic beverages. The production and sale of strong liquors, manufacturing of tobacco products, narcotics, and other dangerous substances, as well as weapons are reserved solely for state enterprises.

The law allows the creation of all enterprises by individual persons, and guarantees all enterprises their independence from the state, which is prohibited from becoming involved in their management. This provision may be of some importance in connection with the operation of state enterprises.

STATE ENTERPRISES
While the Law on Enterprises contains only a few general provisions concerning state enterprises, detailed rules concerning their operations

and governance structure are contained in the Law on State Enterprises of 1990. This law covers all state enterprises except for a special group of firms authorized by the parliament, which are regulated solely by their charters.

The Lithuanian Law on State Enterprises is quite unique among the East European statutes, in that it tries to combine certain features of commercial companies (such as the issuance of shares and certain forms of governance) with traditional forms of state ownership familiar in the region. Consequently, while Lithuania does not have a formal program of corporatization similar to those in the other countries, it permits its state enterprises to become partially privatized without changing their legal form.

The law provides for the existence of two different types of state enterprises:

- state enterprises proper, defined as those firms that either have not issued any shares or have less than 20 per cent of their authorized capital in the form of shares; and
- so-called "state-stock enterprises," defined as firms having more than 20 per cent of their authorized capital in the form of shares. A state-stock enterprise must, however, have a majority of its authorized capital provided by the state, rather than in the form of shares; if the share capital exceeds state capital, the enterprise is required to reorganize within six months into a joint-stock company (the state capital then being exchanged into shares). Likewise, if the share capital falls below 20 per cent of the total, the state-stock enterprise must either sell additional stock or be transformed into an ordinary state enterprise. State capital has separate status from share capital, and does not have the rights associated with the latter; in particular, it does not give the state voting rights or the right to control the commercial activities of the enterprise (the state can, of course, influence the behavior of any enterprises through the use of subsidies, the setting of interest rates, and extending government contracts).[2] Moreover, in cases in which a state-stock enterprise is reorganized into a joint-stock company or another business entity, the state may not control more than one-third of the votes during the first five years.

---

[2] The state does not receive dividends on its portion of the firm's authorized capital. Instead, the enterprise must pay interest on the state contribution. See below.

The shares of a state-stock company may be traded publicly or privately, while those of an ordinary state enterprise cannot be traded on the stock exchange. State enterprises of both kinds can issue preferred shares and other securities, as well as borrow money to finance their operations, but their debts cannot exceed the value of their share capital and they cannot issue bonds. An enterprise can also set up subsidiary state-stock enterprises or become a shareholder in another enterprise or a joint-stock company,[3] but the law limits the extent of cross-holdings among state enterprises:[4] no two state enterprises can own more than 10 per cent of each other's shares.

State enterprises may be founded by an act of government or by an authorized ministry. They do not have title to the property made available to them by the state; their rights are limited to use and management. The bylaws of an ordinary state enterprise, which stipulate the amount and composition of the authorized capital and define the power and composition of the administrative organs, are drafted by the provisional administration appointed by the founder. The bylaws of state-stock enterprises are written by the founding shareholders.

An act of government may suspend the activities of a state enterprise or demand that a state-stock enterprise buy out the state's investment. In case of liquidation of a non-bankrupt state enterprise, its employees and shareholders have a priority right to buy out the state capital within six months of the appointment of a liquidator.

The governing bodies of state enterprises of both kinds are the same: the Management Board, the Supervisory Council, and the general meetings of the employees and the shareholders. An enterprise can operate without a Supervisory Council if the founder (in the case of an ordinary state enterprise) or the shareholders (in the case of a state-stock enterprise) adopt an appropriate resolution. If no council exists, however, the employees of an ordinary state enterprise, or the employees and shareholders of a state-stock enterprise, must elect an auditing committee composed of three members with five-year terms of service.

The Management Board, composed of between three and nine members[5] serving terms of at least five years, collegially manages the

---

[3] An enterprise may not, however, invest more than one-half of its state capital in other enterprises.

[4] Unless indicated otherwise (for example, by referring to it as an "ordinary state enterprise"), the term "state enterprise" will be used below to refer to both state enterprises and state stock enterprises.

[5] In enterprises without Supervisory Councils, the Management Board must have a minimum of six members.

enterprise and deals with all issues not delegated to another body. The board also establishes the enterprise's administrative departments and hires officers to run them. The members of the board are appointed by the Supervisory Council; in enterprises without a council, they are elected in the manner prescribed for the selection of the members of the Supervisory Council. In a state-stock company, the chairman of the board is appointed by the Supervisory Council, while in an ordinary state enterprise he is appointed by the founder. The chairman is also the Chief Executive of the enterprise.

The Supervisory Council, composed of between six and fifteen members serving five-year terms, is elected in separate elections held by the shareholders, administrative officers, and the employees. The number of representatives elected by each of these constituencies varies depending on the capital structure of the enterprise. In state-stock enterprises, two-thirds of the council members are elected by the shareholders, with the employees and administrative officers electing equal numbers of the remaining members. In ordinary state enterprises, the shareholders' representation on the council is reduced: if the shareholders hold at least 5 per cent of the authorized capital, they elect one-third of the council; otherwise, they elect only one member. In all cases, the founder of the enterprise may appoint one member of the council, reducing the representation of the administrative officers by one member. The Supervisory Council appoints the members of the Management Board and reviews all the board's actions. It is also empowered to amend the bylaws of the enterprise, unless the shareholders of a state-stock enterprise reserve that right for their general meeting.

The general meeting of the employees has little role in enterprise governance, except for its role in the election of council members. The general shareholders' meeting, by contrast, has more significant powers, especially in state-stock enterprises. In all state enterprises, the shareholders' meeting, in addition to its electoral functions, must agree to the issuance of preferred shares; in a state-stock enterprise, the meeting can also reserve for itself the power to amend the bylaws, and has the right to remove members of the Management Board, adopt resolutions concerning profit distribution, elect to liquidate or reorganize the enterprise, and reverse a decision of the Supervisory Council.

A number of provisions protect the state from the misuse of its capital. State enterprises are forbidden to use state capital to pay wages, bonuses, and dividends, or to finance non-commercial activities. The state may also refuse to assent to a new issue of securities. The enterprises must pay interest on state property and capital, at the rate set by the government or the Ministry of Finance, or (in the case of municipal enterprises) by the local authorities. The board of a state enterprise can elect to leave up to two-thirds of the accumulated interest in the enterprise in order to increase the state's capital share.

State enterprises may maintain one or two reserve funds: a (tax exempt) reserve fund of nominal share capital, equal to the excess funds received from the purchase of shares over their nominal value (the "nominal reserve fund"); and the profit reserve fund, which is equal to the reinvested portion of profits. The nominal reserve fund and the profit reserve fund may not be more than 10 per cent of the authorized capital, while both reserve funds together must be capitalized at no less than 5 per cent of the enterprise's authorized capital. Until this level of capitalization is reached, the enterprise must place no less than 5 per cent of its after-tax profits in the profit reserve fund.

Should a state enterprise fail to fulfill its financial obligations, including the interest payments on state capital, within three months of their deadline, it can be declared insolvent. In the case of an ordinary state enterprise, insolvency may be declared at the request of the founder, and the founder of an insolvent enterprise has the right to remove the chairman of the board and appoint a new one, and to liquidate or reorganize the enterprise. These provisions also apply in the case of a state-stock enterprise in which the share capital has shrunk to under 10 per cent of the authorized capital.

INDIVIDUAL (PRIVATE) ENTERPRISE
Individual enterprises are unincorporated businesses (sole proprietorships) owned by one person or several persons jointly. The formation, liquidation, and operation of these entities are largely governed by the provisions of the Civil Code. Organizations engaged in non-economic activities can also own individual enterprises, and, unlike other individual enterprises, the enterprises owned by such organizations may acquire juridical personality through a grant from the government. The property of an individual enterprise is inseparable from its owners, who are personally liable for the enterprise's obligations.

GENERAL AND LIMITED PARTNERSHIPS

Partnerships are unincorporated business organizations formed on the basis of an agreement among individuals or juridical persons. In addition to the provisions of the Law on Enterprises and the applicable provisions of the Civil Code, they are primarily governed by a special Law on Partnerships (1990).

A partnership must have at least two, but no more than twenty, members. Governmental entities and state enterprises may not be members. In line with standard practice, Lithuania permits both general partnerships, in which each partner is personally liable for the obligations of the enterprise, and limited partnerships, which have at least one general partner and a number of limited partners, who are basically passive investors[6] with liability restricted to the amount of their contribution. The partnership is not liable for the members' unrelated obligations, but a member's share in a partnership may be reached by his personal creditors, who can move to dissolve the partnership.

Partnership income is distributed among the members at the close of each business year in proportion to each partner's contribution, and changes in profit allocations require a unanimous decision of the members. In general, unless the partnership agreement stipulates otherwise, decisions are made by a majority vote, each partner having one vote, regardless of his contribution.

JOINT-STOCK COMPANIES

In addition to the general provisions of the Law on Enterprises, Lithuanian joint-stock companies (JSCs) are regulated by a special Law on Joint-Stock Companies (1990). This law permits two types of JSCs: regular and closed. The main differences between these two types of firms are the following:

- shares in a regular JSC may be publicly traded, while a closed one may not offer its shares to the public;
- a closed JSC may not have more than fifty shareholders (exclusive of the shareholders who are permanently employed by the company), while regular JSCs are unlimited in size;

---

[6] A limited-partnership agreement may confer a managerial role on a limited partner, to be exercised jointly with a general partner, but the limited partner thereby becomes personally liable for the contracts into which he enters on behalf of the partnership.

- the authorized capital of a regular JSC must be at least Rb 250,000, while no minimum capitalization is required for a closed company;
- a regular JSC must have at least five founders and shareholders, while a closed company needs only two;
- a closed JSC may only issue registered shares, while a regular one may also issue bearer shares;
- a closed JSC may not issue bonds.

A JSC may be founded by any natural or juridical persons, except for banks, which may only found joint-stock banks, and state organs, which cannot be founders of closed JSCs. Banks are also prohibited from owning shares of non-bank JSCs, and state organs are barred from owning more than 50 per cent of a JSC's stock.[7] A closed JSC may reorganize as a public company by re-registering its stock and amending its charter.

The founders of a JSC, who bear personal liability for all acts relating to the formation of a JSC prior to its registration, must prepare the documents needed for registration, and have them verified by an auditor. If the founding capital of a public JSC is not fully subscribed, the registering office may permit a reduction of up to 25 per cent, provided the capital does not fall below 250,000 rbls. The Constituent Assembly (composed of the founders and all subscribers) must be held sixty days after the last day of subscription; it must also approve the audit of the company, and the agreements entered into by the founders, and elect the organs of the JSC.[8]

JSCs may issue both common and preferred shares, but preferred shares cannot constitute more than one-third of the firm's authorized capital. Shares may have different nominal value, but the voting rights of common stock must be proportionate to the nominal value of the shares: unless the charter specifies otherwise, each Rb 100 is entitled to one vote. The charter may also limit the number of votes that a single shareholder may have and stipulate that some shares are non-voting. Shareholders are also precluded from exercising their voting rights on certain matters in which they have a direct interest, such as the valuation of their non-monetary contributions.

The shares of a public JSC (which may be either bearer or registered)

[7] Under the Law on Foreign Investment, state organs are permitted to become founders of JSCs with foreign capital and may hold more than 50 per cent of shares of such JSCs.

[8] The terms of the first Supervisory Council or the Management Board cannot exceed two years.

must be registered with appropriate state agencies; no registration is required for the shares of a closed JSC. No limitations may be placed on the transferability of bearer shares, but the charter of a JSC may require the approval of the Management Board for a transfer of registered shares. Registered shares may also be issued to workers at a reduced price (provided the difference is covered with company reserves) or on an installment plan, and the transferability of such shares may be limited by the charter for a period of no more than three years. (After that period, the shares become ordinary common stock.) A JSC may buy its own shares only in order to avoid losses as a result of a decline in their value, to resell them to the workers, or to decrease its authorized capital. New share issues must be first offered to the existing shareholders on a pro rata basis.

The governing organs of a JSC are: the General Assembly of the shareholders, the Supervisory Council and the Management Board. JSCs with fewer than fifty shareholders and 200 workers may elect not to have a Supervisory Council, and the General Assembly of a closed JSC may decide not to form a Management Board, in which case the company administration or the assembly itself assumes the corresponding responsibilities.

The General Assembly is the highest organ of the company. It must be called once a year, but extraordinary meetings may be called by the council or by shareholders of at least 10 per cent of the shares. A quorum is constituted by one-half of the voting capital (including absentee votes), and the board and council members who are not shareholders have a consultative (non-binding) vote. Proxy voting is permitted, but members of the council or the board cannot serve as proxies. A simple majority is required for most issues, except for charter amendments, a recall of the members of the board or of the council, increasing or decreasing the authorized capital, and company liquidation. In each of these cases, two-thirds of the votes are needed.

The Supervisory Council is composed of between three and fifteen members, but the number of members must be divisible by three. The members are elected for terms no longer than four years, with the possibility of re-election. Except in closed JSCs with fewer than 200 employees, two-thirds of the members are elected by the General Assembly, and one-third by the workers. No person can sit on the councils of more than five Lithuanian companies. The council, which must meet at least every six months, is charged with designating the members of the Management Board and supervising their activities, as well as verifying the company books, and fulfilling other tasks specified in the charter. The council can also designate one of its members to sit on the Management Board for a period of up to six months (but for no more than twelve months in the course of four consecutive years). However, the person so designated cannot simultaneously exercise his rights as a member of the council.

The Management Board is composed of at least three members, who cannot be members of the council or serve on boards of more than two other Lithuanian companies. It is a collegial organ entitled to conduct the company's affairs in accordance with the provisions of the charter, and the decisions of the assembly and the council. The board also represents the company in court proceedings, arbitration, and before state agencies.

A JSC must have an administration, including a chief executive and a chief financial officer, and at least one auditor, who cannot be a member of the board or the council. It must also maintain a reserve fund of at least 10 per cent of its authorized capital; if the reserves are lower than this minimum, 5 per cent of the profits must be contributed to the reserve. In addition to these profit reserves, the company may also keep capital reserves, obtained from the sales of stock at prices above its nominal value.

JSCs may acquire shares of other companies, including controlling stakes of over 50 per cent, but such takeovers are subject to special legislation controls, which require that intent to acquire controlling stakes be disclosed to the target and provide penalties for non-compliance. The law also prevents subsidiaries from holding the shares of their parent companies.

COOPERATIVES
In common with other former republics of the Soviet Union, Lithuania had a substantial pseudo-cooperative sector, primarily in agriculture, housing, and consumer services. As of the autumn of 1992, however, all of these entities have been reorganized, and the Lithuanian law apparently does not recognize cooperatives as a form of economic activity.

The largest pseudo-cooperative sector in Lithuania under the Soviet regime was that of agricultural collectives. The dissolution of all of these entities in accordance with the Law on Agricultural Reform, as well as the transformation of some of them into new "agricultural partnerships" are described in the subsection on privatization in agriculture in Section 4B, below.

The remaining cooperatives in Lithuania, formerly operating under Soviet laws, were forced to change their legal form by the Implementation Decree regulating the entry into force of the Enterprise Law. This decree, which required the restructuring and re-registration of all Lithuanian enterprises prior to October 1, 1990 (July 1, 1990, for individual enterprises), also provided that all cooperatives were to be re-registered as "real economic companies," i.e. entities listed among the permissible business forms under the Enterprise Law.

Bankruptcy

The Law on Bankruptcy of Enterprises in the Republic of Lithuania was passed in September 1992. The law is applicable to economic subjects regulated by the Enterprise Law, but special separate legal provisions may govern bankruptcies of banks and other credit institutions, insurance companies, and agricultural enterprises. The law does not apply to certain state enterprises, as well as budgetary entities, public enterprises, and non-profit organizations. Personal bankruptcy is not covered in the law either.

Bankruptcy proceedings are normally judicial, except when a debtor announces his insolvency in writing to every creditor and establishes a date of a creditors' meeting. The meeting, by a unanimous decision, may then decide upon an extrajudicial mode of proceeding.

A judicial proceeding may be initiated upon a petition by creditors if their claims are three months overdue, if the debtor's assets are insufficient to cover liabilities, or if the debtor is deliberately dissipating its assets. The debtor may also petition for bankruptcy if the enterprise cannot meet its obligations and if its assets are smaller than its liabilities. The court may refuse to accept the petition of a single creditor, or of a group of creditors whose claims are small in proportion to the enterprise's statutory capital. The court may also appoint a temporary administrator, if there is a danger that the debtor's property may be dissipated.

Upon acceptance of the bankruptcy petition (which must be publicly announced), the court appoints an administrator of the bankrupt's property, warns the enterprise about the prohibition against severing work relations with the employees, and inquires with the special state agency charged with "sanation" (see below) concerning the possibility of the enterprise's rehabilitation. (If the enterprise is state owned, the founder must also be informed.) The announcement of bankruptcy also serves to stop all other proceedings against the bankrupt.

The administrator of a bankrupt enterprise is empowered to manage the enterprise, dispose of its property during the bankruptcy proceedings, represent the enterprise in court and at the creditors' meeting, and bring an action to invalidate any transactions entered into by the enterprise within twelve months preceding the bankruptcy proceedings, if such transactions were harmful to the enterprise. The administrator must, on the pain of personal liability, obtain the approval of the creditors' meetings for all transactions that increase the indebtedness of the bankrupt, as well as for sales or transfers of the bankrupt's property.

The meeting of creditors, the chairman of which is appointed by the court, is a body empowered to call the administrator to account for his actions, set his salary (which may be raised by the court) and petition the court for his removal, approve sales and transfers of the bankrupt's property, enter into a compromise agreement with the debtor, propose a reorganization or sanation of the debtor's enterprise, and demand its liquidation. Except when the law provides otherwise, decisions at the meeting are made by the vote of the creditors holding a majority of the claims.

The law envisages the following procedures leading to the satisfaction of the creditors:

- a compromise agreement;
- reorganization of the debtor;
- sanation;
- liquidation.

A compromise agreement between the debtor and the creditors, involving a reduction or deferral of payments on the creditors claims, requires a unanimous agreement of unsecured creditors. A compromise cannot be entered into if the bankruptcy was deliberately provoked by the debtor, and it must be approved by the court, even if the proceedings are extrajudicial.

A reorganization is defined in the Lithuanian law as restructuring involving a division of the bankrupt enterprise, a transfer of its assets, or a change of the character of the bankrupt's economic activity. It can be proposed by the debtor, the administrator, or the creditors' meeting (who must prepare and submit a reorganization project) within three months of the bankruptcy declaration. Reorganization must be approved by creditors representing two-thirds of the claims, and the court can approve the proposal only if it offers a possibility of restoring the debtor's solvency. The terms of the reorganization are determined by the project adopted, which also specifies the respective rights of the creditors' meeting and the bankrupt during the restructuring process. If a reorganization is approved, bankruptcy proceedings are suspended for its duration. If the reorganization is successful, the proceedings are terminated at a successful conclusion of reorganization or restituted if the reorganization fails or is revoked by the court. The latter may be the case when the creditors' meeting decides that the objectives of the reorganization will not be attained, or when the enterprise carries out actions infringing on the interests of other creditors.

The "sanation" envisaged by Lithuanian law is a procedure by which an outside party is allowed to attempt to restore the bankrupt to solvency. The outside party may be a private entrepreneur acting on a commercial basis, or a special state agency designated for these purposes. The process of sanation, which is permissible only if a compromise agreement has not been reached and no scheme of reorganization has been approved, is initiated if the court establishes that such measures may be effective in restoring the solvency of the bankrupt. Sanation is opened with a public tender, in which the state sanation body, as well as private persons, both natural and juridical, may participate. The offers must contain information about the bidder and specify the nature of the proposed restructuring, the required period of time, and the terms on which the creditors' claims will be satisfied. The permissible period cannot be longer than eighteen months, with the possibility of a six-month extension, with no less than one-third of the creditors' claims satisfied within the twelve-month period. (The claims of the creditors are satisfied in the same order as in the case of liquidation.) If the sanation is successful, the bankruptcy proceedings are terminated, and the person who carried out the restructuring receives a property right to the part of the debtor's enterprise corresponding to the sanator's investment. (The law also provides that the state may establish another procedure for the sanation of state and state stock enterprises.)

Finally, liquidation, which cannot take place earlier than three months after the commencement of the bankruptcy proceedings, is begun if no compromise agreement is concluded, the enterprise cannot be reorganized, and sanation cannot be effected. The law specifies the following priorities of the creditors:

1. secured creditors, employee wage claims, and compensation of harms to life and limb;
2. court and administrative expenses related to the proceedings, unpaid bills for commodities delivered during the proceeding, and other claims arising out of the administrator's decisions;
3. taxes and other payments to the budget and social insurance;
4. unsecured creditors.

The claims of creditors in one category are satisfied fully before the next category is satisfied; and if the funds are insufficient to satisfy all creditors in a category, all creditors in that category are satisfied in the same proportion.

Regulations governing foreign investment

Foreign investment in Lithuania is governed by the Law on Foreign Investment (1990, amended 1992) and the Law on Spheres of Business Activity Wherein Foreign Investment Is Prohibited or Restricted (Law Restricting Foreign Business Activity) (1991).

Unlike some other former Soviet republics, Lithuania did not define foreign investment in ways that exclude investment from the other countries of the ruble zone: at least on the face of the legislation, all foreign residents and corporations are treated equally. The law prohibits discrimination against foreign investment, and provides the usual guarantees against expropriation without adequate legal grounds and compensation (which the investor is free to repatriate). A special provision states that the Lithuanian treatment of foreign investment may not fall below the standards defined by international law.

Foreign investment may take the following forms:

- Formation of a joint venture with a Lithuanian partner. Joint ventures are created by a contract, with no minimum foreign investment required. If the local partner is the state, special provisions waive the restrictions on state founding or ownership of joint-stock companies,[9] and require that any joint venture between a foreign partner and the state in which foreign participation exceeds 49 per cent be registered as a joint-stock company,

---

[9] See the subsection on joint-stock companies above, in particular, the text accompanying footnote 6.

rather than as a state or a state-stock enterprise. Also, any branch, workshop, department, or other subdivision of a state enterprise which becomes a part of a joint venture must be disengaged from its parent organization.

- Formation of a company with foreign capital (a wholly foreign-owned company).
- Purchase of shares of a Lithuanian company. If the foreign investor acquires more than 50 per cent of the shares of a Lithuanian company, the firm must be re-registered as a joint venture. Recently passed regulations allow all state enterprises and JSCs to increase their equity capital by selling stocks to foreign investors for hard currency, without any special governmental authorization. However it is necessary for them to inform the appropriate state agencies about the decision.

Foreign investment involving the creation of a new company in Lithuania must be licensed by a special agency of the government. The same rule applies to the purchase of a majority of shares in any Lithuanian company included on a list kept for this purpose by the government. Applications for a license must be processed within thirty days; no provisions for appeal are made in the case of refusals, except to permit the prospective investor to reapply after having taken into account the stated reasons for the original refusal. The investment must be made within twelve months of the issuance of the license, which otherwise loses its validity.

The Law Restricting Foreign Business Activity provides a series of further restraints on foreign investment:

- It bans outright foreign investment in defense-related industries and state enterprises with monopoly positions.
- It allows only state enterprises to manufacture weapons and explosives and to produce and sell narcotics and dangerous biological cultures. This restriction effectively limits foreign investment in such enterprises to 20 per cent of their capital. (See the subsection on state enterprises above).
- It permits only state enterprises and state-stock enterprises (i.e. companies with less than 50 per cent private, including foreign, investment) to manufacture alcoholic beverages and tobacco products.
- It forbids companies with more than 49 per cent foreign ownership to operate oil and gas pipelines, communications systems, electric-

power transmission lines, heating systems, and other facilities related to the functioning of these businesses. It also forbids these companies to operate highways, railways, seaports, airports, lotteries, or gambling establishments.

- It requires special licenses for the exploration and exploitation of mineral deposits and natural resources, the operation of internal transport systems, and the production and sale of poisonous substances.

Foreign investors cannot own land in Lithuania, but they can acquire leases for up to ninety-nine years. All businesses with foreign participation must also be insured with Lithuanian insurance companies.

Foreign investors are granted extensive tax concessions. For all investments made prior to December 31, 1993, the corporate income tax levied on the share of the profits corresponding to the foreign investment will be reduced by 70 per cent for five years from the time the investment becomes profitable, followed by a 50 per cent reduction for the next three years, provided the profits are reinvested in the business. For investments made in 1994 and 1995, the tax reduction will be 50 per cent for six years. There is no reduction in taxes on the profits attributable to domestic investors in joint ventures. In addition, dividends received by foreign investors are free from Lithuanian taxes (i.e. there is no double taxation).

A possible tax problem is created by the required method of accounting, according to which the value of foreign investment is expressed in rubles before taxable profits are calculated. This means that inflation creates paper profits, which are taxed, even if the real value of foreign investment, as expressed in foreign currencies, has not increased.

The law permits full repatriation of profits, both in currency and products or services, without any additional taxation. But no provisions are made for the convertibility into foreign currencies of the income generated by foreign investment in Lithuania.

3B. Structure of ownership

As is true for most of the countries of the region, information on the ownership structure of the Lithuanian economy is scarce and not very reliable. However, several indicators are available which, even if incomplete, shed some light on the relative size of ownership sectors.

Table 3B.1 Number of enterprises by ownership form and sector as of
January 1992

Enterprises and sector	Industry	Agriculture	Total
State-owned	2,192	253	2,445
	5.2%	3.6%	5.1%
Municipal	1,164	–	1,164
	2.8%	–	2.4%
Cooperatives	–	882*	882
	–	12.5%	1.8%
Mixed ownership	113	–	113
	0.3%	–	0.2%
Private**	38,140	5,904	44,044
	91.7%	83.9%	90.5%
Total	41,609	7,039	48,648
	100.0%	100.0%	100.0%

Source: Ministry of Economics; Register of Enterprises; and *Statistical Yearbook of Lithuania*, 1990

* As of January 1991.
** Private sector figures should be treated with caution, as many registered private firms operate either part-time or not at all.

Table 3B.1 shows the number and share of enterprises by ownership (state, municipal, cooperative, mixed, and private) and by main branch (industry and agriculture) in January 1992. Private firms dominate in number, but of course it is probable that they are also relatively small, and many registered units may not even be operating. More recent figures seem to be unavailable, but in October, 1991, just after privatization began, the Lithuanian Department of Statistics estimated that private capital was only 1.5 to 2 per cent of all productive capital. The private sector was estimated to account for 3 to 4 per cent of NMP.

Table 3B.2 shows the distribution of private firms by sector and business form as of July 1991. Most operated in manufacturing, followed by retail trade and catering. Joint-stock companies predominated in the former category, while sole proprietorships accounted for about half the firms in the latter.

Data gathering on private employment has not yet begun, and

Table 3B.2 Distribution of firms by activity and business form as of July 1991

Activity	Joint-stock companies	Sole proprietorship
Manufacturing	39.9	22.3
Construction	24.0	10.3
Retail trade and catering	18.3	36.6
Services (including transportation and communications)	6.6	12.6
Other activities	11.2	18.2
Total	100.00	100.0

Source: Lithuanian Department of Statistics

official employment estimates include only the state and collective farm sectors. A rough estimate of private sector employment, however, can be obtained by extrapolating the employment–population ratio of 1987, before the private sector began to grow, and applying this ratio to the population figures for subsequent years to obtain an estimate for total employment. Assuming no change in labor force participation or in unemployment, the residual after subtracting the official state and collective farm employment from this total is a crude estimate of private sector employment. Table 3B.3 reports the

Table 3B.3 Estimates of private sector employment, 1988–91

(Thousands of persons)	1987	1988	1989	1990	1991
1. Population	3,610.7	3,649.4	3,689.8	3,723.2	3,751.5
2. State enterprise and collective farm employment	1,824.1	1,811.7	1,779.9	1,676.5	1,386.0
3. Total employment under assumption of constant 1987 employment–population ratio	1,824.1	1,842.9	1,863.3	1,880.2	1,894.5
4. Estimated private sector employment (row 3 minus row 2)	0	31.2	83.4	203.7	508.5

Source: Lithuanian Department of Statistics and Privatization Project estimates

results of such an exercise for the years 1987 to 1991: while the population has steadily grown, state employment has fallen, suggesting a rise in private sector employment. Under these assumptions, private employment accounted for well over one quarter of total employment in 1991.

Concerning agriculture, the rapid dissolution of the collective farms has led to enormous growth in the number of private farms, from 5,409 established by the beginning of 1992 to 41,494 by July 1992. The proportion of all agricultural land covered by private farms increased from 2.7 to 10.2 per cent. Under the assumption that each private farm employs an average of three workers, the proportion of primary sector employment accounted for by private farms grew from 4.6 to 35.6 per cent.

Foreign investment has been limited, and moreover, has played a negligible role in the privatization of Lithuanian state enterprises. As of June 24, 1992, there were 1,152 registered joint ventures and 260 wholly foreign-owned firms, up from 596 and eighty-eight, respectively, at the beginning of the year. Foreign investments (53.7 per cent of the ventures' total capital) amounted to Rb 518.5 mln. Almost half of all joint ventures were founded by physical persons, and only a very small number were formed by state bodies. Foreign investment originated mainly from Russia (33.4 per cent), Poland (20.1 per cent), Germany (12.8 per cent), and the U.S.A. (6.2 per cent).

4. THE PRIVATIZATION PROCESS

Introduction

Prior to Lithuanian independence from the USSR, economic reforms were hampered by the necessity for approval from Moscow and by the persistence of the legal framework of the communist system. The realization that real economic reform was dependent on achieving political independence was reflected in the very name of the movement under whose aegis Lithuania proclaimed its independence in March 1990, *Sajudis* (officially, the movement for restructuring). The ensuing Soviet blockade then severely exacerbated the economic crisis in which the country found itself, after already many years of stagnation. Nevertheless, much of the legal basis for privatization policies and the future market economy was put into place under these conditions, even before August 1991, when Lithuania's independence gained general international recognition.

It is difficult to forecast the consequences of the recent elections (late October and early November 1992), in which the Labor Democratic Party, the successor to the Communist Party, won a majority in parliament. While a complete reversal of steps already taken seems quite unlikely, it is possible that the privatization process will slow down, that employees will gain greater preferences, and that other aspects of the reform program, such as price liberalization, will be partially reversed.

4A. Organization of state regulation of privatization

A number of institutions share the responsibility for regulation of privatization in Lithuania. In principle, any of these bodies may propose the privatization of an enterprise, and the controlling body of the enterprise (board of directors or general meeting of employees) may do so as well. In practice, the lists of enterprises to be privatized are assembled by the Department of Privatization in the Ministry of Economy, for property under the jurisdiction of the Republic, and by local councils and commissions, for property under their respective jurisdictions. The government and local councils determine the assets under their respective jurisdictions that will not be privatized.

Special institutions for privatization have been created at both the republican and local levels. Commissions at each level are responsible for approving proposals and setting initial prices, while the actual implementation of privatization is conducted by agencies exclusively at the local level.

At the republican level, the *Central Privatization Commission* was created under the Law on Initial Privatization of State Property, Article 4. The commission is appointed and may be dissolved by the Supreme Council (parliament) on the recommendation of the Prime Minister. The current chairman is the Minister of Economics, while other members are drawn from various ministries, governmental organs, and other organizations, such as unions.

In addition to the legislative proposals on privatization originating with the Ministry of Economics, other ministries, and the government (Prime Minister's Council), the Central Privatization Commission may prepare its own plans for consideration by the Supreme Council. The commission is also responsible for monitoring and regulating the privatization of property under its jurisdiction. More specifically, the

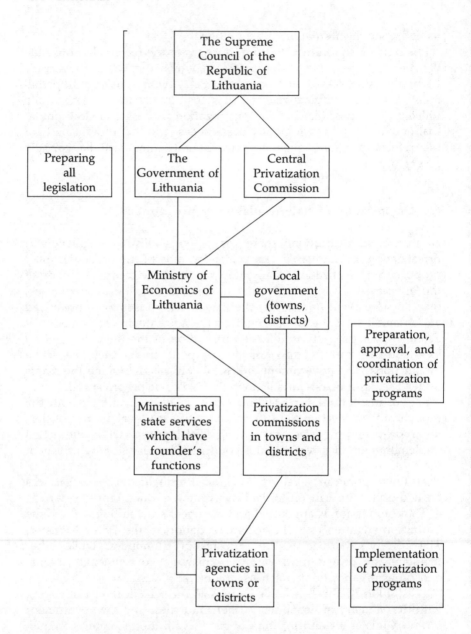

Chart 4A.1 Organizational chart of the implementation of state-owned property privatization

Central Privatization Commission is charged with the following tasks:

a) confirming the national privatization program in coordination with the government (either body can issue decisions on privatization);
b) approving privatization proposals for property under the jurisdiction of ministries and state institutions;
c) certifying the results of privatizations of property under Republic jurisdiction, and issuing titles of ownership;
d) making decisions on initial prices, price reductions (in the event of an unsuccessful auction or undersubscribed share subscription), price increases (in the event of an oversubscription), and other sale conditions;
e) determining privatization procedures for enterprises holding monopolies (defined as over 50 per cent of the output in a given market), if it is not possible to split them up beforehand.

The Central Privatization Commission also approves the list of enterprises to be sold for convertible currency (originally, the task of the Supreme Council).

Also at the republican level, a Privatization Office plays an advisory role with respect to the government, while the Privatization Department of the Ministry of Economy performs the same function with respect to the Central Commission and coordinates the implementation of the Commissions' decisions. The Savings Bank holds the individual voucher accounts. The Ministry of Finance determines the conditions for installment payments.

Branch ministries and other state institutions that founded enterprises prepare privatization plans for property under their jurisdiction, submitting them to the Central Privatization Commission for approval; they are also required to decide how to divide monopolistic enterprises, as well as to provide information for publication, to coordinate with local agencies on sales, and to carry out other decisions of the Central Privatization Commission. Privatization of enterprises in certain branches (culture, education, natural resources, pharmaceutical, transportation, power generation, etc.) may occur "only in coordination" with their founders, according to the Law on Initial Privatization, Article 7. Founders seem to possess the power more generally to block privatization; they certainly also bargain with the commissions over the proportion of the enterprise that is privatized. Lithuania has no special institution that has assumed the state's ownership rights, and these remain instead with the founder, including, notably, the right to sell state shares remaining after "initial" privatization.

Local Privatization Commissions, which have been established in all eleven cities and forty-four districts (*rayon*), play the same role as the Central Commission with respect to municipal property. Local Commissions are appointed by the government, on the recommendation of the Presidiums of Local Councils; a representative of the Central Privatization Commission may be included. The commissions in towns have five members.

Local Privatization Commissions have the following responsibilities:

a) to work out and approve privatization plans for property under the jurisdiction of local government, coordinating with the Central Privatization Commission;

b) to certify the results of privatization in these instances, and issue titles of ownership;

c) to make decisions about initial prices, the sale of shares, etc.

The Central Commission may override the decisions of the Local Commissions, and to some extent, monitors their activities although the right of intervention is rarely exercised.

Both the Central and the Local Commissions are financed through special funds from privatization sale proceeds. When local government property is sold, 30 per cent of revenues go to the Local Privatization Fund and 70 per cent to the Central Privatization Fund. When property under the jurisdiction of the central government is privatized, 5 per cent of the proceeds go to the Local Fund and 95 per cent to the Central Fund.

The actual implementation of both republican and local privatization is carried out by *Privatization Agencies*, which are created by local councils. In each district or town, the agency executes the privatization programs for all the property subject to privatization in that area; prepares the necessary documents, organizes auctions and public subscriptions for shares; and makes suggestions to privatization commissions on discounting the prices of property unable to be sold in the auctions. Vouchers (see below, Section 4B) are distributed to the public through local privatization agencies. The agencies also have an informational role, providing relevant data for publication and for those who need information on enterprises or assets being privatized. They employ a maximum of twenty people in towns and seven people in districts.

Commissions for Agricultural Reform carry out the dissolution of collective farms and organize new legal forms (generally, partnerships) when groups of former collective farm workers become owners of farm assets.

4B. Overview of privatization programs

Primary emphasis in Lithuania's economic transition policy has been placed upon the restructuring of ownership relations, for which the objective is of privatizing two-thirds of state property (including housing, but excluding land) proclaimed in the government's program "Market – Democracy – Freedom." While this goal is unlikely to be fully met in all spheres by the target date of the end of 1992, it nonetheless remains clear that, by many measures and in the words of the IMF, "the initial pace of privatization has been impressive."[10]

The first property transfers in post-communist Lithuania took place towards the end of 1990, when employees were given or allowed to purchase ownership stakes in their enterprises. Three ongoing programs have since been developed: the so-called "Initial Privatization of State Property," the Privatization of Flats, and the Privatization of the Property of Agricultural Enterprises. Lithuania also has four types of vouchers, three of which can be used in all of the programs, and one of which is specifically for agriculture. These policies and programs, together with restitution measures and a special program to privatize bankrupt enterprises, are described below.

Transfers to employees

Two actions by the Supreme Council in late 1990 allowed workers to become partial owners in their enterprises.

Employees of enterprises that were under leasing agreements were given the opportunity to acquire shares in their firms under the Supreme Council Resolution of October 16, 1990. The amount of a given enterprise that could be privatized in this fashion was equal to the sum of the leasing fees paid by the employees or cooperative which undertook the leasing agreement, plus the sum of delayed wage

---

[10] *Economic Review of Lithuania*, International Monetary Fund, Washington, D.C., April 1992, p. 9.

payments invested in production or turned into the stock (venture) fund plus part of the social funds accumulated during the leasing period. Almost sixty enterprises participated in this program and nearly 100 mln rubles of property (book value) was transferred to private employee ownership.

A second measure was the provisional Law on the Accumulation of Private Capital of Employees in State Enterprises, adopted on December 4, 1990. Enterprises with assets whose book value exceeded Rb 330,000 could privatize up to 10 per cent of their capital by the sale of shares to employees.[11] The transfer was subject to a limit of 3,000 rubles per person, of which up to 1,000 rubles could be paid for with vouchers. The shares are nontransferable to outsiders. Between 50 and 60 per cent of Lithuanian state enterprises used this method of privatization, the proceeds from which reached nearly Rb 300 mln, until July 1, 1991, when it was superseded by the "Initial Privatization program" (described below).[12]

Because together these two measures could result in employee ownership of more than 20 per cent of the capital of an enterprise, units with the special legal form of "state-stock enterprise" (described in Section 3A above) were formed even prior to the implementation of the Initial Privatization Program.

Vouchers

Perhaps the most important factor in the fast pace of ownership change in Lithuania is the dominant role played by vouchers. According to the original plans, vouchers were to be the means of payment for two-thirds of the value of all property to be privatized (excluding land), a much higher proportion than in any other country. In addition to large enterprises, both housing and smaller enterprises are privatized using two types of vouchers distributed to all citizens, and compensation vouchers. Furthermore, these vouchers, together with one additional kind, are employed in the privatization of agriculture.

---

[11] Smaller enterprises were excluded because it was planned (and later realized through the Initial Privatization Program) that they would be sold to a single new owner in an auction.

[12] Workers received the additional right, through the Law on Priority of Employees in Buying Shares of Privatized Enterprises, to acquire shares for a price equal to their nominal value up to a limit of 30 per cent of the capital fund of the enterprise (including the earlier share sale).

Unfortunately, a ready answer to the question of the exact extent of privatization through the use of vouchers thus far, is prevented by problems related to changes in asset values, the use of discrete indexation, and a lack of centralized bookkeeping.

The structure of the voucher program in Lithuania is significantly more complicated than in most other countries. There are four types: one transfers some entitlement to all Lithuanian citizens ("one-time investment vouchers"), a second compensates those whose savings have lost real value due to inflation ("supplementary compensation"), a third enables agricultural workers to acquire their enterprises ("supplementary agrarian compensation"), and a fourth compensates victims of property expropriations under Soviet rule. This subsection contains descriptions of these four types; further information about the use of the vouchers in specific programs is provided in the subsequent subsections describing those programs.

None of the four voucher types is material. Instead, an "investment account" is opened in the Savings Bank for each recipient, from which payments can be made for purchases in the privatization program. The original deadline for participation was July 1992, but most individual accounts had been established well before that time. Privately-organized investment stock corporations (intermediaries, described further in the next subsection) also hold such accounts, into which they deposit the investment vouchers and other compensation certificates which citizens choose to place with them. All vouchers held in investment accounts are indexed against the rate of inflation from time to time; for instance, the Government Decree N180 of March 23, 1992 indexed them by a factor of four.

One-time investment vouchers are allocated to all Lithuanian citizens under Article 12 of the Initial Privatization Law. Values of these vouchers are determined as a function of age: those of age thirty-five or older receive vouchers worth 10,000 rubles, those between thirty and thirty-five receive 8,000 rubles, those between twenty-five and thirty receive 6,000 rubles, those between eighteen and twenty-five receive 4,000 rubles, and those under eighteen years of age receive 2,000 rubles.

To compensate for the erosion of real savings due to the high inflation plaguing the economy since early 1991, the government issued special *supplementary compensations* equivalent to 50 per cent of the level of Savings Bank deposits and of life insurance, as of February 26, 1991, but subject to a ceiling of 5,000 rubles. These compensations may be used only as payment in privatization programs and are held together with the one-time vouchers in investment accounts.

Supplementary agrarian compensations are allocated to present and former employees of agricultural enterprises and are also included in the special investment accounts. Their value is calculated as a specific percentage of the value of the one-time vouchers varying with the length of time worked in a state or collective farm: 10 per cent for five to ten years, 20 per cent for ten to fifteen years, and 30 per cent for more than fifteen years.

Restitution vouchers are employed when reprivatization of particular objects or equivalent objects to those expropriated under Soviet rule is not possible. These vouchers are also deposited in the special investment accounts and must be used in privatization purchases. Restitution is further described in a separate subsection below.

Originally, the sale or transfer of all types of vouchers was normally prohibited, except within families, through inheritance, or by investing in investment stock corporations. However, the Law on the Procedure for Using One-time Investment Vouchers and Other Supplementary Compensations for Credits on Construction Cooperative and Individual Houses (flats), passed on May 16, 1991, allowed those who had debts for the construction of their cooperative flat or individual house or who had to pay an initial fee for a cooperative flat, to sell their vouchers at an auction. The proceeds of such sales could be used solely to settle the housing debts. Any Lithuanian citizen with an investment account can purchase vouchers in these auctions, and use them in privatization purchases. In the spring of 1992, vouchers were selling in these auctions for between 1.3 and 1.4 times their face value, on average.

The tradability restriction, however, was difficult to enforce. For instance, the Law on Initial Privatization allowed individuals to form groups and pool their vouchers; in this case, it was a simple matter for one "group member" to contract with the others to buy them out after the sale, particularly after shares became fully tradable after July 1, 1992. Moreover, the price of vouchers in auctions had fallen to below half their face value by early fall 1992. Perhaps for these reasons, the Law on Amendments and Changes to the Law on Initial Privatization (September 17, 1992) lifted all restrictions on the tradability of vouchers. The Government Decree implementing this change was passed in early November 1992.

Vouchers are combined with cash in all privatization sales in Lithuania, with the exception of special decisions of the Central Privatization Commission, as, for instance, in some cases where an offering is undersubscribed. The rules governing the permitted combination of vouchers and cash differ across kinds of assets, and are described for each case below.

The Initial Privatization Program

Its name notwithstanding, the "Initial Privatization Program" is the major program for the privatization of enterprises and enterprise assets in Lithuania. Both small and large enterprises are included, but different privatization techniques are used for enterprises of different sizes. Enterprises which may be privatized under the initial privatization include those in manufacturing and consumer services, as well as commercially run cultural and educational institutions. The government and local councils have excluded those in the energy, transport, communications, and utilities industries.

Two privatization techniques are employed for domestic sales under this program. Auction is the prescribed method for enterprises, subunits, and buildings and equipment with book value under Tls 1 mln. Above that size, and up to a ceiling of Tls 3 mln, the relevant Privatization Commission has the option of using an auction or a public share subscription. Sales of enterprises for which the book value exceeds Tls 3 mln, or where private share capital already exists (for instance, from an earlier sale to employees), must be conducted through public share subscription.[13]

Once the Privatization Commission has approved the privatization of an enterprise, information concerning the enterprise is published in an Information Bulletin. These bulletins, prepared at both the republican and local levels, are issued monthly and contain continually updated lists of enterprises in the privatization process. The information includes data on capital, employment, profitability (according to the Law on Initial Privatization, also "its planned profitability for next year"), output, as well as descriptions of the enterprise's main activity, method of privatization, initial price, and the date of the auction or the beginning of the share subscription.

Auctions are held between fifteen and forty-five days after their

---

[13] The boundaries of these size ranges were originally Rb 330,000 and Rb 750,000, but because of the use of cash and the nominal denomination of vouchers, inflation has necessitated the indexation of these and all other values specified in the program. The transitional Lithuanian currency, the *talonas*, was introduced at parity with the ruble in October 1992; since then, although the official rates have moved in different directions, all nominal denominations in the program are in talonas rather than rubles. This may well change further with the introduction of the *litas*.

publication in the Information Bulletin. The Privatization Commission sets the starting price according to its assessment of the true market value. Participants must register with the Privatization Agency seven days prior to the auction and pay a deposit of five per cent of the initial price of the assets being sold.

An auction may be held if at least two participants have registered, but the sale is valid only if the final bid is at least 5 per cent above the initial price. If these conditions have not been satisfied, the relevant Privatization Commission may order that the sale be allowed with no cash requirement, or it may reduce the initial price by 35 per cent, and, if the sale is still unsuccessful, by 70 per cent. The enterprise may also be liquidated and its assets sold, and it may be withdrawn from the privatization program.

Table 4B.1 Auctions of enterprises, September 1, 1991 to November 24, 1992

	Number	Book value (Tls mln)	Sale price (Tls mln)	Output (Tls mln)	Employ-ment
Central ownership	109	10.5	161.5	328.5	804
Local ownership	1,723	151.7	2,057.7	1,751.3	14,057
Total	1,832	162.2	2,219.2	2,079.8	14,861
Industry	327	31.5	158.8	31.0	3,293
Construction	34	7.3	46.8	32.4	773
Retail trade	807	61.8	1,612.9	1,940.9	6,089
Utilities	107	13.7	106.6	7.6	302
Consumer services	408	34.8	203.7	43.0	3,874
Transport	3	0.9	4.9	0	22
Other	146	12.2	85.8	24.9	508

Source: Ministry of Economics

The first auctions were held in September 1991; the results of the first fourteen months of the program, through November 24, 1992, are shown in Table 4B.1. Some 1,832 units were sold during this period, representing 77 per cent of the number included in the privatization programs and 53 per cent of the original total number of enterprises to be privatized in Lithuania.[14] Nearly all (1,723) of these 1,832 were locally owned. About 44 per cent of the number of auctioned units were engaged in trade. Most of the rest were engaged in industry (18 per cent), and consumer services (22 per cent). The trade units were, however, relatively small on average, accounting for 38 per cent of the state capital privatized and a 41 per cent share of employment.[15]

Table 4B.1 also shows the book value and the value at selling price of the auctioned units. On average prices were bid up significantly during the auctions, particularly in the retail trade sector. Evidently, the prices also exceeded the capacity of single individuals to pay, for although there are no complete data on the new ownership structure, it is generally known that most of the successful bidders were groups, rather than individuals. The governance of these small units may of course be problematic if ownership is excessively dispersed.

In addition to the auction of enterprises, individual assets have also been auctioned under this program. As of November 24, 1992, 1,386 assets had been sold out of a total of 5,152 scheduled to be sold. By contrast with enterprises, few of the assets are in the retail trade sector, and over one quarter are in industry.

Concerning privatization through public share subscription, the other technique in the Initial Privatization Program, the law (as amended) stipulates a subscription period between fifteen and sixty days after the announcement in the bulletin. The price set by the commission must be at least 20 per cent higher than its assessment of the true market value (presumably to prevent underpricing). When the proportion of shares subscribed is between 80 and 110 per cent, the shares are issued at the starting price. If the subscription is outside of this range, the price is adjusted upward or downward by 10 per cent for shorter subscription periods (generally, about twenty days) until the market clears. The shares are issued as ordinary registered shares, which were originally nontransferable, except within families. Since July 1, 1992, the shares have been legally transferable.

Two important differences between this program and the Czechoslovak deserve to be noted. First, the process in Lithuania is not really a mass program in which a large number of enterprises are forced

---

14 A simultaneous "de-monopolization" policy has broken up the original 3,500 enterprises into 5,300 units, 4,400 of which will be privatized.
15 Auctions were temporarily halted during November 1992, to allow the introduction of registration and bidding by mail.

through simultaneously. Second, shares are issued in Lithuania only when the offering is fully subscribed and only for the "equilibrium price," unlike in Czechoslovakia. Both the mass "waves" and the disequilibrium trading of the Czechoslovak program are rationalized on the grounds that they accelerate the process, but it is remarkable that much more rapid privatization seems to have been accomplished in Lithuania without the use of either.

The Law on Initial Privatization treats state enterprises and state stock enterprises differently in terms of the proportion of their value that is privatized through the program. State enterprises (defined as having less than 20 per cent of their value held privately) must issue shares for 25 per cent of their value. It is not completely clear whether further privatization of these enterprises is the decision of the founder or the Central Privatization Commission. On the other hand, the extent of privatization of state stock enterprises is formally the decision of the enterprise managing bodies, with the exception of a requirement for a minimum level of privatization: total private capital must be at least 50 per cent of the total afterward.

Public share subscriptions also began in September 1991; the results to the end of September 1992 are shown in Table 4B.2. Of the total 1,429 enterprises slated for eventual privatization, 906 were privatized by this date, with roughly equal proportions privatized on the local and republican levels. On average, the private share in these firms was 72 per cent. Slightly less than a third of the number of enterprises operated in industry, but in terms of capital, they account for nearly 60 per cent; the second largest group is in construction. It is notable that, on average, the emission share price for republican enterprises was lower than 120 per cent of the enterprise value: there have often been several price-adjusting stages to the subscription, and the price has sometimes fallen.

Participation in most auctions and share subscriptions is restricted to individual Lithuanian citizens, groups of citizens founded by properly notarized agreement, and (as a result of the December 1991 Amendment to the Initial Privatization Law) "investment stock corporations" (intermediaries) in which people may place their vouchers using special investment accounts. Acceptable means of payment include investment vouchers and cash. The cash portion of payment must be at least 5 per cent of the nominal value of the property, but cannot exceed the nominal value of the voucher portion of payment (the so-called "cash quota").

The Initial Privatization Law also provided that some state-owned

Table 4B.2 Privatization by share subscription September 1, 1991 to September 30, 1992

	Number of enterprises to be privatized	Number of enterprises privatized	Book value (Tls mln)	Book value privatized (Tls mln)	Percent privatized	Emission price (Tls mln)
Republic	697	450	8,232.6	5,910.2	71.8	6,697.7
Local	732	456	2,065.2	1,541.2	74.6	1,991.5
Total	1,429	906	10,297.8	7,451.4	72.4	8,689.2
Industry	454	279	5,903.3	4,209.0	71.3	4,824.3
Transportation	69	39	590.9	424.8	71.9	456.0
Construction	357	245	1,842.1	1,354.7	73.5	1,542.4
Trade	269	196	1,305.4	987.7	75.7	1,276.5
Utilities	40	23	106.6	63.4	59.5	108.3
Consumer services	68	41	72.6	54.2	74.6	73.4
Other	172	83	476.8	357.6	75.0	408.3

Source: Ministry of the Economy

property would be sold exclusively for convertible currency, with no limit on the nationality of the purchaser. A list of 114 enterprises to be included in this program, with authorized capital of 1.9 bln rubles, was approved by the Supreme Council in October 1991. The procedures to be used in these cases, however, were only approved in July 1992, with anticipation of assistance from foreign advisers in preparing the enterprises for privatization. In fact, it is an unusual feature of Lithuanian privatization that it is almost entirely domestic: virtually no sales of state-owned property to foreigners have taken place thus far.

As of November 1, 1992, 325 investment stock companies had been established with Tls 12 bln capital of which Tls 2.6 bln had already been invested in privatized companies. These intermediaries are public joint-stock companies registered with the Ministry of Finance. The funds open investment accounts to accumulate the vouchers placed with them by citizens. Shares of some investment stock companies may also be bought for cash, although the total of such cash investments may not exceed 20 per cent of the fund's capital.

Other regulations of the funds include the following. They must use at least 80 per cent of the sum in their investment accounts for the purchase of shares in privatized companies, but are not permitted to acquire more than 50 per cent of any single unit. Their size is restricted to a maximum of Rb 400 mln (now, talonas), the rationale being to inhibit monopolization, although this requirement is easily circumvented through the creation of multiple funds. Cross-investment in other funds is limited to a maximum 10 per cent stake.

An amendment to the implementation of the Initial Privatization Program, under Supreme Council Resolution N1-2444 of March 26, 1992, states that privatized shops and service units must receive permission to make any fundamental change in activity or to close down for repair or reconstruction within the first three years after privatization. During the first year after privatization, no more than 30 per cent of the enterprise's employees may be laid off. This resolution was issued in response to two problems arising when shops and service units were acquired with the intention of using their facilities for other purposes: some areas were left without shops and employees were laid off. Earlier, the first problem was considered sufficiently acute for the government to issue Decree N84 of February 6, 1992, which suspends privatization in cases where the units in question serve social needs not obtainable through other outlets in that district.

The Initial Privatization Law grants no special advantages to employees. As a political response to the layoff problem, however, the

Supreme Council enacted the Law on Priority for Employees in Buying the Shares of Privatized Enterprises in April 1992. State enterprises and state joint-stock enterprises (see sections 3A above and 5 below) undergoing privatization must thereby reserve a proportion of their shares for priority purchase at "nominal price" by employees, retirees and disability pension-holders of that enterprise. The total value of employee shares resulting from this Law and from the 1990 legislation, as described above, must equal 30 per cent of the company's capital.

New methods of privatization were introduced through the Law on Amendments and Changes of the Law on Initial Privatization on September 17, 1992. First, closed auctions and share subscriptions may be held for pharmaceutical, medical, and veterinary units, the right to participate belonging only to licensed practitioners. Second, auctions of blocks of shares may be held for convertible currency. Third, tenders may be held with the participation of foreigners as well as Lithuanian citizens; the quality of the business plan is one of the important criteria for evaluation.

Privatization of insolvent state enterprises

A specific Law on Privatization of Insolvent State Enterprises was passed on July 23, 1991, allowing the sale of such enterprises or their assets with relatively few restrictions, pending the passage of a new bankruptcy law. Individuals or companies registered in Lithuania (but not state enterprises and state joint-stock enterprises) may participate as purchasers, using either vouchers or cash, which in this instance is not subject to quota limits.

Privatization in agriculture

Collective farms in Lithuania were dissolved according to the Law on Agricultural Reform. In many cases, new legal forms, called "agricultural partnerships" and regulated by the Law on Agricultural Partnerships (1991), have been formed on the basis of former collective farm assets. Commissions for Agricultural Reform appointed supervisors to oversee the liquidation and division of each collective farm, and to administer the establishment of the new legal forms. This reorganization of farms began in November 1991, and by the fall of

1992 was essentially complete, although there remain many unresolved problems associated with land restitution.

The new agricultural partnerships, which must derive at least 60 per cent of their income from agricultural production or related services, are organized along the lines of traditional limited-liability companies, the shares being freely tradable among members and third parties, but not publicly tradable. The partnerships are governed by a general meeting of members and a management under a chairman elected for two years. They must also have an auditing commission. Echoing their origin in the former cooperatives, the partnerships must give their members a priority in employment. Foreign persons are allowed as members if they were among the founders.

The Law on Privatization of the Property of Agricultural Enterprises, passed on July 30, 1991, regulates the procedures and terms for closed share subscription sales and auctions of these farms and their assets (equipment, structures, and the land to which they are attached). Only current employees and former employees who retired due to age or disability are allowed to participate; the registration deadline was December 31, 1991. In the event that less than half of the shares in a share subscription for a collective farm or for individual parts thereof are unsubscribed, no partnership is formed, and the assets are auctioned. Any property remaining unsold after these closed auctions is supposed to be sold in an open auction in which any Lithuanian citizen may take part.

Acceptable means of payment in this program are as follows: money (although it is little used in practice), vouchers (including the special agrarian compensation, described above), and "fees" of the agrarian establishment undergoing privatization. These "fees" may be issued to present or former employees, for a value that is somehow meant to reflect the total value of vouchers possessed by those who have registered for the closed auction.

Privatization of housing

The Law on Privatization of Flats, passed on May 28, 1991, pertains to all people permanently residing in Lithuania before March 11, 1989 (thus it is not restricted to Lithuanian citizens), who were renting state-owned housing units at the time. These people now have the right to buy their flats at 1989 prices, either for cash or vouchers, but paying at least 20 per cent of the price in cash. Special rebates (usually applied to the cash portion of the price) are provided to the disabled, the politically oppressed, and the exiled. Installment options are available to all who request them, with a minimum annual payment of 10 per cent of the price, and interest at 4 per cent.

This program is essentially complete. Applications to buy 536,579 units had been received and 468,433 units had been sold (87.3 per cent) by October 9, 1992. Of the total payment, 82.2 per cent was in the form of vouchers. It is also anticipated that up to 5 per cent of the total number of newly contracted flats and empty flats will also be sold, by auction.

Restitution

Under the Law on Procedure and Terms of the Restitution of Owner-ship of Rights of Citizens to their Real Estate, passed on June 18, 1991, the owners and/or heirs of land that was nationalized, confiscated or otherwise taken into the public sector against their will, will receive restitution in one of three ways: return of their land, granting of an equivalent plot, or, where these are impossible, granting of a special restitution voucher, which can be used in privatization sales. The maximum size of plots of land for restitution, as set under the July 1991 Land Reform Law, was raised to 50 hectares of farmland and 80 hectares in total, by amending legislation passed in January 1992.

Agricultural land is supposed to be returned only to those working or planning to work it. Unfortunately, this is difficult to enforce. Furthermore, it seems there are legitimate applications for more land than there is land available, for two reasons. First, expansion of cities has covered land that was formerly agricultural, but urban land is not reprivatized. Second, new agricultural partnerships (described above) have been formed on land that was expropriated. It has not yet been resolved how the former owners of these two categories of land will be compensated.

The restitution program covers not only land, but all physical assets, if they are judged to have changed less than 50 per cent from their pre-expropriation state, according to the Law on Reprivatization. There is a specified maximum area for agricultural land and forests, but no limit of area in the case of industrial, commercial, and residential buildings.

5. CORPORATIZATION

Lithuania does not have a corporatization program in the usual sense of forming wholly state-owned joint-stock companies as a step preceding privatization. However, in enterprises partially privatized through transfers and sales to employees (as described above), hybrid legal forms have been created. The proportion of the value of an enterprise bought by its employees is recognized as an equity stake, defined as share capital, and earns dividends. However, the state's remaining ownership stake in these enterprises is not transformed into share capital. Instead, it is specified as a defined proportion of the enterprise's capital fund, and earns fixed interest payments (currently 7 per cent), rather than dividends.

Hybrid types of state enterprises in Lithuania and their governance structure are described in the subsection on state enterprises in Section 3A, above.